KALI

KALI

The Black Goddess of Dakshineswar

Elizabeth U. Harding

Nicolas-Hays, Inc.
Berwick, Maine

First published in 1993 by
Nicolas-Hays
P. O. Box 1126
Berwick, ME 03901-1126

Distributed to the trade by
Red Wheel/Weiser, LLC
P. O. Box 612
York Beach, ME 03910-0612
With offices at
368 Congress St., 4th Fl.
Boston, MA 02210
www.redwheelweiser.com

Library of Congress Cataloging-in-Publication Data

Harding. Elizabeth U.
    Kali : the black Goddess of Dakshineswar / by Elizabeth U.
  Harding
       p.   cm.
    Includes bibliographical references and index.
    ISBN 0-89254-025-7 : $14.95
    1. Kālī (Hindu deity) 2. Dakshineswar Kali Temple. 3. Kālī
(Hindu deity)--Cult--India--Dakshineswar. 4. Dakshineswar (India)-
-Religious life and customs.   I. Title.
BL1225.K3H29 1993
294.5'2114--dc20   93-15021
                                       CIP
                                        BJ

Cover photograph copyright © 1993 Gandhi Roy

Typeset in 11 point Palatino

Printed in the United States of America

12 11 10
13 12 11 10 9 8 7

The paper used in this publication meets the minimum requirements of the American National standard for permanence of paper for printed library materials. Z39.48-1984.

I offer this book at the feet of Ma Kali with reverence,
and I dedicate this book to my mother, a remarkable
catholic woman who lived through two world wars,
the Great Depression, 45 years of family oppression
and never lost her sweet love, kindness and belief in
the goodness of others.

Contents

List of Illustrations

x ◆ Elizabeth U. Harding

Preface

Kali, the Divine Mother, has been largely misunderstood in the West. As a result, people have labeled her as something evil rather than a source of joy. Up close, the concept of Kali is no more startling than the Christian practice of partaking of Christ's body and drinking his blood during communion. This book attempts to clarify who Kali is and to make the reader feel what it is like to be in India and experience Kali. What does Kali mean to me?

In order to read this book, one does not have to be familiar with Hindu philosophy. I have tried to acquaint the reader with the Hindu concept of God, the Mother, through stories, historic references, an overview of traditional philosophy, and vivid descriptions of the Dakshineswar Kali Temple—the place and its people.

The reader becomes the pilgrim, sharing the excitement and preparation of other pilgrims on the way to see the Divine Mother Kali. Besides getting a glimpse of the Hindu attitude toward this Mother Goddess, one gets useful information about customs at the Dakshineswar Kali Temple—what to do when one arrives there and why.

The third chapter explains the symbolism of Kali and how she is seen by people from different cultures, following different philosophies. It gives a detailed description of the Dakshineswar Kali image and her inner shrine, which is off limits for most people. It looks at the Mother Goddess according to Tantric and Vedantic views. An ongoing commentary by Sri Ramakrishna (taken from *The Gospel of Sri Ramakrishna*), the Kali saint who lived in Dakshineswar, helps the reader perceive the Goddess in her Mother aspect.

The fourth chapter is dedicated to the worship of Kali, the general concept of Hindu worship and the worship as it is performed at the Dakshineswar Kali Temple—on a daily basis and on special occasions.

I found it impossible to write about the Dakshineswar Kali Temple without mentioning Rani Rasmani, the woman who built it. She was a great devotee of Kali. She was very beautiful and, though born poor and of low caste, married an extremely rich man. Upon his death, she decided to take on the responsibility of managing his vast wealth and to build a temple to her beloved Mother Kali. This took tremendous courage since the time was the early 1800s, when women, especially those of low caste, had no place in society except beside their husbands. The Rani's view was catholic—she built a Vishnu temple and twelve Shiva temples in the same compound. (Kali and Vishnu followers often do not get along— Shaktas eat meat while Vaishnavites are strict vegetarians.)

The last chapter is devoted entirely to Kali's mystics, the people who attained the highest realization by worshipping Kali. Though the saints mentioned in this chapter lived mostly in West Bengal in India, their colorful lives, their convictions, and their approach toward the ups and downs of life have a global appeal.

The absence of Westerners among Kali saints in this book does not indicate that great devotees of Kali can only be found in India. Since I began working on this book, I met many wonderful people in the USA who are devoted to Kali. The more I learn about this Great Goddess, the more I feel my understanding of her has just begun and will continue, perhaps, a lifetime.

Elizabeth U. Harding

Jai Kali, Jai Ma Bhavatarini

[Victory to Kali, victory to the Mother, the Savior of souls]

We prostrate before her
who is at once most gentle and most terrible;
We salute her again and again.
Salutation to her who is the support of the world.

Salutations again and again
to the Devi who abides in all beings in the form of consciousness;
to the Devi who abides in all beings in the form of intelligence;
to the Devi who abides in all beings in the form of sleep;
to the Devi who abides in all beings in the form of hunger;
to the Devi who abides in all beings in the form of power;
to the Devi who abides in all beings in the form of modesty;
to the Devi who abides in all beings in the form of peace;
to the Devi who abides in all beings in the form of faith;
to the Devi who abides in all beings in the form of loveliness;
to the Devi who abides in all beings in the form of compassion;
to the Devi who abides in all beings in the form of contentment;
to the Devi who abides in all beings in the form of mother.

May that Devi, the Mother, who appears in the form of all things,
bring forth benefits for all who sing her praises.

—Chandi

Acknowledgments

I am indebted to so many people who gave me support and kindly helped me with my research. I want to thank my spiritual teacher, Swami Chetanananda, for being an inspiration and for making valuable suggestions after reading the manuscript. I want to thank Swami Gambhirananda, the late President of the Ramakrishna Order, who, like a father, blessed me and encouraged me to work on this project. I also want to thank Swami Atmaramananda, Swami Gambhirananda's secretary, who read the manuscript and made corrections.

I am especially indebted to Mrs. Kalpana Biswas, a member of the Rani Rasmani family. Without her help, my photographs of Kali—as well as this book—would not have been possible. My special thanks go to the priests of the Dakshineswar Kali Temple. Pranab Ghosal was of invaluable help. I am indebted to Haradhan Chakraborti, Mohan Chatterjee, Chayan Kumar Ganguly, Dipu, Dwiju and all others who supplied me with valuable information concerning Mother worship at the temple. My thanks also go to the Dakshineswar Kali Temple trustees, to the members of the Rani Rasmani family, the temple office staff and to all Kali devotees who helped with this project.

I thank the publishers mentioned in this book for giving me permission to use their material. I am especially grateful to Swami Adishwarananda for the permission to use many quotations from *The Gospel of Sri Ramakrishna*, Swami Smarananda for quotes from *Sri Ramakrishna, The Great Master*, and Mr. Amiya Kumar Sinha for poems from *Ramaprasada's Devotional Songs*.

INTRODUCTION

The Divine Mother's magic
is ancient as life itself.
She existed before gods and mortals,
and she will still exist even after the great dissolution.
Mother is pure energy in subtle form,
but in times of need
or just out of a desire to play, she manifests.

God, the Mother

When the Gods lay exhausted after warring with the demons, the evil-natured demon king Mahishasura took the opportunity to assemble an army and declare himself Lord of Heaven, Ruler of the Universe.

This blasphemy reached Vishnu's ears and, in anger, he shot forth a terrible light from his forehead. Shiva, too, was angry. He descended from his lofty state of meditation and beamed a sharp ray of blinding light in the same direction as Vishnu. Brahma, Indra and the other mighty Gods did likewise, each issuing forth piercing rays of light. All the Gods' rays joined at one point and, slowly, the blazing concentration of light took shape in the form of a woman.

The light of Shiva formed her face, Yama gave her hair and Vishnu her arms. From the light of Chandra, the moon God, her two breasts were formed. Indra modelled her waist and Varuna her thighs. Earth gave her hips and Brahma feet. The light from the fire God, Agni, fashioned her three eyes. Thus, all Gods contributed their power to manifest the auspicious Devi, the great Mother Goddess.[1]

As soon as the Devi was fully formed, the Immortals prayed to her and worshipped her with praise, ornaments and weapons. Shiva gave her a trident drawn forth from his own, Vishnu a powerful discus, and Indra, the king of the Gods, gave her a thunderbolt identical to his own. Surya, the sun God, bestowed his rays on all the pores of her skin, and Varuna, god of the ocean, gave her a divine crest jewel, earrings, bracelets and a garland of unfading lotuses.

"Victory to the Mother," shouted the Gods as they watched the demon battalions approach with the beating of drums, battle cries, and the blowing of conches. Since the

---

[1] The name "Devi" is derived from the Sanskrit root word "div" which means "to shine"—the Shining One.

Figure 1. Kali.

Devi was of enormous size and highly visible, the demons marched straight toward her, attacking from all sides with arrows, clubs, swords, and spears.

Unperturbed, the Devi roared loudly and laughed a frightening, defiant laugh. Again. And again. And then her ten arms rotated, alternately smashing weapons of the demons and hurling them back at her attackers. With great ease, she picked up dozens of demons at once, killing them with her sword. Some demons she didn't even bother to pick up. She stupefied them with the tremendous noise of her bell and then crushed them with her mace.

The demon Raktabija gave the fierce Mother Goddess a fair amount of troubles. He possessed a special magical power which allowed him to create new demons from his own blood. Whenever the Goddess wounded him, each drop of blood that spilled to the ground sprouted another demon full of strength and brutality. But in the end the Mother outwitted him. She picked up Raktabija and lifted him high into the air to avoid spilling his blood on the ground, and then, gnashing him between her teeth, she drank his blood and swallowed him whole. See figure 1.

Other demons, too, tried to confuse the Goddess with their magical powers. Whenever they were threatened by the Devi, they changed their form and color. But, who can escape the great Mother? Bound by her noose and spitting blood, these demons were soon caught by the Devi. And like a child pulling a toy train, she dragged them over the battlefield where scores of demons already lay split into two by the sharp slashes of her sword.

Snatching some elephants with one hand, the Devi flung them into her mouth and, together with the demon drivers, she furiously ground them up with her teeth. She seized one demon by the hair and another by the neck. One she crushed by the weight of her foot and another with her body.

The Mother's terrible presence filled even the sky. Black clouds gathered and terrifying lightning lit up the ghastly shapes on the ground. There were demons without arms, without legs, demons torn asunder in the middle of their trunks.

When Mahishasura, the king of the demons, saw his army devastated by the blows of the terrible Mother Goddess, his fury knew no bounds. He expanded his body to take on the fierce shape of a giant buffalo. Intoxicated with his own strength and valor, he roared and charged toward the Devi.

"Roar, roar, O fool," shouted the Goddess. "Roar for a moment. When you are slain by me, the Gods will soon roar in this very place."

The earth began to tremble under the stomping feet of the Goddess. Mahishasura fought with all his might but could not conquer the Devi. So he appealed to her sense of justice, complaining that she fought in an unfair way. The Devi, he claimed, received help from so many fierce Goddesses—Durga, Kali, Chamunda, Ambika, and others— and he, Mahishasura, had to fight all by himself.

"I am all alone in the world here," thundered the Devi. "Who else is there besides me? See, O vile one, these Goddesses are but my different powers which again enter into my own self. I stand alone. Don't back off; defend yourself."

The savage fight continued, and the great demon attacked the Mother Goddess with showers of arrows. He hurled discuses, swung his clubs and mace. To no avail. The Devi killed him with her spear, releasing the soul from its evil-natured body and mind.

Dust clouds carried the stench of singed skin and rotting flesh to the blood-red horizon. The demons had been killed, and their blood flowed, accumulating here and there in small pools around carcasses of elephants and horses. Only some headless torsos of demons who refused to give up life still fought the Devi. The battle shrieks had died and the only cries now were those of jackals and hyenas. There was nothing left to kill, but the blood-intoxicated Mother in the form of Kali continued the carnage—smashing and slashing dead demons all over again.

The Gods, who had begun to celebrate victory, became filled with fear. Who was going to stop her? There was only one who could: Shiva, the great God. Besmeared with ashes, the third God of the Hindu Trinity went to the battlefield and lay down motionless among the corpses while the rest of the Gods watched from a safe distance.

The intoxicated Devi staggered across corpses until, suddenly, she found herself standing on top of a beautiful male body—nude and besmeared with white ashes. Awed, she stood still for a moment, looked down at him, and saw straight into the eyes of her husband Shiva. When she realized that she was touching her divine husband with her feet—an unthinkably disrespectful act for a Hindu wife—Kali stretched out her tongue in shame and the destruction came to an end.

The ancient legend of the Devi, the great Mother Goddess, has been handed down by generations of Hindus and stems from a sacred book of the Shakta Tantras, called the Chandi. Although it is understood that the tale's bewildering gore and sentimentality are allegorical, one still wonders what it means to Hindu society today.

From a religious as well as a social standpoint, this legend reaffirms the protecting power of the archetypal Mother who is an integral part of Hindu households. In the West, the woman in the family is mostly seen in her role as the wife, while in India, the woman of the house is always the "mother." Even an unmarried woman without children is often addressed as "mother." It is a gesture of respect, because Hindus consider the position of a mother as supreme.

Hindus, especially in Bengal, worship the great Mother with ceremonies of great splendor. Once a year during an autumn festival called Durga Puja, they reenact the story of the fierce protectress and, side by side, intellectuals and illiterates worship the Mother in temples, homes and in makeshift pandals in the street. In return for their efforts, the great Mother reassures them every year that the good will always overpower the bad—eventually.

From a philosophical standpoint, this legend is an allegorical representation of the constant war going on within all of us—between our divine and demonic natures. In the great Mother Goddess legend, every dominant passion and vice has its special demon representative: Sumbha is the embodiment of lust, Nisumbha is greed, and Mahishasura represents anger.

The Indian scholar Sashi Bhusan Das Gupta wrote an article called "Evolution of Mother Worship in India." He said:

> Whenever our passions are in danger of being erad-icated or suppressed, they change their form and color and try to escape in disguise. This has been illustrated by the story of some of the demons changing their shape when challenged by Shakti, the divine Power.
>
> Our passions and instincts are so deeply rooted in us that they often seem to be indestructible, since one that is killed is replaced at once by another, and so on. This is well illustrated by the Goddess' fight with the demon Raktabija, from whose every drop of blood shed on the ground sprouted a demon with fresh vigor and ferocity. It is the awakening of the Mother within, that is, full consciousness of the divine Power working in and through him, that makes man strong and surcharged with the immense power of God.[2]

Some Hindus talk about their great Mother Goddess with the vehemence of a child who threatens another child while wrestling for a toy: "My mother will punish you if you don't give it to me!" This strong belief in a Goddess that takes care of one's earthly and spiritual wants appears child-ish to some people living in a rational, grown-up world.

But if we dig through our carefully built-up layers of society-dictated values, most of us will admit that some-where deep in the heart is a very soft spot reserved for our earthly as well as archetypal mother. Great people through-out history have believed in a powerful Mother Goddess as

---

[2] *Swami Madhavananda & Ramesh Chandra, Great Women of India* (Calcutta: Advaita Ashrama, 1953) p. 80.

the governing force in the universe. Take, for example, Swami Vivekananda. He became famous in the East and the West for teaching the highest form of Vedanta—Aham brahmasmi (I am Brahman, I am God). Don't bow down to any other God except to the Self within you. Yet, even the high-minded, rational Swami Vivekananda had to acknowledge Mother Kali. On rare occasions, he spoke to special devotees about his inner passion for the Divine Mother. The following is transcribed from a talk that Swami Vivekananda gave to a small group of people assembled in a wooden cottage in Thousand Island Park:

> Mother is the first manifestation of power and is considered a higher ideal than Father. The name of Mother brings the idea of Shakti, Divine Energy and Omnipotence; the baby believes its mother to be all-powerful, able to do anything. The Divine Mother is the Kundalini sleeping in us; without worshipping Her we can never know ourselves. All-merciful, all-powerful, omnipresent—these are attributes of the Divine Mother. She is the sum total of the energy in the universe. Every manifestation of power in the universe is Mother. She is life, She is intelligence, She is love. She is in the universe, yet separate from it. She is a Person and can be seen and known—as Sri Ramakrishna saw and knew Her. Established in the idea of Mother, we can do anything. She quickly answers prayer.

> She can show Herself to us in any form at any moment. The Divine Mother can have form, rupa, and name, nama, or name without form; and as we worship Her in these various aspects, we can rise to Pure Being, having neither form nor name. . . .

> A bit of Mother, a drop, was Krishna; another was Buddha; another was Christ. The worship of even

one spark of Mother in our earthly mother leads to greatness. Worship Her if you want love and wisdom.[3]

The Evolution of Mother Worship in India

Worshipping the mother as God is a most natural thing to do. Belief in a Mother Goddess can be found in almost all races and religions, and especially in ancient history the Mother Goddess played an important role. Considering that the first being a child relates to is its nurturing mother, and considering that primitive people who had no scientific knowledge must have watched the miracle of birth with wonder and awe, it comes as no surprise that our remote ancestors greatly revered the mother. When ancient people began to conceive of a higher supernatural being that would nourish and protect them from evil, they naturally conceived it in the image of a mother.

As we evolved, we began to understand that there cannot be any creation unless there is the union of two—the male and the female. Extending human analogy to the creation of the universe as a whole, we came to believe in a Primordial Father and a Primordial Mother which formed the first pair. All the pairs in the universe are said to be replicas of this original pair.

In India from the age of the Indus Civilization of Mohenjo-daro and Harappa down to the present time, the Father God is represented by the linga (the male symbol) and the Mother Goddess by the yoni

[3] Swami Vivekananda, *Inspired Talks* (New York: Ramakrishna-Vivekananda Center, 1970), pp. 48-49.

(the female symbol). This representation of Shiva-Shakti by the linga-yoni is a popular religious practice in India, and in most of the ancient and modern temples of Shiva, the twins are worshipped in their symbolic representations. In the Tantra literature (both Hindu and Buddhist) the Lord (Bhagavan, the male deity) is symbolically represented by a white dot (shweta-bindu), thus suggesting the likeness with semen, while the Creatrix (Bhagavati, the female deity) is represented by a red dot (shona-bindu), to suggest the analogy with the menstrual blood contained in the ovum.[4]

India has many places famous for Mother worship, but Hindus consider especially sacred those where pieces of the Devi's body fell in her manifestation as Sati.

According to legend, the Divine Mother in the form of Sati married Shiva against the will of her father Daksha. Since he thought of Shiva as a marijuana-smoking, good-for-nothing beggar, Daksha not only refused to accept him into his family, but also denounced Sati and forbade her to return to his kingdom.

For many years, Shiva and Sati lived happily on Mount Kailas, high up in the Himalayas. Until, one day, the sage Narada arrived with the news that Daksha was planning a big festival and sacrifice which all Gods and their families were asked to attend. Neither Shiva nor Sati had been invited. Upon Sati's insistence to attend the sacrifice, Shiva gave in and asked his carrier, the old bull Nandi, to take Sati to her father's court.

Upon arrival, Sati was glad to see her father after such a long absence. She was about to embrace him, but he pushed her away.

---

[4] *Great Women of India*, p. 67.

"Why did you come here? A beggar's wife!" shouted Daksha. He then proceeded to curse Shiva.

Sati blushed deeply.

"Words such as these, the faithful wife must never hear," said Sati. "My ears have listened to you and are now defiled. You gave me life. Now, take it back. I shall not keep it after such dishonor." All color drained from her body and she fell dead at Daksha's feet.

The attendant Nandi sadly returned to Kailas and told Shiva about his wife's death. Shiva's instant grief and wrath were beyond control. He shook his matted locks and out of them leapt a whole army of giants, snakes and ghosts. They turned Daksha's palace to ashes in no time.

Meanwhile, Shiva picked up the dead body of Sati and, bearing it upon his shoulders, he began a terrible dance of destruction. His footsteps shook the world, causing earthquakes and tidal waves that threatened extinction to all.

To save mankind, Vishnu hurled his discus again and again at Sati's corpse until her body fell to the earth, piece by piece. It took fifty-one throws to destroy Sati's body. As soon as Shiva felt her weight gone, he withdrew to Kailas and solitary meditation. He became so absorbed that the Divine Mother, reborn later as Uma, had difficulty in arousing him to forget Sati and marry her.

Wherever the fragments of Sati's body had fallen to the earth, they sprouted sacred Shakti pithas (places dedicated to Mother worship). Ancient temples stand on these spots and, daily, hundreds of pilgrims come to pay their homage to the great Mother. Sati's toes fell to the earth at Kalighat in South Calcutta, and she is worshipped there as Mother Kalika. The gem of Sati's earring fell on Manikarnikaghat in Benares. Sati's right and left breasts fell at Jalandhara and Ramgiri— she is worshipped there as Tripuramalini. Sati's sexual organ (yoni) fell at Kamakhya in Assam.

The Kamakhya Temple is one of the most famous temples dedicated to Mother worship and is especially associated with disciplines practiced according to Tantra.[5] It houses the Mother's image in the form of a yoni-shaped cleft in a rock that hides a natural spring, keeping the cleft moist. Tantrics say that the earth's menstruation takes place there in the Hindu month of Asar (around July/August).

> During Ambuvachi[6] (July-August), after the first burst of the monsoon, a great ceremony takes place, for the water runs red with iron-oxide, and the ritual drink is symbolic of the rajas or ritu of the Devi, her menstrual blood.[7]

Widows do not eat cooked food for three days during this period nor do they cook for anybody else.

In the Shakti pithas across India, traditions differ somewhat and the Goddess' name varies with each location. The Divine Mother likes to play different roles. When Sati had trouble getting permission from Shiva to attend the sacrifice arranged by her father Daksha, she showed herself to him in ten terrible forms, known as the dashamahavidya. Sati became, one after another—Kali, Tara, Sodasi, Bhuvanesvari, Chinnamasta, Bhairavi, Dhumavati, Bagala, Matangi and Kamala. She so successfully terrorized Mahadeva (the great God) that he gave in to her wishes.

Each of these ten Goddesses has a specific universal function. The black Kali is the embodiment of time—the primordial energy. Tara, of dark blue color, personifies the power of aspiration and spiritual ascent. Sodasi represents perfection and Bhuvanesvari the infinite space. Both these Goddesses appear in the color of the rising sun. Sodasi is a

---

[5] A system of religious philosophy in which the Divine Mother is the ultimate reality.

[6] The dark night of the moon.

[7] Ajit Mookerjee, *Kali, the Feminine Force* (Rochester, VT: Destiny Books, 1988), p. 30.

16-year-old girl of reddish complexion who sits astride the prostrate body of Shiva. Bhuvanesvari nourishes the three worlds with her large breasts that ooze milk. Chinnamasta is the end of existence and wears the color of a million rising suns. She stands in the cremation ground on the copulating bodies of Kama, the God of lust, and his wife Rati. Chinnamasta is shown decapitated, holding her own head while drinking her own blood that streams from her neck. Bhairavi is the embodiment of destruction; her complexion is red, and her breasts are besmeared with blood. The ashen-colored Dhumavati, clad in dirty white clothes, is the night of cosmic slumber. Her hair is disheveled; she has no teeth and her breasts are long and pendulous. Bagala, who is the embodiment of illusion, has a yellow complexion, and her head resembles that of a crane. Bagala holds a club in one hand while another pulls on a demon's tongue. Matangi dispels evil, and the color of her skin is black. She is intoxicated, reels about, and frightfully rolls her eyes. Kamala is beautiful, and her complexion is the color of lightning. Kamala, who reveals herself in good fortune, is seated on a lotus. She is surrounded by elephants who pour pitchers of water over her.

Aside from the Goddesses depicted in the dashamahavidya, there are so many other names and forms of the same Divine Mother. In the *Devi-kavacha* attached to the *Chandi*, the Mother Goddess as Navadurga is described as Shailaputri (the daughter of the mountain), Brahmacharini, Chandraghanta, Kushmanda, Skandamata, Katyayani, Kalaratri, Mahagauri and Siddhidatri.

Among the Mother Goddess' many shapes, the most popular are Parvati or Uma, the daughter of the Himalayas; Durga, the powerful protectress who is seated on a lion; Lakshmi, the Goddess of fortune, seated on a lotus; Saraswati, the Goddess of learning, seated on a swan. The Divine Mother manifesting as Chamunda is seated on a corpse, Varahi on a buffalo, Aindri on an elephant, and

Vaishnavi on Garuda—the legendary large bird and carrier of Vishnu. The Divine Mother as Narasimhi, Shivaduti, Maheshwari, and the white Goddess Ishwari is depicted as seated on a bull. As Kaumari, she sits on a peacock, and as Brahmi on a swan.

Hindu imagination is vast, and one wonders how these particular carriers of Hindu Goddesses were selected. Weight seems to be of no importance. For instance, the Goddess Kaumari sits on a peacock, and the chubby elephant God Ganesha has an even tinier carrier. Ganesha's bulky body sits on a mouse.

But what most puzzles people in the West is the Hindu's preference of worshipping Goddesses associated with gore. Even most liberal-minded Westerners look upon Kali as terrible and cruel. She is killing the demons who are also her children if she, indeed, is the Mother of the universe.

"The Divine Mother Kali is ever blissful," says the Shakti worshipper. How can she be cruel? By punishing the demons, she brings balance to this world. Besides, Shaktas (Shakti worshippers) believe that stories about fierce Goddesses stimulate our imagination. They are supposed to horrify and shock, so that we may strip away our pretensions and dare to confront the Cosmic Truth.

What is the truth? According to the Shakta, the truth is that we are all deluded, attached to finite things, and incapable of comprehending the absolute, infinite Truth. And the cause of this illusion is Maya, which is the Divine Mother. Whoever seeks freedom from this dilemma must worship the Mother. By her grace alone can one uncover and regain the Truth. All prosperity comes to the person who worships Shakti—energy.

Aside from the fifty-one Shakti pithas mentioned in the scriptures, India has countless other sacred places associated with

Mother worship. Many came into being through the devotion of a saint who had lived and worshipped the Mother Goddess there and, as a result, had attained illumination. One such sacred place is the Dakshineswar Kali Temple, situated a few miles north of Calcutta. This temple was built by a devout woman in 1847, and the image of Kali in this temple is called Ma Bhavatarini, the Savior of the World. Today, pilgrims from all over the globe flock to the Dakshineswar Temple to see her.

The name of the saint who lived there is Sri Ramakrishna and, for thirty long years, he worshipped the Divine Mother Kali in this nine-spired white temple on the bank of the Ganges. His intense worship awakened the image of Kali and, ever since, she has become a living Goddess.

> The black basalt image of the Mother, dressed in gorgeous scarlet brocade, stands on the prostrate white marble body of her divine consort, Shiva. . . . On the feet of the Goddess are anklets of gold; she wears necklaces of gold and pearls, a golden garland of human heads, and a girdle of human arms . . . . She herself has four arms; the lower left hand holds a severed human head and the upper grips a blood-stained sword. One right hand offers boons to her children; the other allays their fear.
>
> The majesty of her posture can hardly be described. It combines the terror of destruction with the reassurance of motherly tenderness, for she is the cosmic power, the totality of the universe, a glorious harmony of the "pairs of opposites." She deals out death, as she creates and preserves. She has three eyes, the third being the eye of Divine Wisdom; they strike dismay into the wicked, yet pour out affection for her devotees. She is Prakriti, the procreatrix,

nature, the destroyer, the creator. Nay, she is something greater and deeper still for those who have eyes to see.[8]

When visiting a new place, it is wise to take a guide. When going on a pilgrimage, it is wise to follow a holy person. The pilgrim has to deal with strong impressions externally as well as internally, and it's not difficult at all to become side-tracked into emotionalism. But when one keeps company with the holy, one's understanding is largely correct. This is one of the reasons why Sri Ramakrishna appears so often in the pages of this pilgrimage to Kali, the black Goddess of Dakshineswar.

---

[8] *The Gospel of Sri Ramakrishna,* abridged edition, translated by Swami Nikhilananda (New York: Ramakrishna-Vivekananda Center, 1988), pp. 11-12.

Chapter 1

THE DAKSHINESWAR KALI TEMPLE

O Mother! my desires are unfulfilled;
My hopes are ungratified;
But my life is fast coming to an end.
Let me call Thee, Mother, for the last time;
Come and take me in Thy arms.
None loves in this world;
This world knows not how to love;
My heart yearns, O Mother, to go there,
Where love reigns supreme.[1]

---

[1] Dr. Jadunath Sinha, *Ramaprasada's Devotional Songs — The Cult of Shakti* (Calcutta: Sinha Publishing House, 1966), p. 7.

Approaching the Dakshineswar Kali Temple

Though a taxi can drive all the way into the Dakshineswar Kali Temple Compound, it is more interesting to get out where the local buses stop and walk through the lively lane that leads to the temple. The lane resembles nothing a visitor may expect of a modern city street. Yet, it is not so much the poverty and the somewhat chaotic conditions that catch one's attention. One is much more fascinated by the throbbing life in the lane that goes on without shame, indifferent to praise or criticism. Somewhat overwhelmed, one feels mysteriously drawn into the free spirit of the place where people, animals and things live and die, side by side, in unusual harmony.

There are many people walking through the lane. One can distinguish those who have already visited Ma Kali by the large vermilion mark a priest has put on their foreheads. The people who are on their way to see the Mother generally walk faster and only stop at one or two little stalls to purchase a gift or a flower garland for Ma Kali.

A wandering goat trots past the taxi, unconcerned and chewing on something. In front of a little stall across the lane, a few ladies wrapped in brightly colored saris bargain loudly over the price of conch bangles. Their voices intersect with a loudspeaker fastened to a lamppost. Although the sound is turned up full blast, the shrill voice of a female vocalist singing movie songs does not disturb the peace of a dark-skinned, wiry old man with a bright red turban. He calmly squats next to his wares spread out on a mat and looks as if he hadn't moved for years.

A turbanned Sikh taxi driver with a full grayish beard that hangs down all the way to his chest honks his horn—and honks, and honks, and honks—at colorfully-dressed people who walk leisurely in the middle of the lane. In frustration, he spits red chewed-up pan[2] onto the pavement and shouts sharp words at people who pay no attention to him. Very slowly his taxi pushes through the crowd.

Some of the vendors rhythmically shout out their wares—each word, each syllable a beat. Come shoppers, come, come. Other street vendors clank bells, blow horns, or beat upon a surface. Any surface will do. The balloon seller, for instance, makes a noise by rubbing his fingers rhythmically against his balloons. This creates a truly strange sound: "Crrrrrck, crrrrrck, crrrrrck." Never mind that it sounds creepy; the children love it because they associate the "crrrrrck" with the pleasure of possessing a colorful, pretty balloon.

Yes, there is a lot of noise in the lane, but one can't really call it a cacophony. Instead, the combination of the many different kinds of noise rather translates itself in the brain as a steady rhythm, like a beating heart. And listening to it, one can hear what one wants to hear. A devotee passing through the lane perhaps hears "Ka-li, Ka-li, Ka-li," while a merchant may hear "Bak-shish, Bak-shish, Bak-shish."

A young coolie passes. Walking with a fast rhythmic gait, he carries an enormous round wicker basket on his head. Although the basket is covered with a brightly checkered cotton cloth—skillfully knotted at various points—one still sees a fancy Varanasi sari, ripe fruit and flowers peek out here and there. A portly man dressed in silk follows and makes a great effort to keep up with the quick steps of the coolie. He anxiously watches him and, at intervals, he shouts out instructions, "Careful! Don't drop my offering to Kali."

Mangy-looking dogs run in and out of the crowd, eyeing the coolie, looking for food. One dog is placidly chewing on a dead bird lying in the middle of the sidewalk. Perched above the crowd that throngs through the lane sit large,

---

[2] A betel leaf rolled up with spices inside; chewing pan, one's mouth gets stained bright red.

jet-black crows, their sharp claws fastened onto the roofs of little stalls. "Caack, caack," their watchful eyes don't miss any edible morsel that falls to the ground. And if one does, their large black wings swoop down in an instant, and they generally beat the dogs to it. In spite of all the commotion, a small white cow with beautiful, gentle eyes moves languidly through the crowd. A larger brown cow licks a discarded green coconut shell while another probes with its tongue for food among waste lying in the gutter.

There are little stalls on both sides of the lane, one after the other, displaying anything from foodstuff to brass Gods and Goddesses. Colorfully laid out, there are rudraksha beads, glass baubles, lockets, perfume, shawls, little carpets to sit on, incense, conch bangles, iron bracelets, peacock-feather hand fans, vermilion, orange, pink and yellow powder, and little aluminum swords. Numerous posters and small pictures depict various forms of Kali—the supreme energy responsible for the creation and dissolution of the universe. There is Dakshineswar Kali in her benign form, Smashan Kali, fierce and terrifying, and Adyapith Kali, a fairly recent benign form of Kali.

Not only Kali, but also the entire Hindu Pantheon, it seems, is displayed in a stall under the shade of an old black oilcloth. There is Ganesha, the elephant God, made of ivory, a black Shiva linga, and Radha and Krishna in loving embrace. There are brass images of the Goddesses Durga, Lakshmi, and Sarasvati. Parvati, the wife of Shiva, can be seen sitting on his lap.

Since the early missionaries arrived and set foot on India's shores, the Western mind has struggled with this peculiar Indian habit of worshipping a multitude of Gods. Does Kali get insulted if a pilgrim visits her temple and purchases an image of another Goddess? "Of course not," says a Shakti worshipper. To him, Kali, Durga, Lakshmi, Sarasvati are all different manifestations of the same Divine Mother. They are just different names and forms of the Ultimate Force that has brought this universe into existence.

Yet, the popular names and forms of the Goddess make up only a fraction of her portfolio. All women, according to the Hindu, are manifestations of the Goddess, the Shakti (female power), and reverence for the natural mother is really reverence for the Divine Mother. She is the first guru and ought to be honored all through one's life. A Hindu's tale talks about Queen Madalasa, who was greatly responsible for the spiritual realization of her three sons.

Madalasa was a Hindu queen who was blessed, not only with uncommon beauty, but also with divine knowledge. She knew that this world was unreal and illusory and that the only reality was Brahman. When she gave birth to a son, she insisted on nursing the baby herself and bringing him up so that he would attain the highest realization in life. Rocking him to sleep at night, she softly sang into his ear, "Tat tvam asi, Tat tvam asi." Thou art that, that thou art—Thou art Brahman. Madalasa was successful. As soon as the young prince was grown, he realized the emptiness of the material world which he then renounced, leaving the palace to become a sannyasin (monk). King Ritadhwaja, Madalasa's husband, dismayed, could not persuade his son to stay and take over the kingdom.

Two more boys were born to Madalasa and, rocking them in their cradle, she sang softly, "Tat tvam asi, Tat tvam asi." When they grew older, they also renounced the world and left the palace to become sannyasins.

"We have lost all our sons, thanks to your upbringing," said the king to Madalasa. "Promise that the fourth son born to us will be raised elsewhere and groomed to take over the kingdom." The queen agreed.

A fourth son was born, and Madalasa again sang her lullaby, "Tat tvam asi, Tat tvam asi." But King Ritadhwaja took the boy at a very tender age and sent him away to a royal teacher. When her son was leaving home, the queen gave him a piece of paper hidden in a ring.

"My son, a ruler's tasks are difficult and worldly life is full of trouble," said Queen Madalasa. "If you ever get into a dilemma, take off this ring and read the paper hidden within." On that piece of paper was written, "God alone is true. All else is false. The soul never kills or is killed. Live alone or in the company of the holy."

Madalasa's boy grew into a man and successfully ruled the kingdom for many years after his parents had retired to a forest. But as things are in this world, troubles began to set in after some time. One day was especially bad and he remembered his mother. He took off the ring she had given to him, looked inside, and read Madalasa's message. "Tat tvam Asi," rang in his ears and the knowledge of Brahman dawned in his mind. "I am that Infinite Brahman." He handed over the kingdom to a competent minister and, like his brothers, renounced the world to embrace religion.

While dwelling within this world of maya (illusion, worldly existence), Hindus worship many Gods, but when they think of the Infinite, there is only one, all-encompassing God—called Brahman by the Vedas. Brahman is the transcendental all-pervading Reality of the Vedanta philosophy. What Brahman actually is cannot be described, but for the sake of reference, the Vedas refer to Brahman as Sat-Chid-Ananda—Absolute Existence, Absolute Knowledge, and Absolute Bliss. Brahman is the impersonal, sexless, tranquil Infinity. Brahman is. It is "isness" itself, motionless, beyond thought and comprehension.

When the incomprehensible Brahman begins to agitate, it creates and therefore manifests with the help of its own cosmic ignorance. In this state, Brahman becomes Shiva and Shakti, the male and female aspect of being. Shiva and Shakti are two aspects of the same truth—the static and the dynamic, the abstract and the concrete, the male and the female. Creation is not possible without them. Although they differ in form and activity, they are inseparable like the ocean and its waves, the milk and its whiteness. If one thinks of one, one must automatically think of the other.

Hindus also refer to Shiva and Shakti as Purusha (soul) and Prakriti (nature)—the principle behind the pair of opposites, the Yin and Yang. If we accept good, we equally must accept bad—hot/cold, love/hate, war/peace.

Prakriti is Maya, Brahman's veiling power. This world, as we perceive it, is Maya—an illusion—and because most of us cannot behold Brahman, Maya is real to us. But, just like fog that lifts when the sun comes out, Maya disappears when the knowledge of Brahman dawns. One then transcends the pair of opposites, and only the One remains. Only Brahman is.

Prakriti consists of three gunas (qualities) known as sattva (calmness), rajas (activity), and tamas (inertia). Due to the vicinity of Purusha, Prakriti begins to vibrate and the three gunas lose their balance. And then, when the gunas start to vibrate, creation begins. The first manifestation of Prakriti is Cosmic Intelligence, called the buddhi tattva or mahat tattva (Great Principle), and from it arises the individual consciousness, the ego.

From the sattvic part of the individual consciousness come the mind, the five organs of knowledge (eyes, ears, nose, tongue, and skin) and the five organs of action (speech, hands, feet, genital organ, and the organ of evacuation). From the tamasic part come the five tanmatras (subtle elements: sound, sight, touch, taste, and smell) and the gross elements (space, air, fire, water and earth).

The sattva guna is the source of happiness and everything becomes full of delight. A person filled with sattva guna is cheerful. Such a person possesses wisdom, balance, integrity, truthfulness, cleanliness, faith, forgiveness, fortitude, mercy, bashfulness, peace and contentment. The color of the sattva guna is white.

The raja guna is wonderful but not pleasant. Its color is red. A person under the influence of rajas is tremendously active. Although this may be a good thing sometimes, rajas, in general, is the source of many troubles. It brings restlessness, anger, pride, enmity, sleeplessness, egoism, vanity and arrogance to the mind.

The tama guna is black. From tamas arises laziness, ignorance, sleep, poverty, fear, miserliness, insincerity. A person steeped in tamas should try to counteract his or her negative tendencies with rajas. Through work and discipline, one can overcome laziness. Later on, when established in rajas, one can overcome the qualities of this guna through sattva. Referring to the gunas, Sri Ramakrishna said:

Under the spell of God's maya, man forgets his true nature. He forgets that he is heir to the infinite glories of his Maker. This divine maya is made up of three gunas. None of them can reach the Truth; they are like robbers, who cannot come to a public place for fear of being arrested. They rob man of the knowledge of Truth. Tamas wants to destroy him. Rajas binds him to the world. But sattva rescues him from the clutches of rajas and tamas. Under the protection of sattva, man is rescued from anger, passion, and the other evil effects of tamas. Though sattva loosens the bonds of the world and shows him the road leading to the Supreme Abode of God, it cannot give man the ultimate knowledge of Truth.[3]

Sri Ramakrishna attained God through fervent love and extreme longing for a vision of the Beloved. When the tempest of passionate love blows, one need not worry about

---

[3] M., *The Gospel of Sri Ramakrishna,* translated by Swami Nikhilananda, (New York: Ramakrishna-Vivekananda Center, 1969), p. 218.

philosophy, spiritual disciplines, or how to get accepted by a guru. Sri Ramakrishna attained the Divine Mother Kali based on his intense devotion alone. His teachers came later.

But once Sri Ramakrishna had realized God, he thought of the millions of people who never had a chance to hear about Kali. What about them? Could they, following a different religion, also attain God? He stopped visiting the Kali temple and began to practice the prescribed disciplines of other religions. He worshipped according to Christian tradition and saw God; he worshipped according to Muslim tradition and saw the same God. Sri Ramakrishna then realized that all religions lead to the same One Supreme Being, the One God within us all. "God is one, sages call him by various names," said Sri Ramakrishna with conviction.

Time somehow seems to stand still in India—just as it does during the short break when night turns into day or when one breath stops and the next begins. One experiences a kind of dreamlike state while walking through the small lane that leads to the Kali temple—full of anticipation, knowing very well that the Divine Mother Kali is just around the corner.

The warm, gentle air smells of dust, perfume, spices, coconut hair oil, incense and fried grease. One passes tea shops in the lane, shops where one can buy fried things like samosas (deep-fried pastry filled with potato curry) or chops (deep-fried mashed potato balls with spicy fillings), and shops that sell spices and Indian-made cigarettes. A poor rickshaw-wallah, who can only afford to purchase one beedi (a cigarette rolled in a kendu leaf) does not have to pay extra for matches. He can light his cigarette from a long, slowly burning string that hangs next to the shop. There are shops that sell only sweets. Appetizingly displayed behind glass are sandesh (sweet cheese dessert), rasagolla (cheese balls soaked in syrup), sweet curds, gulab jamun (fried lentil-flour

Figure 2. The main gate to the Dakshineswar Temple compound.

Figure 3. Approaching the Dakshineswar Kali Temple from the Ganges.

dumplings soaked in syrup), and jilipis, which are beautifully spiraled golden rings of fried lentil flour soaked in syrup.

The lane dead-ends into the main gate of the Kali temple. While this is the most frequently used entrance, it is not the only one. See figure 2 on page 11. Dakshineswar residents generally enter the temple through the back gate a little further north. The other way to approach the Kali temple is by boat. See figure 3 above. During Sri Ramakrishna's time, many people preferred to come by boat because road conditions were so bad. Today, it is just the opposite. The river has deposited so much silt near the temple ghats that it is impossible to land with a bigger boat. The only boats able to land are small country boats which are typically manned by two bare-bodied, muscular boatmen—a helmsman with a sturdy pole who pushes and guides the boat along in shallow water and a boatman who sits in the back and rows. To the romantic spirit, these boats are wonderful. Non-swimmers may think differently.

The main gate to the Dakshineswar Kali Temple is ornate, arched, fairly high yet narrow—two taxis traveling in opposite directions must pass within inches of each other. The symbolic connotations regarding the passing through an arched gateway or a tunnel are quite stimulating. The gate is a monument that marks the transition from the old to the new, and one almost feels it was built with the moment one passes through in mind. The mindful pilgrim now begins to get ready to meet the Divine Mother Kali.

On the other side of the main gate, one is confronted by beggars who sit lined up on the pavement, one next to the other. They chant with hoarse voices, "Ma, oh Ma, Ma go Ma." Some beggars are hideously deformed and crippled. Their bony hands stretch out toward passers-by; their brown pleading eyes look up from below. And a pilgrim's tossed coin into an empty begging bowl made of tin becomes a cherished treasure, the Goddess Lakshmi herself, to a thin body clad in rags. "Namaskar, God bless you."

Inside the Kali temple compound are more shops and stalls, some of which specialize and sell mainly offerings for Kali. It is considered bad luck and extremely bad manners to visit a deity empty-handed. When visitors select a shop here to purchase something for the Divine Mother, they get an added benefit. The shopkeeper will generally allow them to deposit their shoes underneath his stall free of charge. Some people leave their shoes in their car or waiting taxi cab while others pay a few coins and leave them with a vendor whose sole business is to look after shoes.

Nobody is allowed to wear shoes inside the Kali temple or, as a matter of fact, in any Indian temple. To take off one's shoes is one way to show respect to God and mortals.

The shopkeeper next to the temple parking lot is happy about new business. He greets a pilgrim like an old friend and smiles, exposing a row of white teeth in a handsome brown face. He takes a small brass pot filled with Ganges water and pours some of it over the pilgrim's hands. This water not only washes the dust off the pilgrim's hands but also purifies his or her soul. Hindus believe that the water from the Ganges is holy, and by drinking it or bathing in it, one is cleansed of even the worst sins.

Sri Ramakrishna masterfully cut through hypocrisy but often used humor to soften the blow:

> What is the use of giving an elephant a bath? It will cover itself with dirt and dust again. A bath in the Ganges undoubtedly absolves one of all sins; but what does that avail? They say that the sins perch on the trees along the bank of the Ganges. No sooner does the man come back from the holy waters than the old sins jump on his shoulders from the trees. Therefore I say, chant the name of God, and with it pray to Him that you may have love for Him. Pray to God that your attachment to such transitory things as wealth, name and creature comforts may become less and less every day."[4]

Once the visitor has washed his or her hands outside the little stall and sprinkled some Ganges water on his or her head, the visitor has become pure and is ready to go and see Ma Kali and worship her. A nice thing about visiting a temple in India is that one physically gets to worship the deity and feels a great sense of accomplishment afterward. While the offerings vary, in general, people purchase a hand-woven basket and fill it with sweets, perfume, iron or conch bangles, sindur (vermillion), incense, and a flower garland made of hibiscus or marigolds.

Some devotees prefer to bring offerings from Calcutta where they can get better-quality sweets, but most people purchase gifts for Kali in Dakshineswar. It's more convenient. Besides, in the hot climate sweets may spoil and flowers droop during the long journey. Calcutta is actually only a

---

[4] *The Gospel of Sri Ramakrishna*, p. 190.

few miles away, but poor road conditions and severe traffic can cause delays from 15 minutes to two hours. It's best to travel early in the morning before rush hour. With light traffic one can reach Dakshineswar from Central Calcutta within 30 minutes.

Ma Kali's favorite flower is the red hibiscus, a dramatically beautiful flower of the nightshade family—large and spectacular. Five scarlet petals are fused into a flared corolla, splendid like the skirt of a Flamenco dancer. From its inner lushness arises a narrow single shaft—the pistil—whose crimson head is pointed upward and beyond the petals. "Kali likes red," explains the shopkeeper turned philosopher when asked why this particular flower happens to be Ma Kali's favorite.

Huge garlands of intricately woven hibiscus hang on strings in front of the little stalls. There are also garlands of sweet-smelling jasmine flowers, and inside the shop in the shade stand big pots filled with lotus buds. This royal flower grows wild in the many ponds around Dakshineswar, and flower sellers collect the lotus buds early in the morning when it is still dark outside and bring them to the temple for sale. When a pilgrim has selected and bought one of these lotus buds, the shopkeeper cuts off the stem, and sprinkling a bit of Ganges water onto the bud, he slowly pries it open to unfold the lotus' smooth petals, one after the other.

A lotus in full bloom symbolizes spiritual realization. Hindus say that the six lotuses within the spiritual seeker bloom when the Kundalini, the Spiritual Current, is aroused and moves upward through the Sushumna nerve in the middle of the spinal cord.

Sri Ramakrishna vividly talked about his experience regarding the six centers of the Kundalini:

> Sometimes the Spiritual Current rises through the spine, crawling like an ant. Sometimes, in samadhi, the soul swims joyfully in the ocean of divine ecstasy, like a fish.

Sometimes, when I lie down on my side, I feel the Spiritual Current pushing me like a monkey and playing with me joyfully. I remain still. That Current, like a monkey, suddenly with one jump reaches the Sahasrara. That is why you see me jump up with a start.

Sometimes, again, the Spiritual Current rises like a bird, hopping from one branch to another. The place where it rests feels like fire. It may hop from Muladhara to Svadhisthana, from Svadhisthana to the heart, and thus gradually to the head.

Sometimes the Spiritual Current moves up like a snake. Going in a zigzag way, at last it reaches the head and I go into samadhi.

A man's spiritual consciousness is not awakened unless his Kundalini is aroused.

Just before my attaining this state of mind, it had been revealed to me how the Kundalini is aroused, how the lotuses of the different centers blossom forth, and how all this culminates in samadhi. This is a very secret experience. I saw a boy twenty-two or twenty-three years old, exactly resembling me, enter the Sushumna nerve and commune with the lotuses, touching them with his tongue. He began with the center at the anus and passed through the centers at the sexual organ, navel, and so on. The different lotuses of those centers—four-petalled, six-petalled, ten-petalled, and so forth—had been drooping. At his touch they stood erect.

When he reached the heart—I distinctly remember it—and communed with the lotus there, touching it with his tongue, the twelve-petalled lotus which was hanging head down, stood erect and opened its petals. Then he came to the sixteen-petalled lotus in the throat and the two-petalled lotus in the fore-head. And last of all, the thousand-petalled lotus in the head blossomed. Since then I have been in this state.[5]

The shopkeeper carefully puts the opened lotus—its innocent petals for the first time exposed to the morning sun—on top of the basket filled with Kali offerings. Then he attaches a couple of incense sticks to the side of the basket, lights them, and extinguishes the light with a sharp wave of his hand. A sweet smoke column of perfume rises into the tropical air.

Barefoot and flower basket in hand, one walks west toward the Ganges, passing the once elegant Kuthi on the right where Rani Rasmani, the foundress of the temple, stayed whenever she visited Dakshineswar. This mansion now looks run down and serves as the guardhouse. On the left is a long one-storied building. Wide steps lead up to its long veranda supported by large round pillars. Approximately in the middle of this building, and opposite the entrance to the Kuthi, is a majestic entrance that leads into the inner courtyard of the Kali temple. A couple of guards, who look rather friendly, stand next to the entrance and, lazily, watch throngs of people come and go. See figure 4 on page 18.

In a way, walking over cobblestones with bare feet does something to one's mind. One feels a bit like a child again; one feels very humble and devout; and one definitely becomes more aware of the ground, carefully avoiding little stones, bits of glass, and "brown gold." As it is called in India, "brown gold" is cow dung which is one of the commodities most sought after by the poor. It is collected, usually by a poor woman, as soon as it hits the ground. She will remove every bit of it, and with caring hands knead and form it into small cakes which resemble large hamburger patties. She will then stick these cakes onto a tree trunk,

---

[5] *The Gospel of Sri Ramakrishna*, pp. 829-830.

Figure 4. The Dakshineswar Kali Temple with the Natmandir in front and the Vishnu Temple visible behind.

house, or any other surface she can find and leave them there to bake in the sun. When they are dry, she will collect them and sell them in the market. Poor people use these cow-dung cakes for precious fuel. Cow dung gives them cooked food, tea, and warmth in winter. When one drives in the evening through lanes where poverty dwells, one gets a certain pleasant smell—like bread baking in the oven. And one doesn't turn up one's nose until told that this nice smell is produced by cow-dung burning in a garbage can lined with hardened mud—the poor man's clay oven.

A curious visitor may ask, "What, on earth, is cow dung doing in a temple, and how does it get there?" The answer is simple. Cows walk freely and undisturbed in and out of the Kali temple garden. They eat, sleep, and do whatever they want to do there. The cow is greatly revered in India. She is a symbol of the Divine Mother, a symbol of nurturing and peace.

The cow also is the eternal witness of Lord Krishna's love play with the Gopis, the shepherd girls of Vrindaban. Since the God Vishnu—in his Krishna incarnation—was a cowherd boy and loved cows, a true Hindu will never eat the meat of a cow. But aside from symbolism and religious belief, Hindus also revere the cow out of a sense of gratitude.

People in the West do not understand these feelings for a cow, a dumb animal that is taken for granted. Cattle, in Western consumer terms, are a commodity synonymous with steaks, milk and milk products. This is so because most people in the West no longer have an intimate knowledge of cows. Machines milk them, feed them, kill them, cut them into pieces, and neatly shrink-wrap and package these pieces so that they can be properly displayed in large freezer boxes in supermarkets.

The Hindu, on the other hand, is emotionally involved with the cow not only for religious reasons. This peaceful animal gives him so much; so he loves and honors it in return. In the country, farmers use the strength of bullocks to plough their land and in the city, the government uses cattle as a cheap lawn mower. When one travels through the Maidan, Calcutta's grand central park, one encounters cows grazing at various strategic places where grass had grown too tall.

The cow nourishes like a mother. She gives people milk to drink and to process into cheese and sweet butter. Even the cow's dung is beneficial. Aside from using it as fuel, people in the villages also use it to disinfect their houses. Mixing fresh cow dung with water and clay, women smear it on the walls and floor of the house. They say cow dung and cow urine have medicinal values and disinfect their houses. Do their houses smell bad? No, dried cow dung is odorless. And the cow still serves mankind when dead; its hide is tanned and worked into leather.

But most important of all, the cow's peaceful presence makes Hindus remember God. Still, people in the West have trouble understanding this "holy cow" concept. They say,

"There are people starving to death, yet Hindus won't kill cows and eat their meat to stay alive." Well, it is all a matter of attitude. A tradition that runs as deep as the Hindu reverence for the cow has its roots in mysticism.

Mysticism is always difficult to understand although the mystic's language is usually simple. Ordinary people cannot follow because they are on a different level of understanding, a level not deep enough to comprehend the subtlety of spirit. An ignorant Christian might call a Hindu barbaric for worshipping Kali, a Goddess who accepts animal sacrifice, and an ignorant Hindu might call a Christian barbaric for symbolically drinking the blood and eating the body of a God that hangs crucified on the cross. Neither has grasped the inner meaning of religion. When one worships mechanically, one only cheats oneself. Can one ever feel the excitement inherent in religion or taste the bliss of the mystic if one isn't involved in God heart and soul?

> *How are you trying, O my mind, to know the nature of*
> *God?*
> *You are groping like a madman locked in a dark room.*
> *He is grasped through ecstatic love; how can you fathom*
> *Him without it?*
> *Only through affirmation, never negation, can you know*
> *Him;*
> *Neither through Veda nor through Tantra nor the six*
> *darsanas.*
>
> *It is in love's elixir only that He delights, O mind;*
> *He dwells in the body's inmost depths, in everlasting Joy.*
> *And, for that love, the mighty yogis practice yoga from age*
> *to age;*
> *When love awakes, the Lord, like a magnet, draws to Him*
> *the soul.*

He it is, says Ramprasad, that I approach as Mother;
But must I give away the secret, here in the market place?
From the hints I have given, O mind, guess what that
   Being is![6]

In order to know God, Hindus practice sadhana (spiritual disciplines). Sadhana purifies the mind and gives the aspirant a taste for spiritual joy. With a pure mind, one can attain concentration, yoga, and unlimited power.

Sri Ramakrishna's mind was pure and childlike. He had completely surrendered his will to Ma Kali. He spoke as she bade him speak; he went where she wanted him to go. Later, it became evident to his disciples that Kali had become Ramakrishna, and Ramakrishna had become Kali. Her will and his had become one.

The significance of Mother worship to a real sadhaka (spiritual aspirant) is to feel that he and his universe are nothing but media for the manifestation of one all-pervading Power—the Power of God, the Power that is one with God. Not merely to understand intellectually, but to realize in each and every one of his cells that he lives and moves and has his being in the divine Power that is both immanent and transcendent. All spiritual endeavors of a true devotee of Shakti aim at the realization that his self, including his body, mind and spirit, is an instrument through which the great Mother produces the song of life—a song infinitely varied in tunes and melodies.[7]

---

[6] *The Gospel of Sri Ramakrishna*, p. 107.
[7] *Great Women of India*, pp. 79-80.

It is a hazy morning, and pilgrims crowd through the entrance into the inner courtyard of the Kali temple. Its large wooden doors are open during visiting hours, but when the temple closes during the afternoon siesta, these doors are locked. Only a square hole in the right door remains open all the time, and a determined pilgrim can bend down, squeeze through and get inside.

At last, offerings in hand, one stands in Kali's inner courtyard. Out of sheer awe and admiration one's voice automatically turns into a whisper—yet, there is nothing intimidating about the place. Standing at the entrance, one sees a sunny rectangular courtyard—440 feet long and 220 feet wide—enclosed on all sides by ornate buildings. The courtyard is paved with stone tiles set in concrete that have become smooth from wear. Many, many bare feet have walked over these stones, and the hooves of cows and water buffalo have also left their mark. One's feet feel pleasant, standing on the warm, smooth stone tiles in Kali's courtyard. During the hot season, these tiles get so heated that the feet of pilgrims would blister if temple officials did not create walkways of coarse cloth. See figure 5.

Here and there are flowers and petals strewn over the tiles, dropped by a careless pilgrim or intentionally put there in worship. Near the Shiva temples and the passage to the Ganges, poor women have spread their wet saris over the warm tiles so they may dry quickly. There are priests walking back and forth, and groups of female devotees, each carrying a basket filled with red hibiscus. An old saffron-robed holy man with matted hair leans on a staff while he slowly hobbles toward the northwestern corner of the courtyard.

In the middle of the courtyard are three white buildings. They resemble ornaments made of spun sugar on a wedding cake—white and lacy. The largest in the middle is a nine-spired temple, and one instinctively knows, this is the temple of Kali. The feeling one gets looking at the Kali Temple for the first time is awesome—sheer power and

Figure 5. The line of people waiting to see the Divine Mother Kali winds itself like a snake around the courtyard. Beyond the six Shiva temples in the back flows the serene Ganges.

strength. A vigorous presence radiates over the courtyard and the building itself seems alive with energy, seems to breathe and watch all who enter the courtyard below. Yet, it is not a raw, all-crushing masculine presence; one rather feels it as a capricious cosmic energy, full of flair and intense beauty.

The Kali Temple stands 50 feet square and 100 feet high. Wide, decorative frontal, side, and back steps lead up to a platform surrounding the inner sanctum. The platform allows pilgrims to circumambulate the deity, and, since many people have taken the opportunity to do so, these stone tiles also are smooth from the wear. The platform is wide enough to allow worshippers to stop for a while and pray. It is also wide enough for cows and goats to climb there in search of food although the privilege of their stay is usually of short duration. It lasts only until an irate servant chases them away, shouting, "Hatt, hatt, hatt."

One thin man in a white dhoti has put both his hands on the temple wall and loudly addresses the Mother, speaking to the temple as if it were a person. A family of four sings devotional songs to Kali, and an old woman chants Kali's name loudly as she circumambulates the inner sanctum. One young woman, heavy with child, worships the temple walls with vermilion. Muttering something—a mantra perhaps— she carefully smears the red powder over cracks that have seen plenty of vermilion before. Numerous incense sticks burn along the Kali Temple walls, and here and there, a wor- shipper has hung a marigold garland, some bel leaves and curious little earthen chips. Each chip represents a wish of a visiting pilgrim who has worshipped and propitiated Ma Kali. These walls—painted blood-red for approximately six feet above the platform—bear witness to joy and suffering, birth and death. To some, these outside temple walls are as holy as Kali herself.

The temple's main entrance is from the south since the image of Ma Kali faces south. For some reason, Hindus are very sensitive when it comes to the points of direction. For instance, during meditation they consider it more auspicious to face north or east for, they say, the energy flow is more favorable when one faces these points of direction.

Approaching the Mother: Bhavatarini Kali

If the day of the visit is a Saturday or Tuesday, pilgrims have to wait a long time to see the Divine Mother. A huge crowd lines up in front of Kali's temple, and it may take hours before one catches a glimpse of her. Saturdays and Tuesdays are favorite days of the Mother, and Shakti worshippers come even from distant places to pay their respects.

The line of worshippers wanting to see the Divine Mother Kali today is long and winds itself around the courtyard like a snake. It extends as far as the Shiva temples. Pilgrims patiently wait in the hot sun, each holding a basket of offerings and a garland of red hibiscus flowers. A few have brought black umbrellas and stand in the small round space of shade. Farther on down the line stands a young woman, her hand tightly gripping a naughty-looking boy. Right behind her stand a few girls. They are quite young, and whispering into each other's ears, they giggle loudly, to the dismay of two widows irately watching them. In India, one can tell people's social position by looking at their dress. A widow, for instance, wears white and has no vermilion mark on her forehead.

Dressed in white dhotis and identical looking checkered shirts, several thin men stand very close behind each other. In anticipation, their bony bodies slightly push the people in front, but they don't budge an inch.

It is getting hot, and the sun's strong rays beat down on the tiles of the courtyard. The pilgrims have been standing on the same spot for a long time, and the line of people waiting to see Ma Kali hardly seems to move. Although one's mouth is parched and the feeling of thirst is terrible, one cannot leave one's place in the line lest one would lose it. So, there is nothing else to do but grin and bear it. See figure 6 on page 26.

An old woman in a white sari stands a little farther off in the line. Supporting herself with great effort on a stick, she stands in the hot sun—quietly, without complaint. She must be hot and thirsty and, standing all this time, her bent legs must be giving her a lot of trouble. But whenever her face shows the agony of the body, she closes her eyes and repeats

Figure 6. Devotees, offerings in hand, patiently stand in line for hours to get a glimpse of the Divine Mother Kali.

the name of the Divine Mother Kali. What devotion! Watching this old woman's struggle to see Ma Kali, one's own thirst vanishes and, reluctantly, one relaxes into the extreme heat, the proximity of so many bodies, and into time. The old woman has become a role model. Her steadfastness and renunciation is, at least, sufficient for two. Sri Ramakrishna said in this respect:

> Let me tell you a story about strong renunciation. At one time there was a drought in a certain part of the country. The farmers began to cut along chan- nels to bring water to their fields. One farmer was stubbornly determined. He took a vow that he would not stop digging until the channel connected his field with the river. He set to work. The time

came for his bath, and his wife sent their daughter to him with oil. "Father," said the girl, "it is already late. Rub your body with oil and take your bath." "Go away!" thundered the farmer. "I have too much to do now." It was past midday, and the farmer was still at work in his field. He didn't even think of his bath. Then his wife came and said: "Why haven't you taken your bath? The food is getting cold. You overdo everything. You can finish the rest tomorrow or even today after dinner." The farmer scolded her furiously and ran at her, spade in hand, crying: "What? Have you no sense? There's no rain. The crops are dying. What will the children eat? You'll all starve to death. I have taken a vow not to think of bath and food today before I bring water to my field." The wife saw his state of mind and ran away in fear. Through a whole day's back-breaking labor the farmer managed by evening to connect his field with the river. Then he sat down and watched the water flowing into his field with a murmuring sound. His mind was filled with peace and joy. He went home, called his wife, and said to her, "Now give me some oil and prepare me a smoke." With serene mind he finished his bath and meal, and retired to bed, where he snored to his heart's content. The determination he showed is an example of strong renunciation.

Now, there was another farmer who was also digging a channel to bring water to his field. His wife, too, came to the field and said to him: "It's very late. Come home. It isn't necessary to overdo things." The farmer didn't protest much, but put aside his spade and said to his wife, "Well, I'll go home since you ask me to." (All laugh.) That man never succeeded in irrigating his field. This is a case of mild renunciation.

As without strong determination the farmer cannot bring water to his field, so also without intense
yearning a man cannot realize God.[8]

As the line creeps forward and pilgrims reach the steps
to the Kali Temple, they humbly bend down and touch the
ground with their right hands. See Figure 7. Then, with a
sweeping motion, they touch the crown of the head. This is
called "taking the holy dust." When Hindus visit a deity, a
holy person, an elder or any person of respect, they will take
the dust off the feet in reverence and symbolically put it on
their head. Aside from being the customary way of showing respect, this courtesy is considered to be a great blessing. Children "take the dust off the feet" of their parents,
students "take the dust off the feet" of their teacher, and
younger brothers "take the dust off the feet" of their older
brothers.

As one climbs the broad steps and reaches the platform
of the Kali Temple, the line of pilgrims divides—men go to
the left and around the temple and women to the right
toward the front entrance. With respect to the feelings of
bashful women, Hindus do not like that men should crowd
women. During rush hour in Calcutta, they even established
a "ladies only" car and a special section on trams and buses.

All this sounds very orderly but it really isn't. People
are getting excited now and are starting to push. They have
forgotten the heat and the long wait. They know that there
are only a few more feet left to go, and then they will see the
Divine Mother Kali. In a way, this general excitement of the
impatient crowd is electrifying and, instead of worrying
about being trampled, one feels stimulated and somewhat
wild. Shouts from the crowd echo in one's ears as one is
pushed along by the masses of brown bodies. One cannot
display a will of one's own; the pushing crowd determines

---

[8] *The Gospel of Sri Ramakrishna*, p. 166.

Figure 7. As if they were the feet of the Great Mother Herself, a devotee reverently touches the steps leading to the Kali Temple.

which direction one goes. Like a drifter in a boat, one floats amid the crowd—not quite sure what will happen after the next river bend. See figure 8 on page 30.

The closer one gets to the inner shrine, the louder one hears throaty shouts that echo from within the temple.

"Ma, oh Ma, Ma go Ma! Jai Kali! Jai Kali Ma! Jai Ma Bhavatarini ji ki jai!"

One also hears the loud clanking of a bell that rings in spurts. Yet, one still can't see anything in front besides heads and raised arms.

The front entrance to the Kali shrine has three arched passageways. Because the middle one is blocked, worshippers enter and exit at both sides. Today, it is very crowded, and instead of just entering through the passageway, one is

Figure 8. The closer one gets to the sanctum, the denser gets the crowd. In their excitement, people push towards the front entrance to the Kali Temple.

shoved through. Cold sweat stands on the forehead as one suddenly finds oneself inside a cool covered veranda. It's quite cool although there is no visible air-conditioning system.

Toward the left, suspended from the ceiling, hangs a big brass bell. Every other pilgrim who is pushed past, reaches up and clanks it as loudly as possible at least a couple of times. Parents hold up their children to give them also a chance to clank the bell and thereby proclaim to Ma Kali that they have arrived, that they exist.

Countless bare feet shuffle over the cool, smooth marble tiles. Occasionally one steps on something slippery and wonders what it is. Perhaps it's a flower, spilled water, something indefinable that is better not to know. Whatever it is, one will never know because there is no chance to see the ground. There are too many bodies, pushing, pressing, and crowding like moths in the night toward a light that is still a little farther off.

Everyone's focus is on the lighted entrance in the middle of the covered veranda. A cast-iron gate prevents people from entering, so they crowd before it, half hanging over it, trying to get a little closer inside. Some people kneel, reach through the gate and touch the ground within the sanctum. Immediately behind the gate stand two priests keeping watch. Their white dhotis bear the marks of their profession—red sandalwood paste, vermilion and flower stains. Their foreheads are marked with large vertical lines of vermilion, the signs of a male Shakti worshipper—women wear large vermilion dots.

Pilgrims hand their baskets of offerings to attending priests, who take the hibiscus garlands and expertly fling them into the lighted inner sanctum at Mother Kali's feet. Basket in hand, each priest disappears inside, utters some mantras[9] over the basket and offers it to Mother Kali with reverence. A few sweets from each basket stay with Ma Kali in a box next to the altar, the rest of the offerings, together with flowers taken from the altar, are returned to the pilgrim. These returned offerings are called prasad and considered a great blessing. God has taken the first bite— eaten the subtle essence of the food—and the devotee, swallowing the gross elements of the food, takes the second. See figure 9 on page 32.

Anxiety has reached a fever pitch, and the short distance from the arched passageway to the lighted inner sanctum seems to take forever. But when one finally stands before

---

[9] Sacred words or verse; a particular name of God given by the guru to his disciple during initiation. The mantra, regarded as one with God, represents the essence of the guru's instruction to the disciple who is enjoined to keep it sacred and secret. Repetition of the mantra, performed regularly and reverently, results in purification of the mind.

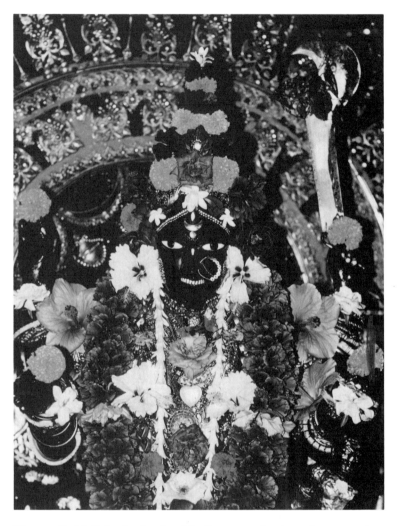

Figure 9. Kali bedecked with flowers during the morning worship.

Kali, time seems to stand still. Everything stops. The people, the noise—all is mysteriously gone. One stares with wide eyes, forgetting even to blink. All one sees is Kali and nothing else. Overwhelmed with feeling one whispers, "I love you." And from within she replies, "You do so much more for I am the source of your being!"

Chapter 2

KALI, THE BLACK GODDESS OF DAKSHINESWAR

She *is all beauty —*
this woman nude and terrible and black,
who tells the name of God
on the skulls of the dead,
who creates the bloodshed on which demons fatten,
who slays rejoicing and repents not,
and blesses him only that lies crushed beneath Her feet.
Her mass of black hair
flows behind Her like the wind,
or like time "the drift and passage of things."
She is blue almost to blackness,
like a mighty shadow,
and bare like the dread realities of life and death.[1]

---

[1] Sister Nivedita, *Kali the Mother* (Calcutta: Advaita Ashrama, 1986), p. 35.

Worship of the Terrible Mother

The scene for true Kali worship takes place in a cremation ground where the air is smoke-laden and little specks of ash from burning funeral pyres fall on white, sun-dried bones scattered about and on fragments of flesh, gnawed and pecked at by carrion beasts and large black birds. A frightful place for most, but a favorite one for the "heroic" Mother worshipper who has burnt away all worldly desires and seeks nothing but union with her. This kind of devotee fears nothing and knows no aversion.

But prone to human emotions, the majority of people are terrified by Kali's awe-inspiring grandeur, back-lit by the fires in the cremation ground. They would much rather worship her in a less threatening place, where stark reality is a symbol rather than the harsh truth. So they flock to temples, worship Kali at roadside shrines or in their own homes. They pray to the Divine Mother to grant them the boon of a child, money to feed the mouths of a hungry family, to grant them devotion and liberation from an existence in misery. "Ma, Ma, Ma go Ma; daya karun; kripa karun." Mother, oh Mother, give me your grace, give me your compassion.

The beauty of the Dakshineswar Kali Temple is far removed from the dreary sight of an active cremation ground. And although the Goddess in this temple is the same Ma Kali as the feared one in the cremation ground, she is regarded as benign—a protectress rather than a destroyer.

How does the Hindu determine whether an image of Kali is benign or fearful? While someone unfamiliar with Shakti worship may perceive all Kali images as equally terrible without making the slightest distinction between them, the Hindu distinguishes a benign (dakshina[2]) from a fearful

---

[2] *Dakshina* translated means an act of gift-giving, especially to a priest for performing a sacrificial ritual.

Figure 10. Shiva never takes his eyes off Kali standing over his heart on his chest.

(smashan) Kali by the position of her feet. If Kali steps out with her right foot and holds the sword in her left hand, she is a Dakshina Kali. And if she steps out with her left foot and holds the sword in her right hand, she is the terrible form of the Mother, the Smashan Kali of the cremation ground. See figure 10.

Now the question arises, why would anyone want to worship the terrible Mother of the cremation ground? According to Tantrics,[3] one's spiritual disciplines practiced in a cremation ground bring success quickly. Sitting next to corpses and other images of death, one is able to transcend the "pair of opposites" (i.e., good-bad, love-hate, etc.) much faster than another who blocks out the unpleasant aspects of life. The cremation ground's ghastly images arouse instant renunciation in the mind and help the Tantric to get rid of attachment for the body.

---

[3] Followers of Tantra.

Actually, to overcome one's attachment is not as difficult as mastering one's aversions. With a bit of discipline and willpower most people can renounce their attractions and desires, but only a rare few can ever overcome their aversions. To conquer both and thereby achieve same-sightedness, Tantrics practice the most extreme esoteric sadhanas. Some of their more gruesome methods include the tasting of excreta and the eating of flesh from a burning corpse.

One of the first things to occur when one tries to understand Tantra, is one's realization of how much Western views on life differ from Indian thought on the subject—in general. In India, the goal of life is God, and the person who has achieved realization of God is the most highly regarded. Kings, queens, and prime ministers bow down to such a person. But in the West, people measure the success of a person's life by his or her worldly achievements. The richest and most famous people are regarded most highly by the rest of society. This fundamental difference in attitude toward the goal of one's life between the West and East has often caused an unfortunate communication gap.

Kali is perhaps one of the most misunderstood forms of God. The ordinary Western mind perceives Kali as hideous and absurd, forgetting that some of the symbols of Western faiths have the same effect on the Hindu. While Christians believe in a God that is all good and a devil that is all bad, Hindus believe in only one Universal Power which is beyond good and bad. To explain this concept, they give the example of fire. The same fire that cooks one's food can burn down one's house. Still, can one call fire good or bad?

Kali is the full picture of the Universal Power. She is Mother, the Benign, and Mother, the Terrible. She creates and nourishes and she kills and destroys. By Her magic we see good and bad, but in reality there is neither. This whole world and all we see is the play of Maya, the veiling power of the Divine Mother. God is neither good nor bad, nor both. God is beyond the pair of opposites which constitute this relative existence.

The Tantras mention over thirty forms of Kali. Sri Ramakrishna often spoke about Kali's different forms. He said:

> The Divine Mother is known as Maha Kali, Nitya Kali, Smashana Kali, Raksha Kali, and Shyama Kali. Maha Kali and Nitya Kali are mentioned in the Tantra philosophy. When there were neither the creation, nor the sun, the moon, the planets, and the earth, and when darkness was enveloped in darkness, then the Mother, the Formless One, Maha Kali, the Great Power, was one with Maha Kala, the Absolute.
>
> Shyama Kali has a somewhat tender aspect and is worshipped in the Hindu households. She is the dispenser of boons and the dispeller of fear. People worship Raksha Kali, the Protectress, in times of epidemic, famine, earthquake, drought, and flood. Smashana Kali is the embodiment of the power of destruction. She resides in the cremation ground, surrounded by corpses, jackals and terrible female spirits. From her mouth flows a stream of blood, from her neck hangs a garland of human heads, and around her waist is a girdle made of human arms.[4]

Tantrics worship Siddha Kali to attain perfection; Phalaharini Kali to destroy the results of their actions; Nitya Kali, the eternal Kali, to take away their disease, grief, and suffering, and to give them perfection and illumination. There are so many forms of Kali. In fact, each district, town, and village in Bengal seems to have its very own Kali, famous for a particular miracle or incident.

---

[4] *The Gospel of Sri Ramakrishna*, p. 135.

Even robbers and thieves have their own Kali. Not so many years ago, robbers lived in Indian woods who had the habit of worshipping Dakait Kali[5] before they went to rob people on highways and in villages. Some of these old Kali images have survived time and are still being worshipped, though for other reasons than originally intended. For instance, a famous old Dakait Kali temple in South Calcutta draws pious pilgrims from all over Bengal.

Kali's Symbols

The name:	*Kali* comes from the word "kala," or time. She is the power of time which devours all. See figure 11 on page 42.
The setting:	A power that destroys should be depicted in terms of awe-inspiring terror. Kali is found in the cremation ground amid dead bodies. She is standing in a challenging posture on the prostrate body of her husband Shiva. Kali cannot exist without him, and Shiva cannot reveal himself without her. She is the manifestation of Shiva's power, energy.
Complexion:	While Shiva's complexion is pure white, Kali is the color of the darkest night—a deep bluish black. As the limitless Void, Kali has swallowed up everything without a trace. Hence she is black.
Hair:	Her luxuriant hair is dishevelled and, thereby, symbolizes Kali's boundless freedom. Another interpretation says that each hair is a jiva (individual soul), and all souls have their roots in Kali.

---

[5] Robber's Kali.

Figure 11. Smashan Kali, with Her left foot forward, dances Her dance of destruction. The Holy Mother, Sri Ramakrishna's wife, worshipped this image of Kali. This picture is still being worshipped in Holy Mother's room at the Udbodhan Office, Calcutta.

Eyes: She has three eyes; the third one stands for wisdom.

Tongue: Her tongue is protruding, a gesture of coyness—because she unwittingly stepped on the body of her husband Shiva. A more philosophical interpretation: Kali's tongue, symbolizing rajas (the color red, activity), is held by her teeth, symbolizing sattva (the color white, spirituality).

Arms: Kali has four arms. The posture of her right arms promises fearlessness and boons while her left arms hold a bloody sword and a freshly severed, bleeding human head. Looking at Kali's right, we see good, and looking at her left, we see bad.

Dress: Kali is naked (clad in space) except for a girdle of human arms cut off at the elbow and a garland of fifty skulls. The arms represent the capacity for work, and Kali wears all work (action), potential work, and the results thereof around her waist. The fifty skulls that make up her garland represent the fifty letters of the alphabet, the manifest state of sound from which all creation evolved.

One should not jump to the conclusion that Kali represents only the destructive aspect of God's power. What exists when time is transcended, the eternal night of limitless peace and joy, is also called Kali (Maharatri). And it is she who prods Shiva Mahadeva into the next cycle of creation. In short, she is the power of God in all His aspects.[6]

---

[6] Swami Harshananda, *Hindu Gods and Goddesses* (Mysore: Ramakrishna Ashrama, 1981), p. 147.

Kali, the Black
Goddess of Dakshineswar

The image of Kali in Dakshineswar has the name
"Bhavatarini"—Mother, who is the Savior of the World.
Although everybody calls her by this name now, nobody
knows who gave it to her and when. Rani Rasmani, the
builder of the temple, signed a Deed of Trust in 1861 in which
Kali's name was recorded as "Sri Sri Jagadiswari Mahakali."
It is possible that Sri Ramakrishna gave her the name
"Bhavatarini" at a later time; though, such an incident was
never recorded by his biographers.

They say that this Mother Kali fulfills all the desires of
her children, be they material wealth or spiritual liberation.
If people pray to her earnestly, the Divine Mother Kali cannot
withhold anything from them. She gave all knowledge and
all power to Sri Ramakrishna. As he tells in his own words:

> I wept before the Mother and prayed. "O Mother,
> please tell me, please reveal to me, what the yogis
> have realized through yoga and the jnanis through
> discrimination." And the Mother has revealed
> everything to me. She reveals everything if the
> devotee cries to Her with a yearning heart. She has
> shown me everything that is in the Vedas, the
> Vedanta, the Puranas, and the Tantra."[7]

When one stands inside Kali's shrine in Dakshineswar,
it is not hard to picture Sri Ramakrishna sitting cross-legged
on the floor, communing intimately with the Divine Mother.
Then one suddenly becomes aware that one stands on the
same floor, sees the same altar and the same image that he
worshipped. And then one feels overwhelmed by a timeless
proximity of a certain sweetness that seizes one's heart.

---

[7] *The Gospel of Sri Ramakrishna*, p. 579.

In comparison to the grand size of the entire Kali temple, Mother's inner shrine is rather small and measures only 15 × 15 feet. The sanctum has blue-tiled walls which bounce off a strong electric light that shines from the ceiling. Standing amid this harsh brilliance, the basalt image of Kali casts no shadows—for they say, God casts no shadows.

Nothing one sees reminds a Western seeker of the places one associates with religion. There is none of the sterile cleanliness of a Western church, no starched robes of priests, and certainly no hushed silence. Instead one sees a sanctum which could be termed neither dirty nor clean. One best calls it active with life. Its animate presence so completely fills the moment in one's mind that it is hard to think of the past, future, or anything else.

Priests in white dhotis[8] and panjabis[9] move busily about. The pujari[10] has climbed up on the steps to the right of the altar and is fastening a lotus onto Ma Kali's right foot. His upper body is bare, and the sacred thread, which all male Brahmins are required to wear, is visible across his shoulder and back. He has bushy black hair and his upper arms and chest bear red sandalwood markings.

The loud, high-pitched voice of an elderly woman echoes within the shrine. Dressed in a white sari, the woman leans over the gate at the front entrance as far as possible, stretching both hands toward Kali. She cries and prays loudly to Ma Kali without a trace of restraint. As far as she is concerned, nothing can hold back her anguished spirit from being heard by the Divine Mother Kali.

The sanctum's marble floor is stained with vermillion, and red hibiscus flowers that have dropped from priests' hands lie here and there. Also strewn about are little iron bracelets, coins and incense sticks—all items thrown from

---

[8] Four yards of cloth wrapped around the waist.
[9] Indian shirt.
[10] Priest.

Figure 12. The inner shrine of Kali in Dakshineswar. It is the same shrine in which Sri Ramakrishna so fervently loved and worshipped God, the Divine Mother. The structure of the shrine is made of silver and so is the lotus on which the image stands. The shrine sits atop an altar, called the bedi, which basically consists of a couple of wide steps. Today, pictures of Sri Ramakrishna and Sri Sarada Ma have been added to the images of Gods and Goddesses residing on the altar. (Photo by Gandhi Roy.)

the outside toward Ma Kali by eager devotees. When the floor space gets too cluttered, a servant comes around, picks up the money, and with a soft broom sweeps all else into the right corner of the sanctum where a small mountain of flowers has already accumulated.

The smells of incense, burning ghee (clarified butter) and flowers, fresh as well as decaying, enter the pilgrim's nostrils, and his ears are full of the sound of gongs, bells, and shouts of an excited crowd. While one's senses take in impressions like a camera with a wide open shutter, one's mind is choked as it were by an indescribable feeling of awe for the Great Mother Goddess in the middle of the holy chamber. See figure 12.

Kali's complexion is black—a shiny black which starkly contrasts with the red lustre of her tongue, palms of her hands and soles of her feet. Her blackness is, at once, strange and familiar. Why is Kali black? It is written in the Mahanirvana Tantra, "Just as all colors disappear in black so all names and forms disappear in Kali." Sri Ramakrishna put the same truth into more colloquial terms:

> You see her as black because you are far away from her. Go near and you will find her devoid of all color. The water of a lake appears black from a distance. Go near and take the water in your hand, and you will see that it has no color at all. Similarly, the sky looks blue from a distance. But look at the atmosphere near you; it has no color. The nearer you come to God, the more you will realize that he has neither name nor form. If you move away from the Divine Mother, you will find her blue, like the grass-flower. Is Shyama male or female? A man once saw the image of the Divine Mother wearing a sacred thread.[11] He said to the worshipper: "What?

---

[11] The images of male deities only are invested with the sacred thread.

You have put the sacred thread around the Mother's neck!" The worshipper said: "Brother, I see that you have truly known the Mother. But I have not yet been able to find out whether she is male or female; that is why I have put the sacred thread on her image."[12]

A priest at the Dakshineswar Kali Temple explains Kali's blackness: "The Devi's complexion changed out of sheer wrath when she heard about the tyranny of the asuras over the Gods. Another interpretation is that she absorbs everything through the process of destruction. She absorbs vices such as hatred, malice, treachery, deceit, anger, passion, etc. Kali's black color means that she is inscrutable and cannot be known by worldly people full of ignorance. Darkness stands for ignorance."

> In dense darkness, O Mother, Thy formless beauty sparkles;
> Therefore the yogis meditate in a dark mountain cave.
> In the lap of boundless dark, on Mahanirvana's waves
>   upborne,
> Peace flows serene and inexhaustible.
> Taking the form of the Void, in the robe of darkness
>   wrapped,
> Who art Thou, Mother, seated alone in the shrine of
>   samadhi?
> From the Lotus of Thy fear-scattering Feet flash Thy love's
>   lightnings;
> Thy Spirit-Face shines forth with laughter terrible and
>   loud![13]

Defiant with vibrant energy, Kali's full-breasted, youthful figure strides forward on the prostrate body of her divine husband Shiva—her right foot on his chest and the left one

---

[12] *The Gospel of Sri Ramakrishna*, p. 271.
[13] *The Gospel of Sri Ramakrishna*, p. 692.

on his right thigh. Shiva lies motionless under her feet, stark nude and very white. His large, serene eyes look up and behold Kali—steady and eternally. Like the yin and yang, Kali and Shiva are one, yet harmoniously different.

Nude and dark, the blissful Divine Mother stands on the white bosom of the blissful Divine Father. Creation is not possible without bliss. Joy never comes from matter. Can anything material ever substitute for the bliss Kali and Shiva experience in their eternal union? Joy comes from the spirit. Kali is the ever-blissful Divine Mother, who gives joy to her divine spouse and to us, her divine children.

The vicinity of Shiva, her divine consort, arouses Kali's excitement. She begins to move and the three gunas[14] begin to agitate rhythmically, creating and destroying. There is rhythm in creation, and there is rhythm in destruction. And it is all done in bliss. Mother loves to play the game of life and death, but once in a while, she stops and releases a soul or two, liberating them from karma and reincarnation. And then she laughs and claps her hands.

Kali is both real and symbolic. But what she is in herself cannot be described. She can only be known through her grace. Kali is self-illumined and beyond the human mind to comprehend. None knows her Supreme Form. Sings Ramprasad, the famous Kali mystic:

Who is there that can understand what Mother Kali is?
Even the six darshanas[15] are unable to describe Her.
It is She, the scriptures say, that is the Inner Self
Of the yogi, who in Self discovers all his joy;
She that, of Her own sweet will, inhabits every living thing.

The macrocosm and microcosm rest in the Mother's womb;
Now do you see how vast it is? In the Muladhara

---

[14] The concept of the gunas is explained in Part 1.
[15] Six major philosophies— samkhya, yoga, nyaya, vaishesika, mimamsa, and vedanta.

The yogi meditates on Her, and in the Sahasrara,
Who but Shiva has beheld Her as She really is?
Within the lotus wilderness She sports beside Her mate,
*   the Swan.*

When man aspires to understand Her, Ramprasad must
*   smile;*
To think of knowing Her, he says, is quite as laughable
As to imagine one can swim across the boundless sea.
But while my mind has understood, alas! my heart has not;
Though but a dwarf, it still would strive to make a captive
*   of the moon.*[16]

For the one she chooses, Kali is an experience, an over-whelming experience. She exists as Kundalini, and like light-ning, she reveals the Great Power. She is the experience; she is the bliss; and she is the giver of bliss. While she can be felt, she can never be defined because to define her would be to limit the Infinite by fitting it according to one's own per-sonality. Kali is infinite and present at all times and at every place. Sri Ramakrishna described his experience of Cosmic Consciousness, thus:

> The Divine Mother revealed to me in the Kali temple that it was she who had become everything. She showed me that everything was full of Consciousness. The image was Consciousness, the altar was Consciousness, the water vessels were Consciousness, the door-sill was Consciousness, the marble floor was Consciousness—all was Consciousness.
>
> I found everything inside the room soaked, as it were, in Bliss—the Bliss of Satchidananda. I saw a

[16] *The Gospel of Sri Ramakrishna*, p. 106.

wicked man in front of the Kali temple, but in him also I saw the Power of the Divine Mother vibrating.

That was why I fed a cat with the food that was to be offered to the Divine Mother. I clearly perceived that the Divine Mother herself had become every-thing—even the cat. The manager of the temple gar-den wrote to Mathur Babu saying that I was feeding the cat with the offering intended for the Divine Mother. But Mathur Babu had insight into the state of my mind. He wrote back to the manager: "Let him do whatever he likes. You must not say any-thing to him."[17]

That which is Brahman is verily Shakti. I address That, again, as the Mother. I call It Brahman when It is inactive, and Shakti when It creates, preserves and destroys. It is like water, sometimes still and sometimes covered with waves.[18]

Shiva, in the Dakshineswar Kali Temple, lies on a "thou-sand-petalled" silver lotus which blooms atop an altar of stone with steps to the front, right and left. This altar is called the "vedi." It has twelve columns made of silver which stand around the holy image of Kali. A costly canopy and a silver cornice hang above the altar. Behind the image of Kali is a decorative silver framework that resembles a burst of light-ning, and behind that is a luxuriously embroidered brocade curtain in which priests hide incense and other offerings used for worship.

The priests had dressed Ma Kali in a red Varanasi silk sari with lavish gold embroidery. Although they dressed the image, they can never dress Kali herself. She is Digambari,

---

[17]*The Gospel of Sri Ramakrishna*, p. 345.
[18] *The Gospel of Sri Ramakrishna*, p. 283.

She who is Naked, She who is clothed in Infinite Space. Kali, the Great Power, is unlimited and can never be contained by anything. She encompasses all but nothing can encompass her. North, east, west, south, up and down—each point of direction has a different deity. But Kali is everywhere.

> She is naked and dark like a threatening rain cloud. She is dark, for she who is herself beyond mind and speech, reduces all things into that worldly "noth-ingness" which as the Void of all which we now know, is at the same time the All (purna) which is Light and Peace. . . . She stands upon the white corpse-like body of Shiva. He is white because He is the illuminating transcendental aspect of Consciousness. He is inert because he is the change-less aspect of the Supreme, and she the apparently changing aspect of the same. In truth, she and he are one and the same, being twin aspects of the One who is changelessness in, and exists as, change.[19]

Kali wears golden anklets, called nupur, which contain little rattles inside. They tinkle every time a priest touches her feet to offer scarlet jaba (hibiscus) and fresh bel leaves, made fragrant with sandal paste.

The actual image of Ma Kali is only thirty-three-and-a-half inches high, yet she appears much taller. Although her golden crown, decorated with countless tropical flowers, adds quite a few inches, it is mostly the emotional impact and awe she creates within the onlooker that magnifies her size substantially.

She is full of majesty. Her posture strangely combines the terror of destruction with the reassurance of motherly love. She is the Cosmic Power, the complete picture. Nothing

---

[19] Sir John Woodroffe, *The Garland of Letters* (Madras: Ganesh & Company, 1985), p. 237.

is missing. All good (symbolized by her right side) and all bad (symbolized by her left side) is within her. She deals out death and terror while she offers fearlessness and boons to her devotees. A glorious harmony of opposites. She is all— energy and power.

Ma Kali looks alive and seems to be listening to the devotees at the front gate. "Ma, Ma go Ma!" they shout, each one trying to outdo the other—like children pulling their mother's skirt in order to get her attention.

Kali is a living Goddess. Once Sri Ramakrishna wanted to check whether the stone image of Kali in Dakshineswar was alive and tested the air under her nostrils. He held a piece of cotton under her nose and found that she breathed into his hand.

Kali has four arms, and each one is adorned with many ornaments made of gold and jewels. Around her wrist jingle bracelets—golden ones, red ones, and some made of conch shell. She has raised her upper right arm and, with this gesture, grants fearlessness to her devotees. Her lower right arm bestows boons. While her right two arms deal out good things, her left two arms threaten. Raised above her head, her upper left arm holds a blood-stained sword, and her lower left one tightly grips a freshly severed human head by its hair.

Golden chains glitter around her waist. Unlike other Kali images, the Kali image in Dakshineswar does not wear a terrible girdle made of severed demons' arms around her hips. The foundress of the temple garden looked upon Kali as Kumari (virgin) and didn't like the idea of demons' hands on her body. Hands are the principal instrument of work, and this girdle of cut-off hands worn by most Kali images represents human action as well as its resulting karma that has been taken back by Kali. At the close of a time cycle, all these merge back into the Great Mother.

Kali's ears are adorned with golden earrings that look like flowers, but upon closer view turn out to be small embryos. All life is Kali's. She gives it and takes it. The Devi says, "It is I who create the whole world and enter therein with prana, maya, and karma."

Attached to the left nostril of her beautiful, slightly arched nose is a golden nose ring with a pearl drop. Kali has three eyes. Between the two large eyes on her forehead is a third one which symbolizes Divine Wisdom. This eye sees all and knows all—past, present, and future.

Around Kali's neck are numerous necklaces. There is the golden cheke,[20] a golden necklace of thirty-two strings, a "chain of stars," various pendants inlaid with precious stones, and a gruesome garland of fifty human skulls. This garland is called the "varnamala."[21] Each skull represents a letter of the alphabet.

The Garland of Letters illustrates this universe of names and forms, that is, speech (sabda) and its meaning or object (artha). Each letter is called an "akshara," which translated means "that which undergoes no change." Combinations of these aksharas become words which are expressed through the mouth. Each akshara has a male and female deity, and through the union of the two, creation evolves. Kali devours all and withdraws both into her undivided Consciousness at the time of dissolution. She wears the letters which she as a creatrix bore and then devours them again when she pleases.

> Indo-European languages branched from the root of Sanskrit, said to be Kali's invention. She created the magic letters of the Sanskrit alphabet and inscribed them on the rosary of skulls around her neck.[22] The letters were magic because they stood for primordial creative energy expressed in sound—Kali's mantras brought into being the very things whose

---

[20] A pearl necklace of seven strings.
[21] *The Garland of Letters*.
[22] Robert Graves, *The White Goddess* (New York: Vintage Books, 1958), p. 250.

names she spoke for the first time, in her holy language. In short, Kali's worshippers originated the doctrine of the Logos or creative Word, which Christians later adopted and pretended it was their own idea.[23]

Kali is Sound, the sound that created this universe. All knowledge is embedded in it. Name and form changes, but sound remains. Within ordinary human beings, three fourths of this sound remains unmanifested, and the only audible part is the gross sound, manifested daily through our mouths. But yogis can also hear the hidden sound, the transcendental sound.

Somehow, there is an irony in the fact that we verbally pray to her to listen to our needs when Kali, herself, is Sound. "Ma, if I express through my mouth, then only will you hear?" Sri Ramakrishna used to cry. "Don't you see into my heart what an agony is going on in there? My mind is panting for you. Ma, don't you hear there?"

Ma Kali's tongue protrudes and blood trickles slowly from the sides of her mouth. Some say Ma Kali sticks out her tongue because she is shy like a village girl. People tell a story how she, thinking him a corpse, unwittingly stepped on her husband's body during the war against the demons, and at the moment of recognition, she recoiled and bashfully stuck out her tongue. Another, more philosophical, explanation says that Kali, through the tongue, is expressing sound and is thereby creating the universe.

And still another interpretation says that Kali's white teeth stand for the white sattva guna, her red tongue stands for the red raja guna, and her black skin stands for delusion which is associated with the tama guna. Kali stretches out her tongue because she wants to conquer her devotees' tama guna by increasing their raja guna. And then she

---

[23] Barbara G. Walker, *The Woman's Encyclopedia of Myths and Secrets*, (San Francisco: Harper Collins, 1983), p. 491.

conquers their raja guna by cutting it with her large white teeth. Through the sattva guna, she leads her devotees toward salvation.

◆ ◆ ◆

There is a lot of noise in the small shrine. Devotees shout, priests shout. "Ma, oh Ma, Ma go Ma!" Attending priests keep flinging so many hibiscus garlands at Ma Kali's feet that Shiva is barely visible. Actually, Kali, also, wears so many flower garlands that it's hard to see her body beneath. Most visitors to the Kali temple rarely ever see the Garland of Skulls because she is so covered with fresh flowers.

On the steps of the altar stand vessels which hold her drinking water, and on the large silver lotus next to the image of Shiva is a small lion made of eight metals, a poisonous gosap (snake) and Shiva's trident. On Kali's left side, next to the silver lotus on the upper step, stands the image of a jackal. The animal's head is tilted upward as if preparing to howl. Staring at Kali in adoration, blood drips out of its slightly open mouth. Also on the upper step but facing front is a small silver throne which holds Ramlala—the boy Ramachandra—made of precious metals. To the left of Ramlala is the image of a black bull. This is Nandi, Shiva's carrier.

Facing front on the altar's upper step is a large photograph of Sri Ramakrishna. Its frame leans against the silver column on Kali's right. Sri Ramakrishna's photo has been decorated with white sandalwood paste and tulsi leaves and is surrounded with a thick flower garland. On the other side of the same step, leaning against the silver column to Kali's left, is a large photograph of Sri Sarada Devi, wife and spiritual consort of Sri Ramakrishna. It also has been decorated with red sandalwood paste and a scented flower garland.

On the altar's lower step, to the side of Sri Ramakrishna's photograph, is a magnificent large shell. It is used to invoke and worship the Goddess Lakshmi, the Goddess of fortune. Priests pour Ganges water into the shell's large mouth and then invoke the Goddess Lakshmi into it. On the same step, but facing front, is Ma Chandi—a copy of the Tantra scripture wrapped in a red cloth. A little farther over is a golden box containing a holy shalagram[24] and a Shiva linga[25] called Baneswar. Next to the golden box, below the photo of Sri Sarada Ma, is a colorful image of Ganesha, the elephant God, whom Hindus consider to be the God of success.

The altar steps on either side are used by priests who climb up to attend to Ma Kali. In great reverence, they stand or kneel on these steps when they need to get close to worship her with various articles or when they need to exchange her fading flowers with fresh ones.

On the marble floor in front of the altar is a clay pitcher filled with Ganges water, which is used in ritual worship. This pitcher is called mangal-ghata and is rarely visible since it is almost always completely covered with garlands, leaves, and flowers. During the morning worship this ghat is surrounded by puja vessels, flowers, and food offerings. The worshipping priest sits on a small mat (called asana) before the ghat, and on his left side is a fairly large glass container which holds a steadily burning ghee light.[26]

Behind the pujari's seat to the south is the front entrance. People rarely enter the shrine from the front except on special occasions, such as Kali Puja. Pilgrims generally are only allowed to come up to the iron gate that blocks the entrance to the inner shrine. There, they get darshan of Ma Kali and hand priests their offerings, who, in turn, throw their long hibiscus garlands with expert precision around Ma Kali's feet.

---

[24] A stone symbol of Vishnu; it is oval and bears certain markings—of natural formation, found in certain river beds in India.

[25] A stone symbol of Shiva.

[26] A wick placed into clarified butter.

In a way, the Kali priests in Dakshineswar appear notice-ably different. They behave with a certain kind of content-ment that reminds one of the satisfied face of a recently-fed child sitting on its mother's lap. There is also something curi-ously striking about their eyes—a kind of brilliant lustre. One could put all sorts of adjectives together and still have difficulty defining exactly what it is that makes their eyes look that way.

As the crowd pushes toward the front gate, a multitude of hands stretches out toward the priests, whose white cloth-ing exhibits numerous flower and vermillion stains. The priests often must shout to keep the crowd at bay. Leaning over the gate and the mass of bodies, they attend to one pil-grim after the other. It's physically exhausting because they have to work very fast. Each pilgrim wants to drink a drop of Kali's charanamrita,[27] be marked with her holy sindur (ver-million paste), and receive prasad from the priest's hands. In return for the favor, priests receive dakshina, a gift of money which is almost their sole source of income. The base salary they receive from the temple is extremely small.

In the southwestern corner of the shrine stands a pail which contains Ma Kali's charanamrita. Next to it, the priests keep a gong and sticks used to beat a large kettle drum during arati (vespers). On the wall a little east of the front entrance, hangs a chamar[28] with a silver handle. The pujari uses it to fan Ma Kali during arati in the hot summer season.

Shoved into the southeastern corner of the shrine lies a good-sized heap of predominantly red flowers. These are flowers which have already been used for worship. Since the constant flow of pilgrims delivers large quantities of

---

[27] The sacred water in which the image of the Deity was bathed.
[28] A fan made of the white hair of a yak's bushy tail.

garlands and flowers for Ma Kali, the priests periodically have to take them off the silver lotus she stands on. Otherwise Ma would disappear behind a mountain of flowers. They toss them into the corner, and when the flower heap becomes too big, a servant comes, puts them into a huge basket and carries them out on his head. Another reason for disposing and sweeping up the offered flowers and leaves is that devotees consider it highly inauspicious to step on Kali's flowers.

A large wooden chest, containing some of Kali's ornaments and some utensils, stands against the eastern wall of the shrine. Right next to it is Ma Kali's bed, where, under a light-green mosquito curtain, she takes rest during siesta and sleeps at night. When it is time to retire, the priests put the Mother to bed by putting a picture of Kali onto the pillow. Then they draw the mosquito curtain, so that Ma Kali may rest undisturbed. They treat Ma Kali as if she were a human being because, this way, they can lovingly worship her. When one considers who Ma Kali really is, one would never dream of offering food to her or making her rest on a bed.

Kali is the Mistress of Time,[29] the cause of worldly change, and as such, she consumes all things. All beings and all things must yield to her in the end—our desires and hopes, our family, romantic ties, our friends, possessions and hard-earned success in business. As the eternal, indifferent Time she confronts man with his pitiful finite attachments, swallows them up, and produces them again in a different form, in a different time.

God created the universe and then entered into it, veiling his divinity with his bewitching maya. Through Kali's grace, a spiritual aspirant can tear those veils.

---

[29] Her name can be translated as the feminine form of "kala" or time.

Hindus view time as cyclical. One cycle is divided into four yugas: krta, or the Golden Age (1,728,000 years), treta (1,296,000 years), dvapara (864,000 years), and kali, the Iron Age (432,000 years). Each cycle of the four yugas is called a mahayuga and lasts for 4,320,000 years. One thousand mahayugas, or 4,320,000,000 years, is equal to one day in Brahma's[30] life which sees the creation of the world in the morning and its dissolution in the evening. Brahma lives for 100 Brahma years or 311,040,000,000,000 human years, and then he, himself, dissolves for a Brahma century during which nothing exists but primeval substance until the great cycle begins again.[31]

Kali is the devourer of Time (kala) and then resumes her own dark formlessness. Each division of time has a different deity, and each smaller division is swallowed by a higher one. Thus, a second is swallowed by a minute, a minute by an hour, a day is swallowed by night and both are consumed by a week. A year disappears into an age which is consumed by a cycle, and a cycle is swallowed whole by Ma Kali.

Taking an example out of everyday life, Sri Ramakrishna explained the dissolution and evolution concept of creation in a way that everybody can understand:

> After the destruction of the universe, at the end of a great cycle, the Divine Mother garners the seeds for the next creation. She is like the elderly mistress of the house, who has a hotchpotch pot in which she keeps different articles for household use.
>
> Oh, yes! Housewives have pots like that where they keep blue pills, small bundles of seeds of cucumber,

---

[30] The Creator, first God of the Hindu Trinity.
[31] Heinrich Zimmer, *Myths and Symbols in Indian Art and Civilization*, ed. Joseph Campbell (New York: Harper & Row, 1962), pp. 13-19.

pumpkin, and gourd, and so on. They take them out when they want them. In the same way, after the destruction of the universe, my Divine Mother, the Embodiment of Brahman, gathers together the seeds for the next creation. After the creation the Primal Power dwells in the universe itself. She brings forth this phenomenal world and then pervades it. In the Vedas creation is likened to the spider and its web. The spider brings the web out of itself and then remains in it. God is the container of the universe and also what is contained in it."[32]

On the northern wall behind the image of Kali hang two swords. They look used. Though the Dakshineswar Temple does not perform animal sacrifices as often as some other temples dedicated to the Great Mother, on a few special days throughout the year, a designated person uses one of these swords to decapitate the animal. These swords have hung there for a long time and were there during Sri Ramakrishna's time. Sri Ramakrishna described a dramatic experience during his early God-intoxicated period. Out of desperation, he almost used Kali's sword:

> I felt as if my heart was being squeezed like a wet towel. I was overpowered with a great restlessness and a fear that it might not be my lot to realize Her in this life. I could not bear the separation from Her any longer. Life seemed to be not worth living. Suddenly my glance fell on the sword that was kept in the Mother's temple. I determined to put an end to my life. When I jumped up like a madman and seized it, suddenly the blessed Mother revealed Herself. The buildings with their different parts, the

---

[32] *The Gospel of Sri Ramakrishna*, p. 135.

temple, and everything else vanished from my sight, leaving no trace whatsoever, and in their stead I saw a limitless, infinite, effulgent Ocean of Consciousness. As far as the eye could see, the shining billows were madly rushing at me from all sides with a terrific noise, to swallow me up! I was panting for breath. I was caught in the rush and collapsed, unconscious. What was happening in the outside world I did not know; but within me there was a steady flow of undiluted bliss, altogether new, and I felt the presence of the Divine Mother."[33]

Three large paintings and a clock hang next to the two swords on the back wall—Ma Tara, Sri Chaitanya, and one picture of Smashana Kali. Mother Kali's shrine hasn't changed much in over a 100 years with the exception of a few commodities that represent technology of our modern age. There are a couple of electric fans that help keep the pujari cool during the summer months, and there is an intercom telephone on the western wall next to the side entrance to Kali's inner shrine. Priests use this phone to communicate with temple authorities at the office.

While the crowd of pilgrims mostly enters Kali's temple through the front doors from the south, priests and the Mother's servants either enter the temple on the side through the western doorway or through the northern entrance in the back. Both these entrances lead into a covered veranda which one first has to pass through in order to reach the inner shrine. Priests often utilize the veranda's cool shade to chat or to take rest between worship services. Servants often

---

[33] *The Gospel of Sri Ramakrishna* , pp. 13-14.

prepare offerings there, and musicians with gongs and large drums wait there for the next arati.

The side entrance is a fairly narrow passageway, and like the inside shrine, it also has blue tiles. It is about three to four feet deep, and on its left side is a closet which serves as temporary storage of flowers offered to Kali. Periodically, a servant empties the closet, carrying the flower offerings in an enormous basket on his head toward the Ganges.

Like the front entrance, the side entrance to the inner sanctum of Kali has a couple of wide steps and a cast-iron gate. But unlike the front entrance, immediately after the gate is a large black step resembling a beam on a ship one needs to climb over to get inside a cabin. This step is made of basalt. All who enter the Kali temple are extremely careful not to touch this black step with their feet, and should somebody's foot accidentally touch it, priests immediately clean it with Ganges water and worship it. In the middle of this step is a large crack.

The story goes that once a tremendous thunderstorm hit Dakshineswar, and Sri Ramakrishna, looking out of his room across the courtyard, observed lightning striking the Kali temple. He knew that one priest was on duty inside the temple and prayed fervently to Ma Kali to save his life. Although the temple shook from the impact of the lightning bolt, it was not destroyed and the priest came out unharmed. The only visible damage was a large crack in the black step of the side entrance leading to the inner sanctum. And since then, people carefully avoid touching it with their feet. Rather, they bow down their heads and touch the step with reverence. Another reason this step is revered is that this same substance, basalt, was used to create the image of Kali.

Both entrances to the inner sanctum have strong cast-iron doors which are closed during siesta and at night to protect Ma Kali from intruders. Vermillion stains are all over these doors—hands have touched them with reverence, and zealous pilgrims have held on to them, trying to feel the Great Mother Goddess Kali.

Kali, the Black Goddess of Yore

Kali is not what one imagines a typical Hindu woman to be. She is neither gentle, bashful, nor subservient toward her husband. She moves around in the nude; her hair is dishevelled; and she gets intoxicated from drinking the blood of demons.

Kali is a Goddess who fights alone. And if she wants help, she accepts it from other females but does not seek it from men. Whenever the male Gods are unable to subdue the demons in battle, they ask the Great Mother Goddess for help, and not until after she has scored a victory can they go back in peace and perform their normal godly duties.

The fact that Ma Kali is black makes one wonder whether this Goddess originated with an ancient African super culture. Most scholars don't believe she is ancient. They call her a relatively "young" Goddess who did not reach full popularity in India until the 18th or 19th century. Their opinion is based on the Vedas which are perhaps the most ancient scriptures in the world. They hardly mention Kali. The earliest references to Kali are found in the Mundaka Upanishad, in the Puranas, dating back to the early medieval period—around A.D. 600.

But, one asks, what about the time before the Vedas were conceived? Could it be that God in ancient times was a She? According to Judeo-Christian tradition, this idea is "unthinkable," but if one seriously studies history with an open mind, one cannot exclude the possibility of a Great Mother Goddess that reigned long before the Father God appeared. Primitive man, observing women giving birth, perceived her as magic and prayed to her to make his tribe strong and give him more sons and daughters.

Dating back to Neolithic times, the most ancient images found were always female and depicted fertility. Many are black and mysteriously related. One can't help but ask, "Was the Black Goddess Kali at one time worshipped by peoples all over the world?" Modern research by Westerners certainly points in this direction.

We find Kali in Mexico as an ancient Aztec Goddess of enormous stature. Her name is Coatlicue, and her resemblance to the Hindu Kali is striking.

The colossal Aztec statue of Coatlicue fuses in one image the dual functions of the earth which both creates and destroys. In different aspects she represents Coatlicue, "Lady of the Skirt of Serpents" or "Goddess of the Serpent Petticoat"; Cihuacoatl, "the Serpent Woman"; Tlazolteotl, "Goddess of Filth"; and Tonantzin, "Our Mother," who was later sanctified by the Catholic Church as the Virgin of Guadalupe, the dark-faced Madonna, *la Virgen Morena, la Virgen Guadalupana*, the patroness and protectoress of New Spain; and who is still the patroness of all Indian Mexico. In the statue her head is severed from her body, and from the neck flow two streams of blood in the shape of two serpents. She wears a skirt of serpents girdled by another serpent as a belt. On her breast hangs a necklace of human hearts and hands bearing a human skull as a pendant. Her hands and feet are shaped like claws. From the bicephalous mass which takes the place of the head and which represents Omeyocan, the topmost heaven, to the world of the Dead extending below the feet, the statue embraces both life and death. Squat and massive, the monumental twelve-ton sculpture embodies pyramidal, cruciform, and human forms.

As the art critic Justino Fernández writes in his often-quoted description, it represents not a being but an idea, "the embodiment of the cosmic-dynamic power which bestows life and which thrives on death in the struggle of opposites."[34]

We find Kali in ancient Crete as Rhea, the Aegean Universal Mother or Great Goddess, who was worshipped in a vast area by many peoples.

> Rhea was not restricted to the Aegean area. Among ancient tribes of southern Russia she was Rha, the Red One, another version of Kali as Mother Time clothed in her garment of blood when she devoured all the gods, her offspring. The same Mother Time became the Celtic Goddess Rhiannon, who also devoured her own children one by one. This image of the cannibal mother was typical everywhere of the Goddess as Time, who consumes what she brings forth; or as Earth, who does the same. When Rhea was given a consort in Hellenic myth, he was called Kronus or Chronos, "Father Time," who devoured his own children in imitation of Rhea's earlier activity. He also castrated and killed his own father, the Heaven-God Uranus; and he in turn was threatened by his own son, Zeus. These myths reflect the primitive succession of sacred kings castrated and killed by their supplanters. It was originally Rhea Kronia, Mother Time, who wielded the castrating moon-sickle or scythe, a Scythian weapon, the instrument with which the Heavenly Father was "reaped." Rhea herself was the Grim Reaper. . . .[35]

---

[34] Frank Waters, *Mexico Mystique: The Coming Sixth World of Consciousness* (Athens, OH: Swallow Press, Ohio University Press, 1975, 1989), pp. 185-186.
[35] *The Woman's Encyclopedia of Myths and Secrets*, pp. 856, 857.

We find Kali in historic Europe. In Ireland, Kali appeared as Caillech or Cailleach, an old Celtic name for the Great Goddess in her Destroyer aspect.

> Like Kali, the Caillech was a black Mother who founded many races of people and outlived many husbands. She was also a creatress. She made the world, building mountain ranges of stones that dropped from her apron.

> Scotland was once called Caledonia: the land given by Kali, or Cale, or the Caillech. "Scotland" came from Scotia, the same Goddess, known to Romans as a "dark Aphrodite"; to Celts as Scatha or Scyth; and to Scandinavians as Skadi.

> Like the Hindus' destroying Kalika, the Caillech was known as a spirit of disease. One manifestation of her was a famous idol of carved and painted wood, kept by an old family in County Cork, and described as the Goddess of Smallpox. As diseased persons in India sacrificed to the appropriate incarnation of the Kalika, so in Ireland those afflicted by smallpox sacrificed sheep to this image. It can hardly be doubted that Kalika and Caillech were the same word.

> According to various interpretations, "caillech" meant either an old woman, or a hag, or a nun, or a "veiled one." This last apparently referred to the Goddess's most mysterious manifestation as the future, Fate, and Death—ever veiled from the sight of men, since no man could know the manner of his own death.

> In medieval legend the Caillech became the Black Queen who ruled a western paradise in the Indies, where men were used in Amazonian fashion for

breeding purposes only, then slain. Spaniards called her Califia, whose territory was rich in gold, silver, and gems. Spanish explorers later gave her name to the newly discovered paradise on the Pacific shore of North America, which is how the state of California came to be named after Kali.

In the present century, Irish and Scottish descendants of the Celtic "creatress" still use the word "caillech" as a synonym for "old woman."[36]

The Black Goddess was known in Finland as Kalma (Kali Ma), a haunter of tombs and an eater of the dead."[37]

The Black Goddess worshipped by the gypsies was named Sara-Kali, "Queen Kali," and to this present day, Sara is worshipped in the South of France at Ste-Marie-de-la-Mer during a yearly festival.

Some gypsies appeared in 10th-century Persia as tribes of itinerant dervishes calling themselves Kalenderees, "People of the Goddess Kali." A common gypsy clan name is still Kaldera or Calderash, descended from past Kali-worshippers, like the Kele-De of Ireland.

European gypsies relocated their Goddess in the ancient "Druid Grotto" underneath Chartres Cathedral, once the interior of a sacred mount known as the Womb of Gaul, when the area was occupied by the Carnutes, "Children of the Goddess Car." Carnac, Kermario, Kerlescan, Kercado, Carmona in Spain, and Chartres itself were named

---

[36] See Sir J. G. Frazer, *The Golden Bough: A Study in Magic and Religion* (New York: Macmillan, 1951), p. 467.
[37] *The Woman's Encyclopedia of Myths and Secrets*, p. 492.

after this Goddess, probably a Celtic version of Kore or Q're, traceable through eastern nations to Kauri, another name for Kali.

The Druid Grotto used to be occupied by the image of a black Goddess giving birth, similar to certain images of Kali. Christians adopted this ancient idol and called her Virgo Paritura, "Virgin Giving Birth." Gypsies called her Sara-Kali, "the mother, the woman, the sister, the queen, the Phuri Dai, the source of all Romany blood." They said the black Virgin wore the dress of a gypsy dancer, and every gypsy should make a pilgrimage to her grotto at least once in his life. The grotto was described as "your mother's womb." A gypsy pilgrim was told: "Shut your eyes in front of Sara the Kali, and you will know the source of the spring of life which flows over the gypsy race."[38]

We find variations of Kali's name throughout the ancient world.

The Greeks had a word Kalli, meaning "beautiful," but applied to things that were not particularly beautiful such as the demonic centaurs called "kallikantzari," relatives of Kali's Asvins. Their city of Kallipolis, the modern Gallipoli, was centered in Amazon country formerly ruled by Artemis Kalliste. The annual birth festival at Eleusis was Kalligeneia, translatable as "coming forth from the Beautiful One," or "coming forth from Kali."

Lunar priests of Sinai, formerly priestesses of the Moon-Goddess, called themselves "kalu." Similar

---

[38] *The Woman's Encyclopedia of Myths and Secrets*, pp. 890-891.

priestesses of prehistoric Ireland were "kelles," origin of the name Kelly, which meant a hierophantic clan devoted to "the Goddess Kele." This was cognate with the Saxon Kale, or Cale, whose lunar calendar or kalends included the spring month of Sproutkale, when Mother Earth (Kale) put forth new shoots. In antiquity the Phoenicians referred to the strait of Gibraltar as Calpe, because it was considered the passage to the western paradise of the Mother.[39]

The Black Goddess was even carried into Christianity as a mother figure, and one can find all over the world images of Mother Mary, the mother of Jesus Christ, depicted as a black madonna.

Kali, the Goddess of Tantra

When a spiritual aspirant has formed a special relationship with Kali, she is no longer just an image in a temple. Her presence fulfills this person's being at all times. In a way, all religions prescribe methods for getting in touch with God. While the methods differ, the outcome is the same. For instance, the person practicing Tantra, in the end, reaches the same goal as the person practicing Vedanta.

A Tantric yogi sees the great Mother present within his human body as the Kundalini. She lies hidden by her self-created ignorance, like a snake, coiled and fast asleep in the muladhara chakra at the bottom of the spinal cord. Through sadhana, the Tantric awakens the Mother and rouses her to go upward. Flashing like a phosphorescent flame through the Sushumna channel, she pierces the various chakras until

---

[39] *The Woman's Encyclopedia of Myths and Secrets*, pp. 491-492.

she reaches the highest plane and unites with Shiva at the crown of the head. At this moment, the Tantric experiences such supreme bliss that his mind cannot contain the small ego-consciousness and becomes illumined. Yet Tantric sadhana does not end there. The perfect realization of the Mother only culminates when one experiences illumination in all planes, even the lowest.

A Vedantist, on the other hand, has a totally different approach. The Vedantist does not like to see Gods and Goddesses and believes that whatever he or she sees in this world is unreal, a play of name and form. He or she even sees the mind as a material entity. Yet, although the mind is devoid of consciousness, it has the ability to function like a mirror and reflect consciousness. For instance, when a pot is placed before one's eyes, one's mind takes its form, and then the light of the Atman (the Self) manifests the pot. One cannot experience or perceive anything without the light of the Atman. The difference between an ordinary person and an illumined soul is that an illumined soul is conscious of the fact that he or she experiences Brahman in every state of the mind, even in the lowest.

Sri Ramakrishna wanted to experience the Truth as taught by different religions. After attaining illumination by worshipping Kali, he practiced the disciplines of other religions, and then said from first-hand knowledge, "As many faiths, so many paths."

Sri Ramakrishna learned Tantra from Bhairavi Brahmani, an attractive female saint who traveled from place to place and taught a chosen few the secrets of Tantra. Sri Ramakrishna sometimes spoke about his Tantric sadhana:

> The Brahmani made me undertake one by one, all the disciplines prescribed in the sixty-four main Tantras, all difficult to accomplish, in trying to practice which most of the Sadhakas go astray; but all of which I got through successfully by Mother's grace.

On one occasion, I saw, that the Brahmani had brought at night—nobody knew whence—a beautiful woman, nude and in the prime of her youth, and said to me, "My child, worship her as the Devi." When the worship was finished, she said, "Sit on her lap, my child, and perform Japa." I trembled and wept, calling to the Mother, "O Mother, Mother of the universe, what is this command Thou givest to one who has taken absolute refuge in Thee? Has Thy weak child the power to be so impudently daring?" But as soon as I had called on her, I felt as if I was possessed by some unknown power and extraordinary strength filled my heart. And no sooner had I, uttering the Mantras, sat on the lap of the woman, like one hypnotized, unaware of what I was doing, than I merged completely into samadhi. When I regained consciousness, I saw the Brahmani waiting on me and assiduously trying to bring me back to normal consciousness. She said, "The rite is completed, my child; others restrain themselves with very great difficulty under such circumstances and then finish the rite with nominal Japa for a trifling little time only; but you lost all consciousness and were in deep samadhi." When I heard this, I became reassured and began to salute Mother again and again with a grateful heart for enabling me to pass that ordeal unscathed.

On another occasion, I saw that the Brahmani cooked fish in the skull of a dead body and performed Tarpana. She also made me do so and asked me to take that fish. I did as I was asked and felt no aversion whatever.

But, on the day when the Brahmani brought a piece of rotten flesh and asked me to touch it with my tongue after Tarpana, I was shaken by aversion and said, "Can it be done?" So questioned, she said, "What's there in it, my child? Just see, I do it." Saying so, she put a portion of it into her mouth and said, "Aversion should not be entertained," and placed again a little of it before me. When I saw her do so, the idea of the terrible Chandika form of the Mother Universal was inspired in my mind; and repeatedly uttering "Mother," I entered into Bhavasamadhi. There was then no aversion felt when the Brahmani put it into my mouth.[40]

Many people ridicule or look down on Tantra as a religion, because Tantra prescribes a non-traditional sadhana they consider blasphemous. The Tantric offers to the Divine Mother panca-makara, or the five items of worship: fish, meat, parched cereals or money, wine and sexual union.

. . . If they had read the Tantra Shastra intelligently and learned its principles from Sadhakas truly versed in it, they would have realized how mistaken were their notions of it, and, instead of despising it, would certainly have admitted that this Shastra is the only means of Liberation for the undisciplined, weak-minded and short-lived. Seeing that wine, flesh, fish are consumed and sexual intercourse takes place in the world at large, I am myself unable to understand why many people shudder at the Sadhana of Panca-makara to be found in the Tantra Shastra. Do these acts become blameable only if made a part of worship?[41]

---

[40] Swami Saradananda, *Sri Ramakrishna, the Great Master*, (Mylapore, Madras: The President, Sri Ramakrishna Math, 1952), pp. 195-196.
[41] John Woodroffe, *Hymns to the Goddess*, (Wilmot, WI:, Lotus Light Publications, 1981), p. 273.

Yet Tantric sadhana should not be mistaken as a license to indulge. Some people forget that the results of Tantric practices can only be obtained if the aspirant resorts to austere self-control as the basis of the disciplines. They engage in promiscuous practices for which the Tantras themselves are being held responsible. One needs a competent teacher to practice Tantra. Great energy, such as lightning, such as the Kundalini, can be a great danger if not channeled properly.

Depending on an aspirant's disposition, Tantra will prescribe a particular method for spiritual practice. In general, the Tantras classify people into three major groups—pasu (animal), vira (hero), and divya (godlike). Inertia is the predominant quality of the pasu, who is deluded, negligent, indolent, and spends an excessive amount of time sleeping. The hero, on the other hand, is full of excessive energy which results in desire, anger, greed, pain, and attachment. He is aggressive and cultivates a fearless stance before Kali, challenging her to unveil her secrets. But the godlike devotee is calm, has wisdom, knowledge and a kind disposition.

Since the pasu aspirant is ignorant of the real meaning of Tantric rites, he or she is not permitted to worship the Divine Mother with fish, meat, parched cereals, wine, and sexual union. Instead, this aspirant is supposed to worship her with substitutes such as eggplant, red radish, lentils, ginger, wheat, beans, and garlic. The pasu is supposed to substitute milk, ghee or honey for wine and meditates on her feet in lieu of sexual union.

The hero, who has acquired purity and strength of character, is permitted by the Shakta Tantras to worship the Divine Mother with fish, meat, parched cereals, wine, and through sexual union. In order to transcend and subdue his restless and excitable nature, the hero aspirant offers these five articles of enjoyment to the Mother while repeating mantras.

The godlike aspirant is self-restrained, tranquil, silent—possessed of a sattvic disposition. He or she is truthful, not

fanatic, compassionate, and respectful to all women as manifestations of the Divine Mother. The godlike aspirant has
firm faith in the guru, mantra, and yantra[42]. This aspirant
performs japam at night and worships the Mother three times
a day, practicing breath control, concentration, and meditation. Through this steadfast spiritual practice, the godlike
aspirant rouses the Kundalini and makes her pierce the six
centers of mystic consciousness.

> A godly aspirant is an adept in meditation on the
> Divine Mother at the centers of mystic conscious-
> ness and experiences Her in them and the universe.
> He transcends the plane of duality and distinction
> and partakes of Her supreme undifferentiated con-
> sciousness and delight. He dissolves his mind, erad-
> icates his ego (aham), and annuls the world of
> phenomenal appearances (idam). He harmonizes
> and synthesizes duality and distinction in unity, and
> attains fulfillment (siddhi). He acquires the integral
> knowledge and the intuitive experience. Saktaism is
> the practical science of attaining the Advaita Vedanta
> knowledge and Absoluteness (sivatva). It is sheer
> nonsense and gross perversion of the truth to brand
> it as gross egoistic hedonism or unrestrained sensu-
> alism. Rama Prasada, Ramakrishna Paramahamsa,
> Bama Ksepa [Bamakhepa], and other Sakta saints
> attained God-realization through the Sakta cult of
> spiritual discipline. Sri Aurobindo based his Integral
> Yoga on this cult, adapted, simplified and rational-
> ized it for the upliftment of humanity to the supra-
> mental level.[43]

---

[42] A mystic diagram.
[43] Dr. Jadunath Sinha, *Ramaprasada's Devotional Songs — The Cult of Shakti* ,
(Calcutta: Sinha Publishing House, 1966), p. 39.

The aim of all Tantric practices is to bring aspirants to the realization that the very objects which tempt human beings and make them experience repeated births and deaths are none other than the veritable forms of God. Contrary to ancient history in which we find that nearly every phase and activity of human life was holy, modern people have moved God to a far-away place called heaven.

Tantric sadhana helps spiritual seekers to bring God back into the human heart and into everything that concerns life—to adore God with body, mind, and words. When we eat, sleep, or go to work, we should do so in worship of God. Every action should be done in glorification of the Divine Mother.

Sri Ramakrishna used to say that true devotees must love and think about God so much that they develop a kind of "love body." This body feels different from the body of an ordinary person. We cannot compare the upsurge of joy we feel during ecstasy with any kind of worldly joy. Sri Ramakrishna said:

> Mad, that's the word. One must become mad with love in order to realize God. But that love is not possible if the mind dwells on lust and gold. Sex-life with a woman! What happiness is there in that? The realization of God gives ten million times more happiness. Gauri used to say that when a man attains ecstatic love of God, all the pores of the skin, even the roots of the hair, become like so many sexual organs, and in every pore the aspirant enjoys the happiness of communion with the Atman.[44]

While Sri Ramakrishna urged his disciples to love God without any reservation, he warned and asked them not to practice the heroic attitude toward the Divine Mother. It is a

[44] *The Gospel of Sri Ramakrishna,* p. 346.

very slippery path, he often said. He asked them to worship Shakti with a mother/child attitude because this kind of relationship kindles purity in an aspirant's mind. It's the safest and easiest path in this kali yuga. The heroic aspirant has every chance of falling and, instead of transcending sense pleasures, becoming very attached and obsessed with them. A pure mind is absolutely necessary to reach the goal. Sri Ramakrishna taught how to worship Shakti as the Divine Mother:

> Shakti alone is the root of the universe. That Primal Energy has two aspects: vidya and avidya. Avidya deludes. Avidya conjures up lust and greed which casts the spell. Vidya begets devotion, kindness, wisdom, and love, which lead one to God. This avidya must be propitiated, and that is the purpose of the rites of Shakti worship.[45]

> The devotee assumes various attitudes toward Shakti in order to propitiate her: the attitude of a handmaid, a hero, or a child. A hero's attitude is to please her even as a man pleases a woman through intercourse.

> The worship of Shakti is extremely difficult. It is no joke. I passed two years as the handmaid and companion of the Divine Mother. I used to dress myself as a woman. I put on a nose ring. One can conquer lust by assuming the attitude of a woman. But my natural attitude has always been that of a child toward its mother. I regard the breasts of any woman as those of my own mother.[46]

---

[45] In this worship a woman is regarded as the representation of the Divine Mother.

[46] *The Gospel of Sri Ramakrishna*, p. 116.

Pray to the Divine Mother with a longing heart. Her vision dries up all craving for the world and completely destroys all attachment to lust and greed. It happens instantly if you think of her as your own mother. She is by no means a godmother. She is your own mother. With a yearning heart persist in your demands on her. The child holds to the skirt of its mother and begs a penny of her to buy a kite. Perhaps the mother is gossiping with her friends. At first she refuses to give the penny and says to the child: "No, you can't have it. Your daddy has asked me not to give you money. When he comes home I'll ask him about it. You will get into trouble if you play with a kite now." The child begins to cry and will not give up his demand. Then the mother says to her friends: "Excuse me a moment. Let me pacify this child." Immediately she unlocks the cash box with a click and throws the child a penny.

You too must force your demand on the Divine Mother. She will come to you without fail. I once said the same thing to some Sikhs when they visited the temple. We were conversing in front of the Kali temple. They said, "God is compassionate." "Why compassionate?" I asked. "Why, revered sir, he constantly looks after us, gives us righteousness and wealth, and provides us with our food." "Suppose," I said, "a man has children. Who will look after them and provide them with food—their father or a man from another village?'" God is our very own. We can exert force on him. With one's own people one can even go so far as to say, "You rascal! Won't you give it to me?"[47]

But in order to get everything from the Divine Mother, one needs to surrender to her. There is one Tantric sadhana,

---

[47] *The Gospel of Sri Ramakrishna*, pp. 629, 630.

called anga-nyasa, wherein the aspirant is asked to conse-crate the different parts of his or her body to the Mother by placing the different letters, both vowels and consonants, on them. During this practice one is to feel that every part of the physical body, with all its biological processes going on within, really belongs to the Mother and not to oneself.

Kali's Mantra and Yantra

Tantric sadhana uses symbols in the form of mantras and yantras. Kali in her seed mantra (bija-mantra) is *KRĪM*. This mantra is a sound representation of the Mother. While the inner meaning of this mantra can only be understood in deep meditation, the word meaning is as follows: *K* stands for full knowledge, *R* means she is auspicious, *Ī* means she bestows boons, and *M* that she gives freedom. Through the repeti-tion of her mantra, OM KRĪM KALI, the aspirant's mind becomes divinely transformed and passes from the gross state of worldly affairs into Kali's subtle light of pure Consciousness. See figure 13.

Kali in her yantra form is the Supreme Generative Energy in the central point, or bindu, enclosed by three pen-tagons (actually five inverted concentric triangles), a circle and an eight-petalled lotus. While the triangle within a female deity's yantra points downward, it points upward

Figure 13. Krīm, seed mantra of the Goddess Kali.

Figure 14. The Kali Yantra.

within a male deity's yantra. But the bindu[48] in the heart of
the Kali yantra is in the same position as the one in the Shiva
yantra. This symbolizes the oneness of the Supreme Female
Principle with the Supreme Male Principle—Kali, as the
energy aspect of material nature, is united with the Absolute
(Shiva) for the sake of creation.

The Kali yantra (figure 14), above is both an object exist-
ing in the external world as well as a subject to be internal-
ized within the human body. Kali is presented here as
Prakriti, symbolized by the eight-petalled lotus, since she is
the cause of material nature. The eight petals stand for the
eight elements of Prakriti—earth, water, fire, air, ether, mind,

---

[48] A black point.

intellect, and ego-sense—of which this phenomenal world is composed. The circle symbolizes the circle of life and death which we must pierce in order to reach the Absolute Reality. The fifteen corners of the five inverted concentric triangles represent the fifteen psychophysical states—five organs of knowledge (sight, hearing, taste, smell, and touch), five organs of action (hands, feet, speech, organ of evacuation, and organ of procreation), five vital airs (prana—upward air; apana—downward air; vyana—air within the body; udana—air leaving the body; and samana—air at the navel which helps to digest food).

Kali within the Human Body

Kali is the mystical indweller in every human body. When she lies in the Muladhara lotus like a sleeping serpent at the base of the spinal cord, she is called Kundalini. When, through yogic disciplines, she becomes aroused, pierces the Sushumna channel and rises upward, she has different names, depending on the chakra in which she resides. In the heart chakra, she is called Hamsa, and in the chakra between the eyebrows, she is called Bindu. Once she reaches the Sahasrara chakra at the crown of the head, she becomes formless, transcendental consciousness.

> A yogin should open the door to liberation through Kundalini. The individual soul should meditate on itself as a spirit in the heart-lotus, on Kundalini in the Muladhara lotus and on the Supreme Self or Parama Siva in the Sahasrara. It should be united with Parama Siva by rousing Kundalini and making her pierce the higher lotuses and ascend to the highest lotus. It cannot be united with Him or become identical with Him without the aid of Kundalini. She is the mediator between the jivatman and Parama Siva although She is non-different from Him. Kundalini, coiled Divine Power, or dormant

power of universal consciousness, exists everywhere in the universe. Matter, life, mind, and super-
consciousness are different degrees of the unveiling
of the dormant power of consciousness. Even in an
atom of matter there is coiled Kundalini in the
nucleus. Matter is dormant power of consciousness.
Divine Power assumes the forms of the individual
souls by limiting Herself, and of matter by coiling
Herself or by becoming dormant.[49]

One's own body is the best place for worship. There is a
unique group of traveling minstrels in Bengal, called Bauls.
They practice their own form of Tantric disciplines. They are
free thinkers who believe that temples, mosques and
churches stand across the path to truth, blocking the search.
They say the search for God is one which everyone must
carry out for himself or herself. It's an inner journey within
one's own body—the greatest temple of all. Sri Ramakrishna
was very fond of Bauls. He told Holy Mother that he would
have to be born again and would return as a Baul in a north-
westerly direction from Dakshineswar.

The human body, according to the Tantricas, is the
best medium for realizing the truth. This body is
not merely a thing in the universe, it is an epitome
of the universe, a microcosm in relation to the
macrocosm. There is therefore nothing in the universe which is not there in the body of a man. With
this idea in view, the Tantrica sadhikas have tried
to discover the most important rivers in the nerve
system of man, the mountains specially in the
spinal cord, and the prominent tirthas (holy places)
in different parts of the body, and the sun and the

---

[49] *Ramaprasada's Devotional Songs,* pp. 6-7.

moon—time element of the exterior universe in all its phases as day and night, fortnight, month and year—have often been explained with reference to the course of the vital wind (prana and apana—exhalation and inhalation). The human form is thus the abode of the truth of which the universe is the manifestation in infinite space and eternal time. Instead of being lost in the vastness of the incomprehensible universe and groping in its unfathomable mystery, a Tantric sadhaka prefers to concentrate his attention on himself and to realize the truth hidden in this body with the clear conviction that the truth that is realized within is the same truth that pervades and controls the whole universe.[50]

Overwhelmed with God-consciousness, Sri Ramakrishna used to say, "I am the machine and She is the Operator. I am the house and She is the Indweller. I am the chariot and She is the Charioteer. I move as She moves me; I speak as She speaks through me."[51]

He saw Kali in all women.

Sri Ramakrishna said to his disciples, "My children, for me it is actually as if Mother has covered Herself with wrappers of various kinds, assumed various forms and is peeping from within them all.

"One day I was sitting and meditating on Mother in the Kali temple," said Sri Ramakrishna. "I could by no means bring the Mother's form to my mind. What did I see then? She looked like the prostitute, Ramani, who used to come to bathe in the river, and she peeped from near the jar of worship. I saw it, laughed and said, 'Thou hast the desire, O

---

[50] *Great Women of India*, pp. 81-82.
[51] *The Gospel of Sri Ramakrishna*, p. 616.

Mother, of becoming Ramani today. That is very good.
Accept the worship today in this form.' Acting thus, She
made it clear that a prostitute also is She, there is nothing
else except Her."[52]

Kali's Boon

The devotee who surrenders to the Divine Mother obtains
everything. Joy in life and joy in death. All becomes bliss,
and all becomes play.

> Kali's boon is won when man confronts or accepts
> her and the realities she dramatically conveys to
> him. The image of Kali, in a variety of ways, teaches
> man that pain, sorrow, decay, death, and destruc-
> tion are not to be overcome or conquered by denying
> them or explaining them away. Pain and sorrow are
> woven into the texture of man's life so thoroughly
> that to deny them is ultimately futile and foolish.
> For man to realize the fullness of his being, for man
> to exploit his potential as a human being, he must
> finally accept his dimension of existence. Kali's boon
> is freedom, the freedom of the child to revel in the
> moment, and it is won only after confrontation or
> acceptance of death. Ramakrishna's childlike nature
> does not stem from his ignorance of things as they
> really are but from his realization of things as
> they really are. He is able to revel in the moment,
> for he knows that to live any other way is a denial of
> things as they are. To ignore death, to pretend that
> one is physically immortal, to pretend that one's
> ego is the center of things, is to provoke Kali's mock-
> ing laughter. To confront or accept death, on the

[52] *The Gospel of Sri Ramakrishna*, p. 577.

contrary, is to realize a mode of being that can delight and revel in the play of the Gods. To accept one's mortality is to be able to act superfluously, to let go, to be able to sing, dance, and shout. To win Kali's boon is to become childlike, to be flexible, open, and naive like a child. It is to act and be like Ramakrishna, who delighted in the world as Kali's play, who acted without calculation and behaved like a fool or a child.[53]

Mother Kali creates when she feels like it and then again destroys her creation when she feels like it. All in fun—just like a child who spends a long time to build a sand castle with great care and, then, on the spur of the moment, destroys it with great delight.

"Bondage and liberation are both of her making," said Sri Ramakrishna. "By her maya worldly people become entangled in lust and greed, and again, through her grace they attain their liberation. She is called the Savior, and the Remover of the bondage that binds one to the world."

> In the world's busy market-place, O Shyama,
>   Thou art flying kites;
> High up they soar on the wind of hope,
>   held fast by maya's string.
> Their frames are human skeletons,
>   their sails of the three gunas made;
> But all their curious workmanship
>   is merely for ornament.
>
> Upon the kite-strings Thou hast rubbed
>   the manja-paste[54] of worldliness,

---

[53] David R. Kinsley, *The Sword and the Flute* (Santa Barbara: University of California Press, 1975), pp. 144-145.

[54] A glue of barley and powdered glass.

So as to make each straining strand
*   all the more sharp and strong.*
Out of a hundred thousand kites,
*   at best but one or two break free;*
And Thou dost laugh and clap Thy hands,
*   O Mother, watching them!*

On favoring winds, says Ramprasad,
*   the kites set loose will speedily*
Be borne away to the Infinite,
*   across the sea of the world.*[55]

The Master said: "The Divine Mother is always playful and sportive. This universe is her play. She is self-willed and must always have her own way. She is full of bliss. She gives freedom only to one out of a hundred thousand."[56] That's a fairly slim chance but no reason to give up.

An ancient Hindu story tells about two men practicing spiritual disciplines under a tree. When the first man, by divine intervention, found out that he had to live two more lives before he could attain liberation, he sat down in despair. When the second was told by a divine voice that he had to be born as often as there are leaves on the tree, he began to dance with joy. "I will be liberated so soon," he shouted. At this, the divine voice said, "My son, I have just tested you. You are liberated right now."

We all worship God, knowingly or unknowingly. Satyam shivam sundaram—God is Truth, God is Beauty, God is Bliss. When we have removed all the noise and static, we find that it is our nature to love God—passionately. Jai Kali.

---

[55] The allusion of Ramprasad's song is to the kite-flying competitions in India. Several people fly their kites and try to cut one another's kite strings. Whoever has his string cut loses his kite and quits the game.
[56] *The Gospel of Sri Ramakrishna*, p. 136.

Chapter 3

WORSHIP OF MA KALI

Awake, Mother! Awake! How long Thou hast been
    asleep
In the lotus of the Muladhara!
Fulfill Thy secret function, Mother:
Rise to the thousand-petalled lotus within the head,
Where mighty Shiva has His dwelling;
Swiftly pierce the six lotuses
And take away my grief, O Essence of Consciousness![1]

---

[1] *The Gospel of Sri Ramakrishna,* p. 182.

The Nature of Worship

The search for God begins when one's soul is no longer satisfied with worldly enjoyments and becomes restless for a deeper, more intense joy. This spiritual journey is often agonizingly painful until the unfulfilled soul finds its maker.

We all instinctively know God, but having enmeshed ourselves within the cocoon of sophisticated complexity, we need to rediscover our primal instincts. It's not easy to develop one's instincts to be like those of a calf that will find its mother's udder even blindfolded. Every sincere devotee must find the Great Mother—eventually. But the ones who want to speed up this process should block out the world's noise and distractions and focus the mind onto their own Self. From the many methods that teach people how to achieve good concentration, the path of devotion is perhaps the easiest.

Prayer, when intensely practiced, gradually merges into meditation. But few people are capable of praying with such intensity as to convert it into meditation. For most people who follow the path of devotion an intermediate discipline is necessary in order to attain and sustain the state of meditation. This intermediate discipline is worship.

By worship we mean not only external ritualistic worship but also mental worship, japa, stuti (adoration), even work done as service to the Lord. In other words, by worship we mean the cultivation of a worshipful attitude—an attitude of offering everything to God. Since human nature is self-centered, this attitude of giving develops only slowly. The natural tendency of the mind is to be always at the receiving end. That is why asking, or prayer, comes first. It is only when, as a result of prayer, the soul starts receiving grace in the form of faith, love and strength that it can truly start offering everything including itself to God.[2]

According to Swami Bhajanananda, a scholarly monk of the Ramakrishna Order, worship is a special kind of I-Thou relationship between the soul and God. It should have the following characteristics:

1. SACRIFICE—True sacrifice should be an act of giving without expectation of return. It does not matter what we offer but how we offer it. Giving up selfishness is the best sacrifice.

2. ADORATION—Love plus reverence is adoration. Love becomes Bhakti only when it is sublimated by the highest reverence for the Supreme God. And this reverence comes from the awareness of God's transcendental nature and supernatural glories. In Hinduism, adoration takes the form of chanting the names of God. The main purpose of sankir-tan[3] is remembrance and adoration of God. Some people put an overemphasis on meditation, but, studying the lives of the great saints of India, one ultimately finds that most of them spent their time singing the glories of God.

3. SACREDNESS—Everything connected with worship is sacred, and worship itself imparts sanctity to the worshipper and the articles of worship. According to Hindu belief every organ of the body and every object has a subtle Divine Form or Presiding Deity. And by invoking these deities, the body as well as the articles become sanctified. A major part of Hindu worship is devoted to the symbolic purification of the mind so that the Atman may manifest itself in all its intrinsic lustre and glory.

---

[2] *Prabuddha Bharata*, May 1980, editorial by Swami Bhajanananda, pp. 202-203.
[3] Group singing of divine names as popularized by Sri Chaitanya.

4. CULT—While most people associate cult with sectarianism and fanaticism, spiritual seekers see it as entering into a relationship with a God or Goddess. However, it is not easy to establish an intimate, personal relationship with such an intangible Spiritual Being, and whenever someone is successful, it is mostly based on the worshipper's own psychic makeup. There must be some similarity between the adorer and the adored. For instance, a worshipper of Kali has some attributes of Kali in him or her, and likewise, a worshipper of Shiva, has Shiva's attributes. Otherwise, he or she wouldn't feel attracted toward that particular deity. This is the rationale behind the concept of ishta devata (Chosen Deity)—the God one loves the most, naturally and without being told to do so. Cult expresses itself in two ways: myth and ritual. While myths are sacred stories about Gods and Goddesses, ritual is a symbolic act which expresses a mystic relationship between man and Deity.

> Ritual is a kind of sacred language. Man is not only a knower but also a doer. He can express his feelings through words as well as through actions, perhaps more eloquently through the latter. However, religious rituals are not artificially coded. Like music and dance, ritual, too, springs spontaneously from a deeper layer of consciousness where man touches the divine harmony of the rhythms of life. Says Susanne Langer in her celebrated book, "Ritual is a symbolic transformation of experience that no other medium can adequately express. Because it springs from a primary human need, it is spontaneous activity."[4]

Worship, as a spiritual discipline, prepares one's mind for higher meditation because, during worship, one needs

------

[4] *Prabuddha Bharata*, May, 1980, p. 206. Susanne Langer's book is called *Philosophy in a New Key*, published by Harvard University Press, 1980.

to focus one's will on a particular Divine Form. When worship is performed wholeheartedly, one feels a sense of accomplishment, a sense of assurance that one's life and actions are sanctified. Of course, the ultimate purpose of worship is the direct vision of the Deity, and all worship is based on the belief that one, indeed, can contact the Divine through it.

Daily Worship at the Dakshineswar Kali Temple

It is still dark outside and the birds are yet asleep when a shout, "Ma jago, " breaks the stillness of the early morning hour.[5] The time in Dakshineswar is shortly before 4 A.M. A lone priest walks past a dim lantern toward the Kali temple, and when he reaches the cast-iron temple door, there is already a small crowd of pilgrims waiting to see the Divine Mother Kali.

Why do they get up so early to see Kali when they can comfortably get up later and see her just the same?

Hindus say that there are three times a day which are most favorable for spiritual practices. These auspicious times occur during the morning and evening twilights and at midday. The morning sandhya (worship) should be performed while the stars are still visible, the midday sandhya when the sun is in the meridian, and the evening sandhya when the sun is visibly disappearing. According to the *Srimad Devi Bhagavatam*, a Tantric scripture on Devi worship, the morning and evening sandhyas should last 48 minutes. During this time Brahmins recite the Gayatri Mantra.

> The sandhya performed in dwelling houses is ordinary; in nature among cows it is good, and better

---

[5] Ma Jago means: Mother, wake up!

still on the banks of a river. But sandhya performed
before the Devi's temple or the Devi's seat is best.
The three sandhyas done before the Devi bring
excellent results.[6]

The priest opens the side gate to the Dakshineswar Kali
Temple with a jerk and slips into the dark veranda, closing
the door behind him. As soon as they see the priest go inside,
all pilgrims rush toward the main entrance. The fortunate
ones in the front cling to the gate with anticipation. At four
o'clock sharp, the priest, now joined by another, opens
Mother's large iron doors from inside. A great commotion
sets in among the pilgrims.

"Jai Ma, jai Ma, jai Ma, jai Ma, jai Ma, jai Ma, jai Ma,
jai," chant Kali's devotees with fervor as soon as she becomes
visible.

The priest blows into a conch shell, signaling the start of
the mangalarati.[7] As one listens to the soft cooing of the conch
shell, one feels enchanted and acutely aware of one's privilege to be part of a magic moment—so beautiful that it seems
unreal. The air is warm and moist and drifting past are
clouds of sweet-smelling incense which burns somewhere
nearby. Standing outside in the darkness, Ma Kali's devotees look intently at the softly-lit inner shrine. A new day is
about to start, and they are the first ones to see the Divine
Mother Kali. They start the day with an impression of Kali on
their minds and pray, "Ma, may you always be on my mind."

The arati, or aratrikam, is a rite which involves the waving of a lighted lamp before the Deity as a symbolic act of
the soul's surrender to God. The arati is perhaps the only ritual which allows collective participation, and devotees chant
the divine name, clap their hands or sing bhajans while the
priest performs the rite.

---

[6] *Srimad Devi Bhagavatam*, translated by Swami Vijnanananda (New Delhi:
Munshiram Manoharlal, 1986), p. 1099.
[7] Early morning service.

Lest he rudely awake Ma Kali, the priest carefully avoids touching the altar. His bare upper body glistens in the yellow, flickering light. His right arm shoots up, snakelike, with a dancer's elan as he rhythmically waves the pancha-pradeep (a brass vessel holding five ghee lights) in front of Kali—waking her softly.

Devotees believe that a special manifestation of the Divine Presence in the image occurs during the waving of this light. They feel a direct communion with Kali at this time. After the five lights, the priest waves a conch filled with water, called pani sankha, in front of Ma Kali, followed by a red cloth, a red flower and a chamar (fan).[8]

"Ma, you have given these five elements to me, so I am worshipping you with them."

The priest completes the worship with great devotion, offering ghee (clarified butter), rock candy and other sweets to Kali. Being relatively short—it doesn't last much longer than ten minutes—the morning worship ends when the priest blows the conch. The doors to the Kali temple close again for another couple of hours since Mother Kali is still resting. She does not officially wake up until a priest lifts the mosquito curtain off her bed and removes her picture which is lying on the pillow. This is usually done around 6 A.M.

Priests begin their daily routine by cleaning Mother's vedi (altar). Once the shrine is clean, they attend to the Great Mother herself. Ma Kali gets bathed with Ganges water and covered with scented oil and perfume. While one priest stands on the side steps of the altar and washes her, another holds out a small pail in an attempt to collect Kali's bath water without spilling. These priests have done this many times and their knowing hands wash and dry Kali carefully, yet with speed. Her bath water is called charanamrita—nectar from the feet of the Divine. It is precious. Devotees believe

---

[8] These items symbolize the five elements—fire, water, ether, earth, and air.

that whosoever sips this sacred water will attain supreme love and Kali's grace.

To the unbeliever, charanamrita is just water, but to the devotee, the power of charanamrita can move mountains. It's a matter of faith.

There is a Hindu story about a faithful milkmaid, whose guru once severely scolded her for being late in delivering his milk. When she replied that she was delayed crossing the river because the ferry boat broke down, the angry guru shouted, "Chanting God's name, one can cross the ocean, and you can't even cross the river?" The simple milkmaid took his words to heart and, when one day the ferry boat was inoperative again, she thought, "My guru, who is akin to God, said that I should cross the river chanting the name of the Lord. If he says I can walk on water, it must, indeed, be so." Thinking thus, she chanted God's name and put one foot forward and then the other. She managed to cross the river on foot. When she narrated this to her guru, he didn't believe her. "Show me," he said, and followed her to the river. The milkmaid had no trouble walking on water, but when the guru attempted to do likewise, he sank knee-deep into the muddy river. "How is it," cried the guru, "that I, who commanded you to chant the name of the Lord and gave you the power to walk on water, cannot do it myself?" The milkmaid turned her head, looked at him and smiled. "My dear guruji," she said. "My faith in the Lord's name and your words gave me this power. But you don't have the same faith, because when you first stepped out onto the water you lifted your cloth lest it should get wet!"

Faith, undoubtedly, is a great virtue, but sometimes, common sense can save a spiritual seeker a lot of trouble. For instance, someone with a sensitive stomach unaccustomed to Indian water may avoid stomach problems by not drinking charanamrita. One can also show respect by touching the sacred water to one's lips and then pouring it over one's head. It's the attitude that counts.

In the course of one week, Ma Kali generally wears two or three new saris that were given to her by loving devotees. And once she has worn them, they become eagerly-sought-after prasad. Kali's saris usually get changed in the morning before the crowds of pilgrims arrive. A priest first drapes a long cloth around the pillars of Ma's shrine, hiding her nakedness just like women do when they change their wet saris to dry ones at the bathing ghat—their faces visible but their bodies hidden by a cloth held up around them.

Why should anyone want to hide the body of a Goddess whose essential nature is as naked as space? One explanation may be that the priests who lovingly serve her on a daily basis look upon her as their very own mother. And who would want to see their mother exposed naked to the eyes of strangers?

As soon as Kali's sari is properly draped, priests offer flowers to her. They decorate her with fragrant flowers of various colors by attaching them to her feet, head, and body. Then they offer flowers to all the other deities on the altar.

Around 6:30 A.M., Ma Kali is ready to receive the devotees who have been waiting patiently at the main entrance. People squeezing through the frontal archways into the covered veranda get a chance to watch the dhup-arati. A priest waves dhup (incense) in front of Kali for a few minutes until the inner shrine is filled with perfumed smoke.

Kali's garland-maker arrives a little after 8 A.M. to prepare her mala (garland). Although Ma receives many flower garlands made by many different people throughout the day, she generally only wears one very large garland around her neck. Mother's special garland-maker, a tall soft-spoken man, works near the back door within the closed veranda. Sitting cross-legged on the marble floor, he carefully examines the various brilliantly-colored flowers spread on a mat next to him. When his work is done, the lavish flower garland he just created is at least four to five inches thick.

This large mala is generally offered to Kali around 9 A.M. Many priests have arrived by this time. They are busy exchanging faded flowers with fresh ones. They change the flowers Kali holds in each of her hands and the ones stuck into her crown while the priest in charge of the Kali Temple stands back and oversees all the activities.

The head priest in charge of all temples in the entire Dakshineswar Temple compound is the oldest member of Sri Ramakrishna's family. While most of the priests are members of Sri Ramakrishna's family, the trustees of the Dakshineswar Temple have also appointed staff priests who serve Kali and conduct her worship when the members of Ramakrishna's family are not available.

About 9:30 A.M., the daily worship of Kali begins with the first food offering of seasonal fruits, sweets and uncooked rice. These items were prepared in Kali's kitchen, located in the long row of buildings behind the Kali Temple. Servants begin early in the morning to wash and cut fruits for God. One of these sevaks (servants) then carries the fruits, rice and sweets on a huge silver plate to the Kali Temple. He crosses a small portion of the courtyard and walks up the wide back steps, entering the Kali Temple through the back entrance.

The offering is put in front of Kali, and the pujari (priest who performs the ritual), sitting cross-legged on a small mat, called asana, rearranges the puja vessels around him to make room for the food. The pujari is an attractive, tall, thin man with bushy hair. He sits facing Kali. His forehead has a vertical mark of vermillion, and his upper body is bare except for a thin, loosely draped shawl and a holy thread, which indicates that he is a brahmin.

Like a surgeon about to perform an operation, the pujari shifts things around and properly establishes the location of each vessel and plate. Then he takes the food offering and divides the entire volume into five little mounds—one for Ganesha, the elephant God; one for Narayana, the "Mover on the Waters" (another name for Vishnu); one for Ma Chandi, the Mother of the Shakta Tantra; one for Lakshmi, the Goddess of fortune; and one for Kali and Shiva.

Before the actual morning worship begins, the pujari has to perform a lengthy purification ceremony. He follows ancient Hindu rituals which were influenced by the Tantras. According to some scholars, the most systematic form of worship was developed in Bengal. Swami Bhajanananda explains the daily ritual as follows:

> The normal daily puja consists of six steps: preparations, purifications, divinization of the worshipper, invocation in the image, service to the Deity and conclusion. Every ritual act is followed or preceded by the utterance of a mantra.

Preparations

> Before the puja proper begins certain preparations are made. The ground is washed or wiped clean and the vessels, including a lighted lamp, are arranged on it. The various articles of worship such as water, sandal paste, flowers, etc., are kept ready for use near the worshipper who squats on the ground facing east or north.
>
> The very first ritual is achamana, or purification of the mouth, without which the sacred mantras should not be uttered.
>
> Then the worshipper makes the samkalpa, or sacramental intention. This is a declaration of the purpose of the worship, which may be worldly prosperity or liberation. This connects the will to the act of worship, which thus becomes a conscious, self-directed, goal-oriented discipline.

The next step is the consecration of the water to be used in worship by invoking in it the presence of the seven holy rivers of India from the solar orb. This consecrated water, called samanya arghya, is used for all the remaining rituals.

The worshipper then salutes the various deities and the line of teachers.

Purification

Everything relating to the Deity is sacred and every object connected with puja must be separately sanctified by ritual purification. The removal of various psychic obstacles and the expulsion of evil spirits are also parts of the purification process.

Divinization of the Worshipper

The worshipper must symbolically destroy his papa purusa (sinful self) and let his pure, self-luminous, true self shine forth. For this the worshipper first does pranayama to purify his subtle body. Then follows an important ritual called bhuta shuddhi. In this the worshipper meditates on the kundalini power rising from the base of the spine to the head where it gets united with the light of the Supreme Spirit. He now imagines that his impure gross and subtle bodies are dried up and burnt by this mystic fire. Then he thinks that he is putting on a new divine body, free from all taints of sin, created out of his luminous true self.

After bhuta shuddhi the worshipper invokes the divine Presence in the heart of the new ethereal body. The Deity thus invoked within is then worshipped mentally.

Invocation in the Image

The worshipper has now acquired a divine body and feels the divine Presence in his heart. Next, he has to infuse divine power into all his limbs and organs. This is done by a process called nyasa, which literally means "laying hands on." The worshipper, chanting certain mystic syllables, touches various parts of his body. This gives him the necessary power and fitness to do the next ritual called avahana or invocation of the Deity in a metal image or a stone emblem or a flower. In this process the worshipper imagines that the Deity who is seated in his heart comes out through his breath onto the flower in his hand which is then laid on the head of the image. This is followed by the infusion of power called prana pratistha in the image through special invocatory mudras (gestures).

Thus, puja involves double invocation—first in the heart of the worshipper and then in the image.[9]

Service to the Deity

The worship of Spirit is only possible by the Spirit, and to worship Kali, the pujari must first become Kali. He meditates on Kali in order to acquire her attributes. In a way, one's destiny is determined by the soul's intense aspiration. But, wishful thinking or daydreaming is not enough. One must strengthen one's will so that it becomes powerful and strong enough to transform one's character.

---

[9] *Prabuddha Bharata*, May, 1980, pp. 246-247.

After the pujari has purified everything—the flowers, fruits, vessels, himself—he prepares a paste[10] by grinding bel leaves, hibiscus, and red and white sandalwood, rice, and durva grass in a sparkling copper pot in front of him. First, he worships the Guru and then Ganesh, the God of success. "May my worship be successful," he prays.

Then the pujari bathes an egg-shaped black stone. This is Banalinga, a name of a particular Shiva linga. After Shiva has received his bath, the pujari bathes two round black stones. These are sacred shalagrams and the priest refers to them as Vishnu and Narayan. When the linga and shalagrams are not being worshipped, they are kept in a decorative golden box on Ma Kali's altar. The pujari dries each holy stone with a clean cloth and worships it with arghya, putting the paste on a bel leaf for Shiva and on tulsi leaves for Vishnu and Narayan. By means of a silver ring, the pujari attaches the arghya around the stones.

Sri Ramakrishna's picture and Sri Sarada Devi's picture also get worshipped with arghya. The pujari uses the stem of a leaf as a paint brush and creates a decorative dot pattern of arghya on the pictures. Sri Ramakrishna, who is said to be an incarnation of Vishnu, is also worshipped with a tulsi leaf that the priest glues onto the picture by means of the arghya paste.

Once the pujari has put arghya on all deities—including the mangal-ghat, Shiva's trident and the gosap[11]—he climbs up the side steps of the altar and offers the arghya to Kali's murti (image), touching her feet, forehead, arms, etc. All the while chanting mantras in a melodious voice, the

---

[10] The Dakshineswar Temple priests refer to this paste as arghya. In general, arghya is not ground into a paste. Instead, it represents a respectful offering to the Deity and consists of bel leaves, red hibiscus and red and white sandalwood paste, rice, and durva grass.

[11] A lizard-like extremely poisonous snake.

priest smears the paste onto bel leaves and flowers, and by means of a special red string, ties the arghya to Kali's feet. It will remain there for 24 hours until the next morning when it is replaced with a new offering.

Lastly, the priest worships himself with arghya, offering it to the God within himself. He puts the paste on his forehead, throat, back and arms—three horizontal stripes on each upper arm. Sometimes, a visiting pilgrim is fortunate enough to catch the pujari in a special mood and receive a dot of arghya on the forehead.

After the offering of arghya, the actual worship begins. Worshipping a conch filled with water, the pujari invokes the deity into the water, and then, uttering mantras, he sprinkles this holy water over himself and all other articles. With a sudden abrupt motion, the pujari knocks on one of the puja vessels. The fairly loud, tinny sound produced symbolizes that the Deity has been invoked. Everything is pure and ready for the puja to begin.

The actual Kali worship is not performed on the Kali image but on the mangal-ghat, an earthen vessel filled with Ganges water, that stands on the floor in front of the pujari. This pot-like vessel is a representative of the Great Mother, the cosmic womb. It is within easy reach of the pujari, who will not leave his seat during the ritual.

Worship of miraculous vessels is by no means unique to Hinduism and exists in nearly all mythologies. Celtic European pagans worshipped the "mother-pot" of Cerridwen, a cauldron fundamental to Druidic belief.

The pujari makes offerings and treats Kali in the mangal-ghat in front of him as one would an honorable, beloved guest. In formal worship, offerings can include anywhere from five to ten, to sixteen or more articles. Various Tantras prescribe different articles for the worship of Kali, but all external articles are used only as symbols for the real offering, namely that of the human body and mind.

The Mahanirvana Tantra says, "The Heart-Lotus" should be offered as a seat, the nectar [amrita] shed from the Sahasrara as water for washing the feet, the mind as the oblation [arghya], the memory [citta] as flowers, and the vital airs [prana] as incense.

The Jnanasamkalini Tantra says, "Libation to the Supreme Liberatrix should be made from out the vessel of the Moon, and arghya should be given from out the vessel of the Sun. Compassion, wisdom, and forgiveness are flowers as is also the control of the senses. So, too, are charity [daya] and religious merit. Non-injury [ahimsa] is an excellent flower. Bliss is a flower, and so, too, is the worship of the Sadhaka. Whoever offers these ten flowers attains to the feet of the Liberatrix."[12]

While the puja is going on, there are about four or five priests in Mother's inner sanctum. They attend to the many pilgrims that come to the front and side entrances to worship Kali with their offerings. There is much noise in the small shrine—shouts, clanking bells, and the footfall of thousands of pilgrims echo over the marble floor.

People in the West have been taught to whisper in churches, but in India, people don't equate respect with silent behavior. Everyone at the Dakshineswar Kali Temple seems to shout, even meek-looking little old men and women. Once they see Kali, they shout, "Ma . . . Ma go Ma . . . Jai Kali, Jai Kali," as loud as their voices permit. In contrast to Sri Ramakrishna's room where people sit quietly and meditate, Kali's inner sanctum is rarely quiet.

---

[12] *Hymns to the Goddess*, p. 319.

The Conclusion of the Worship

The conclusion of the morning puja is marked by an arati. After waving the traditional panchadip,[13] the pujari ignites a small bowl of camphor by means of a ghee light kept in an open-ended glass box to his left. He chants with a melodious voice, "Jai Jai Kali, Jai Shiva Kali, Shiva Kali, Kali Durga. . ." while his right hand shoots up and down with the brightly burning camphor. Little black soot specks splutter here and there over the marble floor. A handsome attending priest with short-cropped hair, takes the burning camphor light as soon as the pujari puts it down onto the floor. With a loud "Jai Kali," he runs and carries the large burning flame from person to person. All stretch out their right hands, touch the flame and then the crown of their heads. As one devotee touches Kali's flame and puts his hand on his heart, he feels a divine scorching heat going straight through his body— all the way to the backbone.

The pujari continues to chant while he waves a panisankha[14] before Ma Kali. Then he waves a red cloth and then a flower. And when he blows into a conch, the puja is officially over. All noise stops, and one can hear only the haunting sound of the conch. All heads—pilgrims, priests, servants—are on the floor, bowing down before the Divine Mother Kali. They remain this way and don't look up until the pujari stops blowing the conch. It is now about 11:30 A.M.

The pujari concludes the ritual by offering handfuls of flowers, thereby surrendering himself and the fruit of his worship at the feet of Kali. This ritual is called pushpanjali, and on festive days or special occasions, others also are permitted inside the inner shrine to offer pushpanjali to Kali.

Descendants of Rani Rasmani, the foundress of the Kali Temple, are permitted to enter Kali's inner sanctum whenever the temple is open. As part owners of the temple, they

---

[13] The panchadip is five burning ghee lights on a decorative brass vessel.
[14] A conch filled with water.

enjoy certain privileges, and to be able to offer pushpanjali is one of them. Today seems to be a special day for one attractive, middle-aged lady dressed in an elegant white sari with a decorative black border. She excitedly makes her way into the inner shrine and gives last minute instructions to the pujari, who will make a special offering in her name. Today, she is arranging a thank-you offering to Kali because, by Mother's grace, her son got accepted into a medical college.

A few guests in festive attire follow her into the inner shrine, each one carefully avoiding the black basalt step at the side entrance. They group themselves behind the pujari, their faces solemn, their hands folded in prayer. An attending priest, dressed in a white Indian shirt and vermillion-stained dhoti, distributes handfuls of flowers and bel leaves into each person's right hand. The pujari softly utters a mantra, barely loud enough for others to hear. But the small group of people in the inner shrine know the holy words and repeat the mantra in unison. A few more mantras are repeated in this fashion, and then all offer pranams to Kali. They lift their flower-filled hands to their foreheads and then with a "Jai Ma," they toss the flowers and leaves at Kali. Some land at her feet, some hit Shiva's head, and others never make it as far as the altar. One thin man, eager to get Kali's attention, aims his flowers like darts, throwing them with a velocity worthy of an American basketball player. He succeeds in hitting Kali's garland with a large orange marigold, thereby knocking off a few other flowers. An uninitiated onlooker may think that Kali would become angered by this, but judging by the elated face of the "marigold thrower," hitting Mother's garland must be an achievement rather than a disgrace.

Ma Kali receives an offering of cooked food anywhere between noon and 1:30 P.M. depending on the cook who doesn't always finish cooking the meal at the same time. Compared to Western institutions, Hindus are a lot more

relaxed when it comes to timeliness. At the Dakshineswar
Kali Temple, rituals and the way they are performed are also
a bit more relaxed. There are a few standard rules, but the
finer nuances and length of time a particular rite should take
are left up to the officiating priest.

Between the morning puja and the cooked food offering, priests have some time to relax, and they do so on the
western covered veranda outside the inner shrine. They sit,
leaning against the blood-red, glossily painted wall, reading
a newspaper, gossiping, or slightly dozing off until they
hear a shout from the back entrance.

When this shout is heard, all jump up quickly and move
to the side and out of the way. The shout alerts everyone that
the cook is coming with Kali's food. A servant appears first
and sprinkles Ganges water all the way from the kitchen to the
temple to purify the passage. Then the cook appears with
quick steps, carrying a huge tray. Clad only in a dhoti, he runs
along the covered veranda from the back toward the side
entrance and jumps over the black step into Ma Kali's inner
sanctum. He is followed by an assistant who also runs, carrying an equally large tray of food items. Both shout, "Jai Ma,"
as if to alert the Divine Mother that food is coming. Kali's
musician, who lazily leaned in one corner, waiting for the
bhog arati to start, comes to life and hits his large drum.
"Bong, bong," echo the temple walls.

The cook places Kali's food tray on a small stand located
on Ma's right side. Her food generally consists of rice, fried
vegetables, vegetable curry, dal (Indian lentils), ghee, fish
curry, sweet curds, and rice pudding. As soon as the food is
appetizingly arranged, the priest offers it to Kali by uttering
a mantra. Then, everybody vacates the inner shrine, and the
pujari closes the large iron doors behind him. Kali eats alone
and undisturbed.

The pujari stands facing the shut cast-iron door, his back
turned toward the other priests on the covered veranda. His
eyes are closed and he mutters mantras while slowly turning

his beads. After some time, he claps his hands thrice, and shouting "Ma! Kali Ma!" he pushes open the large iron doors. Ma has finished eating.

Now the bhog arati begins in the Kali temple. Accompanied by a musician on a large drum and another beating a gong, the pujari first waves a panchapradip before Kali. Then he continues the arati with a conch filled with Ganges water, a brilliantly-colored red cloth, a flower, and a chamar. During the morning puja, the priest had purified the five elements (fire, water, earth, air, and ether) by worshipping the Divine Mother with them, and now he is offering them at her feet.

All attending priests and servants stand against the walls of the inner shrine, rhythmically clapping their hands, shouting, "Jai Ma, Jai Ma!" Devotion is written all over the face of one tall young priest who has managed to worship Kali with all sorts of articles while keeping his clothes immaculately white. His eyes are closed while he claps his hands and one can tell his mind is focused within. Ma! Ma! Ma! Kali Ma! The cooing sound of a conch being blown signals that the arati has ended and Mother Kali is about to take her midday rest.

Servants enter the shrine to pick up the food trays next to Kali's altar. This food is considered her leftovers and has now turned into prasad. Upon the question whether Kali has really eaten some of this food, the priests reply that God eats only the subtle element of the food and leaves the gross portion for the devotees. Some of the prasad goes to the priests, who take it home to their families during siesta. The main portion goes back to the kitchen where it is added to the rest of the food steaming in big cauldrons, turning all into prasad.

The temple doors close, and the Dakshineswar Kali Temple compound quiets down under the scorching heat. The priests, who live nearby, go home to their families to eat lunch and sleep for a while. The others eat and take rest on bunk beds in rooms along the row of buildings surrounding the temple courtyard. During the summer months when it gets too hot, they sleep on the open veranda in front of their rooms, softly snoring until it is time to open up the Kali Temple again.

The part-owner of the Kali Temple, together with her little festive group, goes to the VIP trustee room across the courtyard. There, on an open veranda, she will entertain her guests with a sumptuous meal. Servants will walk from guest to guest, offering a rich, elegant pillau, various courses of delicate curries made of rare kinds of fish and meat, curds and sweets. While they serve, the hostess will sit at the end of the row, fasting and watching her guests eat with great delight.

On the other side of the courtyard behind the Kali Temple, pilgrims have lined up, each carrying a previously purchased ticket. They are waiting for the distribution of Kali's prasad.

No puja is complete without the joyful sharing of prasada, the offered sacramental food, by the devotees. It is held that worship without distribution of prasada becomes ineffectual. Prasada is considered so sacred that it should be treated with respect, and holding it in hand one is not expected to salute [take the dust off the feet of] another person. Partaking of prasada is done not merely to gain a psychological sense of participation in worship. Its main purpose is to purify the body and mind, as the root-meaning of the word indicates. The word also means Grace, and so, partaking of prasada is in act of accepting divine blessings.

It is believed that when food materials are offered to the Deity, some changes take place in the subtle elements constituting them. How this takes place is a mystery. The Chandogya Upanisad says: "The Gods do not eat or drink; just by seeing this nectar they become satisfied." Sri Sarada Devi used to say that when she offered food to the Lord, she saw a ray of light coming from the eyes of the Deity and touching the offered materials.[15]

The hungry pilgrims pile into a long covered veranda in front of the kitchens. Sitting cross-legged next to each other, they form a straight line along the cool walls of the veranda. Servants walk back and forth in between the lines of pilgrims, putting down earthen cups filled with fresh water and leaf plates—the disposable "paper plate" of the Orient. Poor people make up these leaf plates by sewing together a number of smaller leaves. A fancier version sometimes used is a cut portion of the tender, green banana leaf.

Preparing themselves for Kali's deliciously spiced prasad, people go through the ritual of sprinkling their leaf plates with water to wash the dust off. One servant carries a large bucket and a ladle, and walking bent between the pilgrims, he dishes out big heaps of steaming rice. The servant wears a dhoti which flimsily covers his thin loins and legs, and his bare upper chest exposes the holy thread that indicates he is a Brahmin and belongs to the highest caste. Other servants follow him, each ladling out different preparations—lentils, curries, fried vegetables, fish, and chutney.

As soon as they are served, people start eating with their hands—no forks, spoons, or knives are used. Their chatter has calmed down now, and one can hear a soft "Soop, soop," as food enters their mouths. It is most interesting to watch Indians scoop up food—which is sometimes of fairly liquid consistency—and fling it expertly into the mouth without dripping food over their clothes. Hindus only use the right

---

[15] *Prabuddha Bharata*, May, 1980, p. 247.

hand to eat. They use the left hand for dirty jobs, such as cleaning the body after having used the rest room. Only the right hand is used to offer food to a guest, to God, and to oneself.

Sweet curds and rice pudding are served at the end of the meal. After they have finished eating, pilgrims pick up their leaf plates and earthen cups to toss them outside near the water fountain where cows, dogs, cats, goats, and crows already wait to finish off the leftovers. Nothing goes to waste. Garbage heaps in India don't get a chance to become large. There is always someone poorer who will pick up what another has thrown away.

In front of the water fountain, pilgrims noisily splash water all around while they wash their hands and rinse their mouths. Hindus always rinse their mouths after each meal. The mouth must be clean when one chants the holy name of God. It is hot, and dozens of pilgrims lazily move toward the Natmandir where they settle down to sleep a little or just to take rest until it is time for the Kali Temple doors to swing open again.

Immediately south of the Kali Temple, connected by a platform is a spacious music hall, called the Natmandir. It has no walls. Only huge pillars support its ornate, stuccoed roof. Four Bhairavas[16] carved of stone, each facing a different point of direction, sit high up on the Natmandir's outer walls. Trident in hand and fierce looking, these Bhairavas are said to protect the sanctity of the place. Whenever Sri Ramakrishna visited Ma Kali's inner shrine, he used to look up and salute one of the Bhairavas as if asking for permission to enter.

When the temple door is open, Ma Kali can see directly into the Natmandir, where musicians and theatrical groups

---

[16] The guardian angels of the Lord Shiva.

perform for her on special occasions. She can see the pilgrims who sit there on their asanas (small prayer rugs), eyes shut, meditating on her. And she can see whenever a sacrifice takes place beyond the Natmandir at the sacrificial place.

Devotees are generally not allowed in the inner shrine of the Kali Temple, and meditation on the platform surrounding the temple is difficult because of the tremendous crowd. Therefore, people come to the Natmandir. Everyone has a right to perform worship in the Natmandir: holy men with matted hair, businessmen, housewives, students, young girls, old men and children alike. Some bring their own utensils and perform ritualistic worship, reading loudly from the Chandi. Mothers bring their small babies for blessings—their doll-like tiny faces made up with sandalwood and their large eyes outlined with kajal[17]. Old women dressed in white, the color of the widow, do japam here hour after hour, invoking blessings for a grandson, a daughter full with child, or a departed husband.

The amalgamation of daily prayer and worship for decades has given the Natmandir a special serenity, a holy atmosphere that is tangible and can be experienced. Resting in the Natmandir's cool shade after the temples close for siesta, devotees enjoy the sacred peace. Everybody who comes to the temple feels a special something. Just as a person visiting a perfume shop can't help but smell the sweet fragrance, like it or not, a person visiting the Natmandir feels the peace and serenity.

Sri Ramakrishna spent many hours in the Natmandir, often pacing back and forth in front of the Kali Temple. One day, in a state of ecstasy, he embraced one of the Natmandir's large columns because he perceived it as full of consciousness. Using the Natmandir's inner and outer columns as an example, Sri Ramakrishna would tell his disciples that it is better to belong to the inner circle because the guru provides

---

[17] Collirium made out of charcoal.

full protection to those close around him while those belonging to the outer circle have to weather storm and wind by themselves. People who sometimes dwell in God and sometimes in the world have to put up with nature's blows just like the outer columns of the Natmandir.

M., one of Sri Ramakrishna's householder disciples, describes a particular mood during one of his first meetings with the Master in the Natmandir:

> It was now late in the evening and time for M's departure; but he felt reluctant to go and instead went in search of Sri Ramakrishna. He had been fascinated by the Master's singing and wanted to hear more. At last he found the Master pacing alone in the Natmandir in front of the Kali temple. A lamp was burning in the temple on either side of the image of the Divine Mother. The single lamp in the spacious Natmandir blended light and darkness into a kind of mystic twilight, in which the figure of the Master could be dimly seen.

> M had been enchanted by the Master's sweet music. With some hesitation he asked him whether there would be any more singing that evening. "No, not tonight," said Sri Ramakrishna after a little reflection.

> M bowed low before him and took his leave. He had gone as far as the main gate of the temple garden when he suddenly remembered something and came back to Sri Ramakrishna, who was still in the Natmandir.

> In the dim light the Master, all alone, was pacing the hall, rejoicing in the Self—as the lion lives and roams alone in the forest.[18]

---

[18] *The Gospel of Sri Ramakrishna,* p. 92.

Immediately south of the Natmandir is the bali, the sacrificial pole. Most temples dedicated to Shakti, the Divine Mother, have a sacrificial place either near or in the Natmandir. It is a two-forked wooden pole used during the ritual wherein an animal, generally a goat, is beheaded and sacrificed to Kali—an act which completely horrifies our pet-conscious western society. How terrible, how barbaric! But, what about our slaughterhouses? One wonders what the answer would be if a goat or sheep bred for food could speak and were asked what it prefers: to die in a modern slaughterhouse or at the sacrificial pole of Kali? To be distributed in freezer boxes or to be cooked and eaten after the worship by devotees with reverence?

Suppose people in the West were to be asked, "Is it wrong to kill an animal in a temple and offer it to God?" Ninety-nine, if not one-hundred, percent of them will say, "Yes." Then, suppose all the people who said, "Yes," were to be asked: "Is it wrong to kill an animal in a slaughterhouse?" Only the vegetarians among them could say, "Yes," with a clear conscience. Most of us do not kill animals and probably never will, but if we eat meat, we kill by creating a demand for meat. It is easy to judge foreign customs, yet it is very difficult to look objectively at one's own habits.

The question arises, is Ma Kali cruel to animals? The answer is, no. Throughout history the Great Goddess was considered the Mother of all and this includes wild animals. All animals belong to her, and to this day, nobody is allowed to wear leather in her presence in the temple. Animals are offered to Kali as a sacrificial rite and afterward they are cooked and distributed as prasad (sanctified food)—as a gift from the Goddess.

The Goddess is not only the Mother of all animals but is also present in each of the animals. Once her son Ganesha, the elephant God, hit a cat and when he came home, he discovered in horror that the injury he had done to the cat appeared on his mother's body.

Sri Ramakrishna, who perceived Mother in all, could never bear cruelty to animals and showed love for all creatures. Once a pregnant cat took refuge at his feet. Sri Ramakrishna himself found the cat a home, asking one of his devotees to take care of the cat and kittens. Whenever this devotee visited the Master, he would inquire about the welfare of the cats.

Ma Kali is awakened from her midday rest at 3:30 P.M. by a priest who serves her a cup of cool green-coconut milk, fruits, and sweets. Immediately after, the temple doors open, and people lined up outside may come in and offer their worship to Ma Kali.

The constant stream of devotees does not end until the evening arati which is held at 6:45 P.M. in summer and at 6:15 P.M. in winter. This arati basically is the same ritual as performed in the morning, except that it lasts longer—about three quarters of an hour. Accompanied by loud drums, gongs, and cymbals, the pujari performs the ceremony with great intensity.

After arati, the iron doors close again. Now the priests are busy taking all flowers off Ma Kali and cleaning her altar. They clean and wash off everything except the arghya on Kali's and Shiva's feet. Around 8 P.M., Kali is served dinner, which generally consists of luchi (fried bread), fried eggplant, fried potatoes, milk, and sweets. At night, Kali only eats vegetarian dishes.

Before the priests close the temple for the night, Ma Kali is put to bed. A priest puts a picture of Ma Kali onto the small bed next to the altar, pulls the mosquito curtain and tucks it in lest mosquitos should disturb the Mother's sleep. Miraculously, there are no mosquitos in Kali's inner sanctum although there are countless mosquitos in Dakshineswar. They don't frequent the inner shrine of Kali and seem to prefer the VIP trustee lounge. See figure 15.

Figure 15. A rare photo of the Goddess Kali taken in the evening after arati, and here you see her without flowers. (Photo by Gandhi Roy.)

After Ma Kali has been officially put to bed, the priest in charge of locking up purifies the inner shrine by sprinkling Ganges water all around. He waves incense in front of Kali's bed and bows down to her, his head touching the marble floor. Then he closes and locks the inner and outer doors to the Kali Temple. Now, Mother will sleep until a priest awakens her at 4 A.M. with a "Ma Jago!" Get up, Mother!

Special Worship

Contrary to the Western calendar which is calculated according to the position of the sun, the Bengali calendar is lunar. Auspicious days for festivals, even birthdays, are based on the position of the moon. Although the Bengali lunar calendar also has twelve months, it does not correspond with the Western calendar. For instance, the Bengali New Year is celebrated in mid-April, and Vaisakh, the first month in the year, begins mid-April and ends mid-May. Festivals, also, do not fall on the same days as those in the West.

Throughout the year, there are various seasonal celebrations and special worships dedicated to Kali. Mother is treated like a living person and her comfort is of utmost importance. During the winter season, for instance, the pujari, afraid that Mother might feel cold, does not use a chamar to fan her while performing the arati. He also covers Kali and the other deities on the altar with woolen shawls when he puts them to bed at night.

The Dakshineswar Kali Temple opens at 4:00 A.M. for mangal arati, which generally lasts for 15 minutes. Then the temple closes again and does not reopen until 6:00 A.M. The daily morning worship starts around 9:30 A.M. and, after the food (bhog) offering which happens around noon, the Kali Temple closes again until 3:30 P.M. The evening arati is being held at 6:30 P.M. The temple closes for the night at 8:30 P.M. during the winter months.

During the summer season, the Kali Temple remains open until 9 P.M. On Sundays and holidays, the temple is open an hour longer in the afternoon—from 3:00 P.M. to 9:00 P.M. in winter and from 3:00 P.M. to 9:30 P.M. in summer.

The darkest night of the moon is of special significance for Kali worship, and a festival held the day before the night of the new moon (amavasya[19]) is repeated every month. During this special worship, an animal is sacrificed to Ma Kali. The morning worship draws thousands of people to the Dakshineswar Kali Temple. They come for various reasons. Some come to get darshan[20] of Kali while others come to see the excitement and to watch a priest sacrifice a male goat.

Before the animal is sacrificed, priests bathe the goat in the Ganges while the morning puja is still going on. Then they carry the animal up the steps, past the Natmandir and into the Kali Temple. The pujari performs a short ritual, and worships the goat by putting vermillion and flowers on its head. Then he walks behind Kali's altar and takes down one of her swords, handing it to a small, thin man who humbly accepts it.

Meanwhile, the goat is carried outside, through the Natmandir and to the sacrificial place (bali[21]). Priests and assistants follow in procession, carrying incense and items for worship—a casket containing vermillion and an earthen pot covered with a banana leaf and one ripe banana. Their faces solemn, the priests wave incense in all directions as they walk from Kali's shrine to the bali. They pay no attention to the intermittent shouts, throaty and brutal, that arise from within the assembled crowd. The pujari worships the sacrificial pole and then purifies the surrounding area by uttering holy mantras.

Although people crowd and push to get a closer look, nobody dares to block Ma Kali's view. They leave room for a

---

[19] Amavasya = new moon.
[20] See a holy face.
[21] Bali = to cut; bali-sthan = cutting place.

narrow lane which starts at the inner sanctum of Kali and runs straight to the sacrificial place. When the thin man in charge of the execution worships the sword and then lifts it up high for Kali to see, there is a hushed, tense silence. Pilgrims, priests, businessmen, beggars, and children alike, all seem to hold their breath. But when the head of the goat comes off with one strike and rolls in the sand, a tremendous noise breaks loose. Drums, gongs, and cymbals herald the sacrifice's completion. Women produce a high-pitched sound by singing a high note while wagging their tongues. It's an eerie sound, but considered auspicious when performed at important moments. Adding to the general excitement, men shout, "Jai Kali," and children peek around the saris of their mothers to see something they are not sure they want to see.

After the sacrifice, one priest takes the head of the goat, puts it on a silver plate and carries it back into the inner shrine of Kali. The small man who beheaded the goat is busy worshipping the bali with vermillion and flowers, while servants carry the body of the goat to the kitchen where it will be cleaned, cooked, and served to Kali during the food offering. Inside Kali's shrine, priests perform a ritual on the head of the goat. Uttering mantras, they light a small ghee light on the goat's head, and then offer it to Kali.

Before the goat was sacrificed, priests had covered the image of Gopala on the altar with a red cloth. Since Gopala (baby Krishna) is a vegetarian, he is covered because he cannot stand the sight of animal sacrifice. The red cloth stays on Gopala until the goat's head has been carried outside the inner sanctum of Kali.

But every seventh year, Gopala does not need to be covered during amavasya worship because there are no animal sacrifices throughout the entire year. One son-in-law of Rani Rasmani, the foundress of the Kali temple, was a Vaishnava and vegetarian. Upon his pleas, the Rani promised him that every seventh year, nobody at the Kali Temple would be allowed to sacrifice animals to the Goddess. This custom still prevails, and every seventh year, Kali becomes a vegetarian.

Animals throughout history have given their lives so that human beings can live. We have slaughtered animals for food as well as for salvation, and the belief that the killing of life can eradicate one's sins is not unique to Hinduism. The "scapegoat," in some form or another, appears in most religions. Christians believe that through the death of Christ, they were given eternal life and their sins were eradicated. By sacrificing animals in front of Ma Kali, Hindus believe they have symbolically chopped off their lust, greed, anger, jealousy, selfishness and ego.

Right or wrong? One could debate endlessly on this subject and still never reach a conclusion. There will always be people who think it their right to eat meat, and there will always be others who refute them. One may take the middle road and point out that anything carried to excess is bad. Fanaticism is a bane that has plagued this world too long, and people who were so sure that they were right have done massive evil throughout history. Evil rarely comes dressed as evil and often appears in the form of a powerful, "virtuous" leader. And what can be more deadly than virtue carried to excess?

In an effort to obtain God's grace and go to heaven, Hindus at one time performed an excessive amount of animal sacrifices. They killed herds of goats and sheep and, still, they did not stop. One day Buddha observed a shepherd boy chasing a lame goat. The boy hit the animal because it couldn't run as fast as the others. Buddha said, "Why are you hitting this poor creature?"

"Well," replied the shepherd boy, "we have to reach the sacrificial place at a certain time and this goat is holding us up."

Buddha said, "Don't hit the goat. I shall carry it." Saying so, he took the goat on his shoulders and followed the shepherd boy. They walked for a long time, and when they came to the sacrificial place, Buddha began to argue with the brahmin priests.

"Why are you performing this cruel sacrifice?" asked Buddha. "Our king will go to heaven," said the priests. "If by killing these innocent creatures your king will go to heaven, then kill me," challenged Buddha. "Your king will go to a better heaven."

There was a big debate and even the king came to listen. In the end, Buddha defeated the brahmins, and the king stopped all animal killing in his kingdom.

The morning ritual of amavasya ends with the pujari performing a Vedic ritual—the homa fire. During the Vedic period, all offerings to Gods were made to fire, which was regarded as the mouth of the Gods. Agni, the fire God, was believed to act as a messenger who would carry the offerings to the God propitiated. Later on, people began to believe that Gods directly accept offerings, and so the rituals changed. Nevertheless, homa fire is still practiced, especially on auspicious days when large pujas are performed.

Sitting on the marble floor of the Kali Temple's northern covered veranda, the priest builds an intricate pattern with pieces of wood on a square metal tray filled with white sand. Then, while reciting mantras, he lights the wood and pours clarified butter on it to make it burn better. The fire burns brightly, and flames shoot high. Smoke fills the veranda, but although some cough uncontrollably, the devotees watching the event do not leave the veranda. The thick smoke travels around the corner and enters Kali's inner sanctum. Looking through the heavy haze, a devotee might see the face of Ma Kali, looking pleased and radiant.

Besides amavasya, Hindus celebrate many other festivals in honor of Kali. During Jaistha, the second Bengali month, which starts around the middle of May, Phalaharini Kali puja is held during the new moon night. Priests begin the Phalaharini Kali puja after 9 P.M., and the worship continues until one or two o'clock in the morning. During this ritual, not only one goat is sacrificed but also vegetables. Along with the goat, priests also behead one long spear of sugar cane and a football-size chalkumra, which is a kind of pumpkin.

The snana-yatra, the bathing ceremony day of Lord Jagannath, is also celebrated during the month of Jaistha. It is a big festival at the Dakshineswar Kali Temple because it falls on the day when the temple was dedicated in the Bengali year of 1262—May 31, 1855. The snana-yatra is celebrated in the morning. During the morning worship in the Kali Temple, two goats, one chalkumra and one sugar cane are sacrificed to Ma Kali.

Besides amavasya, there are no special festivals held at the Dakshineswar Kali Temple during the next three Bengali months—Asarh, Shravan, and Bhadra—which end around the middle of September. But in the following month, Aswin, a major Bengali festival takes place. It is the autumn festival of Durga Puja which gets celebrated with great pomp and splendor. And a few weeks later, during the month of Kartik, people celebrate Kali Puja, the greatest night of the year for Kali worshippers. Jagaddhatri Puja, celebrated in the same month, is held in the morning. One goat, sugar cane, and chalkumra get sacrificed during the worship.

The months of Agrahayan and Poush, which end around the middle of January, have no special festivals other than the monthly ritual of amavasya. During the month of Magh, the Dakshineswar Kali Temple celebrates Ratanti Puja during the night before the day of the new moon. This puja lasts until 1 or 2 A.M., and one goat, sugar cane, and chalkumra get sacrificed.

The following month, Falgun, does not have any special festivals dedicated to Ma Kali. Nevertheless, it is a month that calls for a great celebration at the Dakshineswar Kali Temple. The great saint of Kali, Sri Ramakrishna, was born during this month, and devotees come from far to witness the special worship in his room near the Ganges. Throughout the year, Sri Ramakrishna is worshipped and served cooked food in the Vishnu temple, but on his birth anniversary, priests worship him in the room in which he lived and saw God for fourteen years.

During Chaitra, which is the last month of the Bengali calendar and begins around the middle of March, people observe the festival of Basanti Puja. This puja is similar to Durga Puja, but it is performed on a much smaller scale.

Durga Puja

During the Durga Puja festival, the image of the Divine Mother is worshipped day and night in temples, homes, and in temporarily erected pandals on the street. Priests perform elaborate rituals and recite ancient Sanskrit texts, depicting the bloody victory of the Mother Durga over the hosts of demons. Offices and shops close for four to five days, and people fast and keep vigil. Half of Calcutta is in the street, and people walk from place to place to see who has the most beautiful image of Mother Durga. They come from all over and walk miles to see the living Divine Mother in so many forms, in so many clay statues.

While Calcuttans are in a mad frenzy, each and all seeking to find the most beautifully modeled image of Durga, the Dakshineswar Kali Temple does not take part in the competition. Priests there do not worship Durga in a specially created image of the Goddess and, instead, perform the traditional Durga worship in front of the Kali image.

Durga Puja is a five-day celebration, starting with Mahalaya, a ritual during which the Mother Durga is petitioned to come to Earth and take part in the festivities. Mahalaya coincides with the amavasya celebration during the month of Aswin (sometime between the end of September and beginning of October). And since Durga Puja is perhaps the most widely celebrated religious function in Bengal, it may be appropriate to describe this festive season although it does not directly relate to Kali worship.

Weeks before Durga Puja, peasants dig up clay from the Ganga and sell it to sculptors who build beautiful Durga images according to ancient traditions. Mother in her earthen image is generally represented as Mahishasura-mardini, killer of the demon Mahishasura. To visually describe her power, the Hindu sculptor gives Ma Durga ten arms, each holding a different gift from the Gods. One arm holds a conch, another a discus, a bow and arrow, a sword, dagger, shield, rosary, cup of wine and a bell. One of her arms strikes the demon Mahishasura with a trident. He looks up and his last glimpse of the world is the face of the Divine Mother. Struck by the blow of the Goddess, the demon has shed his buffalo head which lies bleeding on the ground. His face has become serene before death, and he looks at Durga with awe, wonder and surrender.

Durga's face has a golden-yellow complexion. She has three eyes—the middle one in her forehead is the eye of Knowledge. She is adorned with a crown, jewelry, and garlands. Durga wears a gorgeous Varanasi sari and stands on a lion, her official carrier. She is flanked by her children—Ganesha, the elephant-headed God, and Lakshmi, the Goddess of wealth, on her right and Sarasvati, the Goddess of learning, and Kartik, a handsome warrior God, on her left.

On the first day of Durga Puja, the priest symbolically takes his own life energy out of his body and installs it in the clay image. After four days, when the puja is over and before the image is immersed in the river Ganges, the priest will again symbolically take back his life energy into his own body.

On the third day of Durga Puja, the Divine Mother is worshipped as Kumari (virgin) in a 5-year-old girl. Only girls that are healthy, graceful, beautiful, and born into a pious family are selected for the worship of the Kumari Puja. The Srimad Devi Bhagavatam emphasizes that the pujari should utter the proper mantra while he worships the little girl. He should give her presents of costly garments, precious jewelry, garlands, and scents. He should offer her the finest sweets and cool milk of the green coconut. And if he worships Kumari properly, there will never be misery or poverty for him. His enemies will be undone, and he will enjoy riches, a long life and power.

Belur Math, headquarters of the Ramakrishna Order, annually celebrates this Kumari Puja on the western platform of the Ramakrishna Temple on the bank of the river Ganges. A pretty girl, decorated with jewelry, sandal paste, and garlands, and dressed in a costly red silk sari, is placed on an altar and worshipped in traditional fashion by a monk.

During the worship, people see the girl no longer as a little girl belonging to such and such parents. She has become the Divine Mother herself. Although the ceremony lasts over an hour, a curious Westerner was told that never has a little girl become restless, jumped off the altar and run to her parents. That alone seems a small miracle. Somehow, the worship transforms the child, and she instinctively understands the significance of the moment. At the end of the worship, the priest bows low before the girl. And when she stands and raises her tiny hand in blessing, the thousands of people watching from the lawn cheer with tears in their eyes.

The Srimad Devi Bhagavatam lists in detail at what age girls ought to be worshipped and what results the worshipper may obtain. When one worships a 3-year old girl, for instance, the puja is called Trimurti Puja and is supposed to yield longevity, the acquisition of dharma, wealth, and the fulfillment of desires. If the girl is 4 years old, she is called Kalyani, the fructifier of all desires. While some people propitiate a virgin to bestow prosperity, to cure diseases, or to destroy obstacles, the sincere spiritual aspirant worships the Universal Mother within the little girl, asking for nothing but devotion to her lotus feet.

When all the demons—all vices within us—are killed, Mother Durga goes back to her home high up in the Himalayas, and her clay image is immersed in the Ganges. Of course, at the Dakshineswar Temple there is no image to be immersed, because Mother Durga is worshipped in the living image of Kali. But all over the city of Calcutta, clay images of Durga are assembled and made ready for the immersion. In the evening, it seems as if the entire population of Calcutta has come out into the streets to watch the various Durga images go by. They are carried on trucks toward the grand river Ganges while people sing and dance in the street, feed each other, give gifts and then go home to write each other cards like people in the West do at the Christmas season.

Kali Puja

About three weeks after Durga Puja, during the month of Kartik, the long awaited, favorite night of the Shakti worshipper arrives. The Kali Puja is performed during the dark night of the new moon. Traditions have remained the same throughout history, and today's Kali Puja differs little from Kali Pujas performed over one hundred years ago. M., the recorder of *The Gospel of Sri Ramakrishna*, described the Dakshineswar Kali Puja festivity on Saturday, October 18, 1884.

It was the day of the worship of Kali, the Divine Mother. The worship was to begin at eleven o'clock at night. Several devotees arrived at the temple garden early in the evening. They wanted to visit Sri Ramakrishna during the holy hours of the night of the new moon.

M. came alone to the garden about eight o'clock in the evening. The great religious festival had already begun. Lamps had been lighted here and there in the garden, and the temples were brightly illuminated. Music could be heard in the nahabat. The temple officers were moving about hurriedly. There was to be a theatrical performance in the early hours of the morning. The villagers had heard of the festive occasion, and a large crowd of men and women, young and old, was streaming in.

In the afternoon there had been a musical recital of the Chandi by Rajnarayan. Sri Ramakrishna had been present with the devotees and had enjoyed the recital immensely. As the time for the worship approached, he was overwhelmed with ecstasy. . . .

It was the awe-inspiring night of the new moon. The worship of the Divine Mother added to its solemnity. Sri Ramakrishna was seated on the couch, leaning against a pillow. His mind was indrawn. Now and then he exchanged a word or two with the devotees. . . . Haripada was gently stroking the Master's feet. The Master was humming some of the songs he had heard that evening during the recital of the Chandi. He sang softly:

Who is there that can understand what Mother Kali is?
Even the six darsanas are powerless to reveal Her . . .

Sri Ramakrishna sat up. With intense fervor he began to sing about the Divine Mother:

All creation is the sport of my mad Mother Kali;
By Her maya the three worlds are bewitched.
Mad is She and mad is Her Husband;
mad are Her two disciples!
None can describe Her loveliness,
Her glories, gestures, moods;
Shiva, with the agony of the poison in His throat,
Chants Her name again and again.

The Personal does She oppose to the Impersonal,
Breaking one stone with another;
Though to all else She is agreeable,
Where duties are concerned She will not yield.
Keep your raft, says Ramprasad, afloat on the sea of life,
Drifting up with the flood-tide,
drifting down with the ebb.

The Master was quite overwhelmed with the song.
He said that songs like this one denoted a state of
divine inebriation. He sang one after another:

This time I shall devour Thee utterly, Mother Kali!
For I was born under an evil star,
And one so born becomes,
they say, the eater of his mother—

Then:

O Kali, my Mother full of Bliss!
Enchantress of the almighty Shiva!
In Thy delirious joy Thou dancest,
clapping Thy hands together! . . .

Ramlal entered the room. The Master said to him:
"Please sing something about the Divine Mother.
It is the day of Her worship." Ramlal sang:

> *Who is the Woman yonder who lights the field of battle?*
> *Darker Her body gleams even than the darkest storm*
> *   cloud,*
> *And from Her teeth there flash the lightning's blinding*
> *   flames!*
> *Dishevelled Her hair is flying behind as She rushes*
> *   about,*
> *Undaunted in this war between the Gods and the*
> *   demons.*
> *Laughing Her terrible laugh, She slays the fleeing*
> *   asuras,*
> *And with Her dazzling flashes She bares the horror of*
> *   war. . . .*

Again Ramlal sang:

> *Who is this terrible Woman, dark as the sky at mid-*
> *   night?*
> *Who is this Woman dancing over the field of battle?*

Sri Ramakrishna began to dance to the song. Then
he himself sang:

> *The black bee of my mind is drawn in sheer delight*
> *To the blue lotus flower of Mother Shyama's feet,*
> *The blue flower of the feet of Kali, Shiva's Consort.*
> *Tasteless, to the bee, are the blossoms of desire.*
> *My Mother's feet are black, and black, too, is the bee;*
> *Black is made one with black! This much of the mystery*
> *These mortal eyes behold, then hastily retreat.*
> *But Kamalakanta's hopes are answered in the end;*
> *He swims in the Sea of Bliss, unmoved by joy or pain.*

After the music and dancing, Sri Ramakrishna sat
on the couch. Some of the devotees went to the temple to salute the image of the Divine Mother. Others

sat quietly performing japa on the steps leading to
the Ganges. It was about eleven o'clock, the most
auspicious time for contemplation of the Divine
Mother. The flood tide was rising in the Ganges,
and the lights on its banks were reflected here and
there in its dark waters.

From outside the shrine M. was looking wistfully at
the image. Ramlal came to the temple with a book
in his hand containing the rules of the worship. He
asked M. if he wanted to come in. M. felt highly
favored and entered the shrine. He saw that the
Divine Mother was profusely decorated. The room
was brilliantly illuminated by a large chandelier
that hung from the ceiling. Two candles were burning in front of the image. On the floor were trays
full of offerings. Red hibiscus flowers and bel leaves
adorned Her feet. She wore garlands round Her
neck. M.'s eyes fell on the chamara. Suddenly he
remembered that Sri Ramakrishna often fanned the
Divine Mother with it. With some hesitation he
asked Ramlal if he might fan the image. The priest
gave his permission. M. joyously fanned the image.
The regular worship had not yet begun.

The devotees again entered the Master's room. . . .
Sri Ramakrishna sat on the small couch, and the
devotees on the floor. . . . Ramlal entered the room
and saluted Sri Ramakrishna, touching the ground
with his forehead. Then with great respect he
touched the Master's feet. He was ready to worship the Divine Mother in the temple.

Ramlal: "Please permit me to go to the shrine."

The Master twice uttered the words "Om Kali" and
said: "Perform the worship carefully. There is also a
sheep to be slaughtered."

It was midnight. The worship began in the Kali temple. The Master went to watch the ceremony. During the worship he stood near the image. Now the sheep was going to be slaughtered. The animal was consecrated before the Deity. People stood in lines watching the ceremony. While the sheep was being taken to the block, Sri Ramakrishna returned to his room. He could not bear the sight.

Several devotees remained in the temple till two o'clock in the morning. Haripada came and asked them to take the prasad to the Master's room. After finishing their meal they lay down wherever they could for the remainder of the night.[22]

Kali Puja in Dakshineswar today is as exciting as it was during the time of Sri Ramakrishna. A devotee still perceives the Godman and his disciples singing and dancing—oblivious to the world and completely absorbed in bliss—on the old stone tiles of the Dakshineswar Kali Temple. The feeling of joy is intoxicating, and one experiences the saying, "True religion isn't taught; it's caught." It seeps in as in osmosis, and one doesn't need to do anything but be there. As a person who enters a perfume shop smells perfume, liking it or not, a person entering the Kali Temple during the Kali Puja night picks up a tangible spirituality.

Before the vesper service begins—around 6:30 P.M.—a priest ignites pieces of fragrant bark from the chal tree in a small bowl. And then waving the bowl in a circular motion, he circumambulates Kali's altar until the whole inner sanctum fills with smoke. Images look as hazy as in a steam bath, and from somewhere, a mystical glow pierces the smoke. Golden, diffused light falls on the marble floor, on the blue-tiled walls and on devotees who stand in awe outside the inner sanctum.

---

[22] *The Gospel of Sri Ramakrishna* , pp. 617-621.

Kali's face glistens in the soft light. Every year, a few days before Kali Puja, priests put a new coat of paint on her image and clean all her jewelry until it shines. They dress her in a new Varanasi silk sari, and amid the luxurious red silk, her face looks flushed like a young girl about to go to a dance. Kali wears numerous thick flower garlands around her neck and holds one white lotus in each one of her four hands. One white lotus is tucked into the anklet on her right foot and another blossoms on her left foot. The lotus on which the image of Ma Kali stands has been recently coated with silver, and it sparkles in the light.

Instead of the regular panchadip[23], the pujari has picked up an elaborate brass receptacle somewhat resembling a chandelier or a small brass Christmas tree of lights. On numerous tiers flicker countless ghee lights as the pujari slowly raises his arm and waves all these lights before Kali in a circular motion. While his right hand waves the lights, his left hand rings a big brass bell with a constant, rhythmic motion—a clank . . . a clank . . . a clank . . . a clank. Outside the shrine on the covered veranda, musicians beat a large drum and a brass gong, creating such noise that the sheer loudness makes it impossible for the bystander to think of anything other than the immediate moment.

Ringing the brass bell without missing a beat, the pujari puts down the chandelier of lights and picks up a bowl of burning camphor. As he gracefully waves the bowl in front of Kali, her face reflects the yellow light, and she looks benevolent. The flame leaps up into the air two feet or higher, and specks of black soot fly in all directions. When the pujari has finished worshipping the Great Mother with the burning camphor, an assisting priest carries the flame from person to person. Wherever he stops, people hold out their right hands as if to caress the flame, and then in reverence, they touch their heads and hearts.

---

[23] Vessel holding five ghee lights.

The pujari picks up a large conch shell filled with holy water. A red hibiscus flower is stuck on top of the shell. He cups his right hand over the conch shell and waves it in front of Kali while his left hand continues to ring the big brass bell. One feels mesmerized following the snakelike motions of the pujari's arm. After waving a red cloth and then a white lotus before Kali, the pujari fans her with the chamar. This is the last time this year that he will fan Ma Kali with a chamar. He won't use the chamar again until after Shiva Ratri (during March) when the cool winter season ends.

Once the arati is finished, many priests and attendants enter the inner shrine and immediately busy themselves with cleaning. They sweep and wash the marble floor with Ganges water. Then they clear the altar, removing all flowers and leaves. One priest, who has an unusually striking face and jet-black wavy hair, is carefully taking all the flowers and garlands off the image of Kali. Another priest sits cross-legged next to the altar and mixes red powder with ghee in a brass container. He is preparing vermillion, the red color Hindu women use to decorate their foreheads.

The earthen pitcher (ghat) which symbolizes Kali and stands in front of the altar is entirely without flowers now and looks bare. On other days, it is covered with so many garlands, flowers, and leaves that people can hardly see it, but tonight it has been scrubbed and all vermillion removed. All must be spotless before Kali Puja begins.

Servants load huge baskets with flowers that were previously offered to Ma Kali. One old servant winds a towel and puts it on top of his head in a circle. The towel will protect his head and balance the enormous basket while he carries it out of the temple to the Ganges. Every time the doors open and a priest or servant goes in or out, the crowd outside the temple pushes a few inches closer and shouts. While a few devotees have managed to come inside and bring baskets of offerings, most stand outside and hope to get at least a glimpse of Kali.

As soon as the inner shrine is washed and cleaned, Mother's cook arrives with her dinner and puts the tray on the sparkling tiles. Tonight, her dinner consists of fried bread, potatoes, fried vegetables, milk and some sweets.

The outside platform surrounding the temple is lit up by countless tiny candle lights. Tonight is not only Kali Puja but also the Festival of Lights. The whole of India celebrates this Festival of Lights, and thousands of tiny butter lights float down the Ganges, put there by loving hands and sent off with a prayer. It is truly a thrilling experience to stand on Kali's platform in the warm night air and watch the devotees as they circumambulate the Great Mother Goddess— their intense, prayerful faces lit by hundreds of flickering lights. The smell of exotic incense is everywhere. Kali worshippers have inserted burning incense sticks into cracks of the outside walls of Mother's temple. All but the moment is forgotten, and the onlooker feels transported into some sort of twilight zone.

A pleasant breeze comes from the Ganges, and melodious voices fill the night air. These come from the Natmandir where a kirtan party sings Kali bhajans without pause. The group of men and women started singing earlier in the evening and are scheduled to continue throughout the night.

The evening is progressing fast and it is now past 8 P.M. Ma Kali's dinner is over and servants have removed her tray. Numerous priests are busy decorating the entire inner shrine. In an intricately interwoven pattern, resembling a curtain of exquisite lace, they hang fragrant garlands of jasmine and tuberoses around Kali's silver altar. Kali, herself, is decorated with a thick, beautiful white and yellow garland.

The head priest from the Vishnu temple enters the shrine and bows before Ma Kali. A few devotees and descendants of Rani Rasmani, the temple foundress, also enter and are permitted to make pranams before Kali. Since the front entrance is locked for preparation of the puja, priests open the side entrance to the Kali temple at intervals to give devotees a chance to bring their offerings and, in turn, receive prasad. Some devotees arrive with huge baskets laden with presents—flowers, fruits, sweets, ornaments, and small tin swords resembling Kali's large sword.

When the crowd pushing toward the entrance gets too large and rowdy, a crew of volunteers with red armbands tries to push people back in an attempt to close the doors again. The volunteers are mainly young men hired by temple officials to keep law and order during Kali Puja night. Without the help of these volunteers, things could become unruly since many male Mother worshippers drink wine during this night and, not being accustomed to doing so, become boisterous. Hindus, in general, do not drink alcohol, and drinking wine during Kali Puja night is a fairly recent custom. Besides intoxicated Kali worshippers, volunteers also have to control hordes of exuberant young devotees who celebrate by throwing firecrackers—frequently and loudly.

Although the doors to Kali's temple are closed now, a few devotees have managed to stay within the boundary of the covered veranda. As a volunteer opens the door to let one devotee out, one rowdy young man enters the veranda by slapping his way through the door. Two offended volunteers immediately charge after him and try to lift the unruly fellow outside, but he slips through their arms and sinks to his knees with utter humility and devotion. Before Kali, the Great Mother, the big bully turns into a harmless little boy.

There is much noise of drums near the front entrance. This indicates that Ma Kali's earthen pitcher is being carried to the Ganges where it will be filled with fresh water. And, at the sound of more drums, priests and servants return with the earthen pitcher which contains the "liquid Mother." The little procession is accompanied by gongs, shouts, and cymbals. "Jai Ma, Jai Ma, Jai Kali Ma i ki jai!" Once it reaches the inner shrine, a priest welcomes the Mother by ringing a big brass bell. As soon as the earthen pitcher is placed before the altar, the pujari covers it with a fresh coconut.

The main pujari sits on an asana flanked by two assistant pujaris in front of the altar. His upper body is bare except for a silken yellow cloth wrapped diagonally around his shoulder and waist, half covering the holy Brahminical thread. Large rudraksha beads hang round his neck, and his forehead is marked with a vertical line of vermillion. The upper bodies of the two pujaris on either side of him are also bare and their Brahminical threads are visible.

Before the actual Kali Puja, the pujari must first go through a series of purification ceremonies. The first purification rite is called acamana—the sipping of water. Repeating mantras, the pujari inhales and sips Ganges water while envisioning that this water has come from the feet of Vishnu. He purifies himself by identifying with the drops of water he drinks, and his individual soul merges with the cosmic soul. After worshipping the Guru and various deities in a few lengthy rites, he performs sankalpa—the resolution. The worshipper makes a conscious resolution wherein he states the purpose for the worship.

A few more rituals follow, and then he is ready to "establish the pitcher." The main pujari invokes Kali into the water inside the earthen pitcher after he has shaken it and thereby symbolically has put his own consciousness into it. He proceeds with the worship by sprinkling rice and throwing it into all corners to feed evil spirits that may dwell in the vicinity. "May all spirits be pacified."

Some more purification rites follow. The pujari purifies the earth, his asana, his hands, his body, the flowers for offering and utensils to be used. He worships the ingredients themselves. Then he imagines a wall of fire, surrounding him and Kali, and prays that outside influences may not disturb the worship. Then follows pranayama, a process of breath control which purifies and calms the body. The pujari breathes in through the left nostril, holds his breath, and then breathes out through the right nostril. All this is done according to a specific count. For instance, one may count to 4 when breathing in, count to 16 when holding the breath, and count to 8 when breathing out.

The pujari must go through all these purification rites in order to destroy, symbolically, his karma-tainted body and create a new divine body. Otherwise, he cannot worship Kali. This process is called bhuta shuddhi, the purification of the old and the formation of the celestial body. As love is only possible between equals, so worship also has to be performed by those of equal standing. Devo bhutva devam yajet (One has to be God to worship God).

Once the pujari has purified his body and mind, he rouses his kundalini and invokes the living presence of Kali into himself, using select mudras[24] and mantras. He begins to consecrate his entire body and being. Using his hands to make a specific mudra, he places the mantra onto a particular part of his body. He imitates the gestures of Ma Kali—holding a sword, a demon's head, granting boons, fearlessness, etc.—thereby awakening her power within himself. This he continues until his body and all his senses have become one with Kali.

Then the pujari picks up a conch shell filled with Ganges water and asks Ma Kali to reside there. As a symbol of her all-pervading formless presence, the pujari sprinkles this

---

[24] A symbolic gesture made with the hands during worship. To give an example of a mudra, the pujari performs the kurma mudra, also called the tortoise mudra, when the worship calls for meditation. Holding a flower between his two palms, the pujari joins the tips of his forefinger and thumb of the left hand with his little finger and forefinger of the right hand and then stretches the right thumb horizontally over the wrist of his left hand. He folds the middle and ring finger of his right hand downward and the last three fingers of his left hand upward over the back of his right hand. The back of his right hand is curved like the back of a tortoise.

water over everything, including himself. He then sits very still, preparing for the physical worship by first mentally worshipping her. Instead of perfume, he offers his power of smell. Instead of light, he offers his own power of sight. He meditates on Ma Kali within the shrine of his heart. But in order to worship her for the world to see, he has to take Kali out of his heart and transfer her onto the image on the silver lotus. He does this symbolically by breathing out onto a flower which he then puts on the black basalt image of Kali.

Up till now, the pujari has prepared himself for the actual ritual through purification rites and mental worship of Ma Kali. Now he is ready to perform the external worship. Kali Puja calls for a sixteen-item worship. A variety of articles are offered to Kali: asana (seat); padya (water for washing the feet); arghya (respectful offering of hibiscus, bel leaves, durva grass and uncooked rice); achamaniyam (water to rinse the mouth); gandha taila (oil for the body and hair); snaniya (water for bathing); vastra (clothing); abharana (jewelry); gandha (perfume); pushpa (flowers); vilvapatra (bel leaf); mala (garland); dhupa (incense); deepa (light); naivedya (fruit and candy); paniya (water for drinking); punarachamaniyam (water to rinse the mouth again).

Every time the pujari waves light before Kali, a musician standing behind a large drum responds by beating it a few times. The crowd also responds and shouts outside the temple, "Jai Ma Kali, Jai Ma Kali." Firecrackers explode periodically in the distance.

The priests have drawn two thick ropes from Ma's inner sanctum to the sacrificial place south of the Natmandir, thereby creating a straight walkway. And volunteers see to it that nobody enters this roped-off area or the section cordoned off with bamboo poles around the sacrificial place.

The crowd is restless, waiting to witness the animal sacrifices. Body against body, they press against the ropes to get a glimpse of Kali within the brightly-lit inner shrine. The excitement in the air is tangible, and one can see it in the faces of people. Some openly express it while others silently experience behind hooded eyes. Frequent shouts of "Jai Ma" come from the masses.

Inside the shrine, Ma Kali looks beautiful. It is hard to describe her primal beauty because one sees her with one's instincts rather than using one's reasoning power. Kali is adorned with magnificent garlands of different hues, and a giant wreath made of bel leaves hangs between her lower arms. She seems to be holding it.

Being there—at the Dakshineswar Temple—during Kali Puja night is an experience one will not forget throughout a lifetime. While, surely, all people assembled feel this definite spiritual excitement, the pujari worshipping Kali seems to feel the most. Maybe it's the mystical radiance emanating from Kali or it's the pujari's own excitement that has put him into a noticeable swoon. Whenever he gets up, another priest has to support him so he won't fall. By now, he has shouted mantras for hours, and his voice has become very hoarse.

The night is black, and although it is getting late, nobody looks tired. About 1 A.M. the animals are brought into the temple. Four attendants walk in succession within the roped-off area toward the Great Mother Goddess, each carrying a goat. Stroking the animal he carries with intimate affection, one attendant stands in line waiting to show the goat to Kali. The goats are wet and look somewhat dazed. They have been bathed in the Ganges and now face a tremendous crowd, cheering them and shouting excitedly. The kirtan party in the Natmandir has been singing without break since early afternoon and has now reached a fever pitch.

One by one, each goat enters the inner sanctum where the pujari performs a ritual and worships the goat. He utters mantras, puts vermillion on the animal and offers it to Kali. Once the rite is performed, an attendant dressed in a dhoti from the waist down, picks up the animal. "Jai Ma," he shouts as he runs between the ropes toward the sacrificial place. The masses yell as he lifts the goat high above his head and shows it to the crowd.

Another attendant is walking a wet sheep toward Kali's inner shrine. Gently stroking the animal, he pushes it forward and inside the inner sanctum. After some time, the attendant and sheep come back outside. Without looking right or left, the sheep runs straight between the ropes and the shouting mass of people, toward the sacrificial place.

All this is quite shocking to an onlooker who has not grown up with this custom. In the West, one rarely sees death because people cover it up the instant it occurs. But if one thinks about this Western custom, it's rather amazing that death should be so scary to people who do not mind—some even enjoy—to look at violence and gore. To the Hindu, on the other hand, all is worship—life, death, business, sex, birth—all are God-given. And tonight, these animals have become God. God is being offered to God while loud drums and the strange, high-pitched sound women produce with their mouths and consider auspicious echo across the dark Ganges.

A servant runs between the ropes toward the inner sanctum, carrying the head of a goat on a platter. Now, the goat has become a statue—far removed and impartial. Other servants carry the other goat heads, the head of the sheep, sugarcane and pieces of squash which also have been sacrificed at the bali into the inner shrine of Kali.

Farther down toward the Natmandir, a tall man, dressed like a Calcutta gentleman, moves through the crowd and freely distributes water from a bottle. The water looks clear but it contains blood. The man has washed the blood off the holy sacrificial place and desires to share the treasure. Hands stretch toward him, and he puts a few drops into each. People devoutly drink the water and wipe the remaining drops on top of their heads. "Jai Ma."

A small man, his body and clothes blood-stained, staggers between the ropes toward the Kali shrine. In his right hand he holds the bloody sword used to behead the animals and vegetables. On Kali's front steps, the man collapses into a shastanga pranam.[25] The animal sacrifice is over.

Close to 3 A.M. the pujari begins the worship of Kali's husband, and Shiva Puja starts inside the Kali sanctum. He worships Shiva in traditional style and offers a fragrant garland of white flowers.

After the Shiva Puja, servants enter the inner shrine, carrying large trays with food offerings. The animals which had been sacrificed earlier are now offered to Kali in cooked form. Tonight is Kali's big night and she gets served a multitude of delicacies—steaming curries, Basmati rice, vegetables, fried bread and pastries, chutney, yoghurt, salad, and many different kinds of sweets. There are dainty sandesh (made of cheese) decorated with silver foil and pistachio, golden-colored spirals called jilipis, toast-brown gulab jamuns in sweet syrup and much more.

Shortly after the food offering, a commotion among the priests signals to people outside that a new phase of the Kali worship is about to begin. Priests run here and there between the two ropes that separate them from the masses. They carry asanas, wood, and various utensils. Outside the Kali temple, right below the wide front steps, servants throw buckets of Ganges water, washing the area and at the same time drenching people sitting nearby.

The last ritual of Kali Puja night, the homa fire ceremony, takes place outside the shrine of Kali. Three asanas are spread before a fairly large, square brass vessel containing sand. The main pujari, flanked and supported by his assistants, slowly walks out from the temple and takes his seat before the square vessel. His voice is so hoarse by now that he can no longer shout. Nevertheless, he utters the

---

[25] A full prostration wherein a person lies down on the floor, head down and arms stretched toward the object of worship.

appropriate mantras and uses a stick to draw a yantra into the sand. Then the pujari places flowers onto the yantra and worships it. One attending priest takes his seat on the pujari's side while the other, black curls falling into his face, brings out wood from a huge bag and stacks it on the sand where the pujari had drawn the yantra. Shouting out mantras, both attending priests pour ghee over the wood while the pujari lights the pile. Flames shoot high into the black night sky, and sparks fly above the heads of people in the crowd.

After staring into the leaping flames for a while, one needs little imagination to see Ma Kali dancing in the flames. The crowd around the fire sits quiet now, spell-bound. There are no more firecrackers going off; people have stopped shouting "Jai Ma"; and even the kirtan party has stopped singing devotional songs. Only the crackling fire and the hoarse voice of the pujari can be heard.

The blaze is very high now, and a breeze, coming from the Ganges, pushes the flames close to the crowd sitting on the other side of the sacrificial fire. Although they come dangerously close to some people and almost seem to touch them, nobody moves or leaves their seat. Their desire to see the homa fire and be spiritually cleansed by taking part in the ceremony is greater than their fear of getting burned. Observing one lady's contorted face, one can guess that the heat is intense. Yet withstanding her agony, she sits still and stares into the dancing, leaping flames.

The smell of burning wood has brought out one giant cockroach. The insect first takes its place on top of a wood pile but then reconsiders and runs toward a lady in a red-and-white sari. With a suppressed squeak, she tosses the cockroach in a different direction toward another lady devotee who flings the large insect into the air with a disgusted "Heigh!" The frightened cockroach is being tossed from one to the other until it lands under the assistant priest, who has lifted his body to put more wood on the fire. When he sits back down the cockroach is gone and does not reappear.

As soon as the ritual is completed, the pujari douses the flames with yoghurt and Ganges water. He takes a few smoking embers from the brass vessel and puts them onto a large banana leaf, where he crushes them with a tonglike tool. Then, with a copper spoon he takes some of the crushed embers, puts them into a copper pot, and, adding ghee, he grinds them into a paste.

Meanwhile, the crowd has stood up, and people rush toward the pujari to receive blessing. The pujari dips his finger into the paste he has created and, uttering a mantra, he puts a dot on the pilgrims' foreheads. May the fire of Brahman cleanse us of all our sins.

The pujari and priests move back through the crowd into the inner shrine of Kali, and a few lucky devotees, mainly descendants of Rani Rasmani, manage to follow and squeeze in before the front gate closes. The people locked outside shout, "Jai Ma, Ma, Ma, Ma, Ma Go Ma." The atmosphere in the inner shrine is electric, and during pushpanjali, one can feel the hair on both arms stand on end. A priest hands flower petals and leaves to people inside the inner shrine, and holding these between their folded hands, they repeat mantras after the pujari. At last, they throw the flower petals toward Kali with a prayer.

Outside, the crowd is getting restless. People are hungry and anxiously waiting for prasad. Soon after pushpanjali, priests and attendants walk around and freely distribute different kinds of prasad to devotees. They hand out food, flowers, garlands, little bracelets and fruit. Happy recipients hold up the articles to their heads in reverence. The crowd is still busy eating and fondling their cherished prasad when the pujari, accompanied by attending priests, comes out of the Kali Temple. One of the priests carries a large brass pot filled with Ganges water, the water that was used to worship the Great Mother Goddess throughout this night. Using palm leaves, the pujari sprinkles this water onto the devotees. All bow their heads and accept the blessing of shanti jal, the water of peace.

It is now 4 A.M. A priest shouts, "Ma jago." It is time for mangal arati. The pujari waves the traditional five lights in front of Ma Kali while the crowd outside shouts with an intensity that does not reflect the strain of staying up all night.

"Jai Kali, jai Kali, jai Kali, jai Kali, jai Kali!"

A new day is dawning, and the birds begin to sing and chatter in the trees.

Chapter 4

DAKSHINESWAR KALI TEMPLE HISTORY AND SURROUNDINGS

O *Mother! How shall I call Thee?*
Sometimes Thou sittest on Shiva's left[1]
and sometimes Thou standest on Shiva's chest.
Sometimes Thou art in cosmic form
and sometimes Thou art a nude Woman;
Sometimes Thou art Krishna's sweetheart
and sometimes Thou art Krishna fallen at Radha's feet.
Sometimes Thou art Mother of the universe
dwelling in the five elements;
Sometimes Thou art Kulakundalini on the four-petalled
      lotus.
Prasada says, "I shall listen to none."
The name "Mother" is peerless.
Therefore, Mother, I call Thee "Mother" to get Thy
      secure feet.[2]

---

[1] Shiva's wife Durga.
[2] Dr. Jadunath Sinha, *Ramaprasada's Devotional Songs—The Cult of Shakti* (Calcutta: Sinha Publishing House, 1966), p. 33.

The Temple

Standing in the courtyard in front of the Kali Temple, one is amazed to see the different kinds of people, worshipping in a variety of ways. One man with the sandalwood markings of a Vaishnava looks up at the Kali Temple and loudly chants, "Hare Krishna, Hare Krishna, Krishna Krishna, Hare Hare; Hare Rama, Hare Rama, Rama Rama, Hare Hare." Nobody stops him or tells him he had better chant a Kali mantra. An elderly woman shouts, "Jai Ma!" in front of the Vishnu Temple, and nobody turns to look at her or finds it unusual that she would address Krishna as "Ma."

A great harmony prevails on the grounds of the Dakshineswar Kali Temple. Every sincere devotee is welcome here to worship the God of his or her own choice. Although there are guards and priests who watch to ensure order is maintained, there is none who tells another how to worship God or which God to worship. This religious tolerance and idea of oneness is infectious, and one is impelled to begin one's own form of worship, calling the God one has always felt dwelling within one's heart. Figure 16 shows a map of the temple grounds that we will be discussing in this chapter (see page 148).

North of the Kali Temple stands the Vishnu Temple, also referred to as the Temple of Radhakanta. This temple is dedicated to Radha and her beloved Krishna—the God who manifested himself as an Incarnation of Divine Love. Krishna is looked upon as the beautiful cowherd boy who played with the Gopis in a lush, pastoral setting. Out of love and reverence for this divine cowherd boy, Vaishnavas[3] never kill Krishna's friends—the cows or any other animals. No meat or fish is ever offered to Vishnu—only vegetarian dishes.

---

[3] Hindus who worship Krishna.

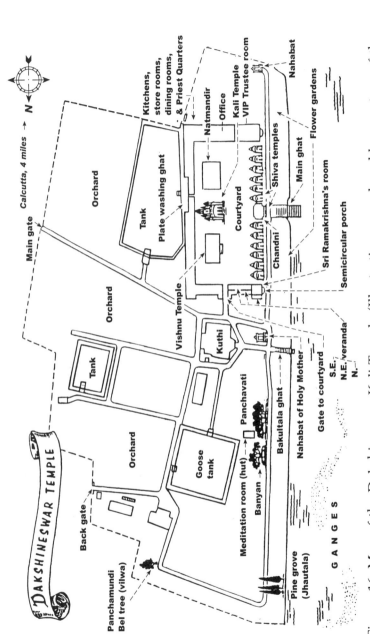

Figure 16. Map of the Dakshineswar Kali Temple.(Illustration reproduced by courtesy of the Vedanta Society of Southern California.)

   Like the Kali Temple, the Vishnu Temple is also built
upon a platform. Wide steps lead up to a veranda supported
by a row of columns. See figure 17. Past the veranda is the
sanctuary, a silver shrine with the images of Radha and
Krishna, and an adjacent room which contains another image
of Krishna. See figure 18 on page 150. The temple staff tells
the following story about this particular image, which is lovingly referred to as the "Broken-Image Krishna."

Figure 17. The Vishnu Temple where Sri Ramakrishna began
his service as a priest in Dakshineswar.

Figure 18. Raghuvir shalagram, the Rasmani family deity kept in the Vishnu Temple. A shalagram is a stone emblem of God, particularly Vishnu.

Three months after the temple's dedication in 1855, a mishap occurred which upset the proprietress, Rani Rasmani, and sent the priests scurrying. The priest at the Vishnu Temple fell when carrying the image of Krishna. It fell on the marble floor and Krishna's leg was broken in several places.

According to Hindu custom, a broken image cannot be worshipped. So, the pandits suggested immersing the image in the Ganga and installing a new one. Rani Rasmani felt sad because she had developed a special liking for this particular Krishna image. What was to be done?

Sri Ramakrishna solved the problem. He said to the Rani, "Why will you throw away this image? When your son-in-law breaks his leg, do you throw him away into the Ganges? No. You go to a doctor and fix his leg."

Figure 19. After a priest had accidentally dropped this image of Krishna, Sri Ramakrishna mended it. This image is preserved in the Vishnu Temple.

The Krishna image was then repaired by Sri Ramakrishna himself. See figures 19 and 20 on pages 151 and 152. He told the Rani that he would glue the image so that nobody would detect the break. This same image is still worshipped in the Vishnu Temple today in the room next to the main shrine.

Two priests sit cross-legged at the doorsill of the Radha-Krishna shrine and offer charanamrita, a few drops of the

Figure 20. The break in Krishna's leg can still be seen today.

sacred water, into the right palms of visiting pilgrims. For this service, they receive a few coins. Some devotees also ask for a sacred Tulsi leaf—this plant is Vishnu's favorite—and once given, they eat it with great reverence.

The shady veranda is fairly large and gives pilgrims a chance to sit for a while, meditate and think of the Lord. One old woman comes here every day and sits before the "Broken-Image Krishna." Her face glows with joy and her lips move as she reads from a scripture that barely holds together. Its cover is completely faded, and the inside pages are falling apart from so much use. The book, itself, is a monument to love. Looking at the old woman reading her old scripture, one's fire of devotion is kindled and one becomes acutely aware of how much more one must do to earn the love of God. On the southernmost side of the platform of the Vishnu Temple is a basin full of water. Pilgrims wash their hands and feet there before visiting the Lord. Next to it is a sacred Tulsi (Basil) plant.

Opposite the Vishnu and Kali temples, enclosing the courtyard from the west, is a row of twelve identical Shiva temples. See figure 21 on page 154. Six to the south and six to the north. In the middle is a portico called the Chandni from which broad brick-built steps lead to a ghat on the holy Ganges where Sri Ramakrishna used to bathe.

Pilgrims of all ages mount the spacious steps leading up to the Shiva temples and visit one temple after the other. Each Shiva in each temple bears a different name and has a different aspect of God, the Father. Although the lingas in each temple look alike at first, after careful observation, they all differ slightly. The names of the twelve Shivas are: Yogeswar, Jatneswar, Jatileswar, Nakuleswar, Nakeswar, Nirjareswar, Nareswar, Nandiswar, Nageswar, Jagadiswar, Jaleswar and Yajneswar.

Figure 21. The Shiva temples of Dakshineswar. There are 6 Shiva temples on either side of the Chandni, a portico above the steps leading down to the bathing ghat and the Ganges.

God, the Father

Shiva, third God of the Hindu Trinity, is the Supreme Reality. He is the Destroyer, Death, and when countless births have taught us all the lessons we need to learn and renunciation becomes natural, Shiva then is Resurrection, too.

All that is born must die. All that is produced must disintegrate. This is the law. And to reinforce the law, Hindus have three main Gods, each responsible for one of the main departments in our life cycle.

Brahma is the Creator and responsible for all creation and production. Vishnu is the Preserver and is responsible for the welfare and maintenance of life. It is always Vishnu who reincarnates as an avatar (God in human form) to save mankind from doubt and sin. Shiva is the Destroyer, the power behind destruction. And he is more than that. When, at the end of a cycle, he disintegrates the universe into a boundless void, he becomes this void. This void, the substratum of all existence, gives birth again and again to this apparently limitless universe, which is Shiva. Therefore, Shiva is thought of as the God of Destruction and also of Resurrection.

Hindus worship Shiva in the linga, a simple stone shaft which horrified early Missionaries because of its likeness to a phallic symbol. See figure 22. Hindus do not worship sex; they worship the motherhood and fatherhood of God. Hindu children are taught from early on to worship their parents as living Gods. Without the parents' loving care and protection, none could survive.

Figure 22. Devotees are allowed to enter each Shiva temple, worship and encircle the Shiva-Linga within.

Swami Vivekananda[4] gave a lecture at the Paris Congress in 1900 during which he vehemently refuted the statements of some Western scholars that referred to the Shiva linga as phallic worship.

His [Swami Vivekananda's] first words at the Congress were in connection with the paper read by Mr. Gustav Oppert, a German Orientalist, who tried to trace the origin of the Shalagrama-Shila and the Shiva-Linga to mere phallicism. To this the Swami objected, adducing proof from the Vedas, and particularly the Atharva-Veda Samhita, to the effect that the Shiva-Linga had its origin in the idea of the Yupa-Stambha or Skambha, the sacrificial post, idealized in Vedic ritual as the symbol of the Eternal Brahman. "As, afterwards," said the Swami, "the Yajna (sacrificial) fire, its smoke, ashes and flames, the Soma plant, and the bull that used to carry on its back the wood for the Vedic sacrifice, gave place to the conceptions of the brightness of Shiva's body, his tawny matted hair, his blue throat and the riding on the bull of Shiva, and so on; just so, the Yupa-Skambha gave place in time to the Shiva-Linga, and was deified to the high Devahood of Shri Shankara." Then, also, the Shiva-Linga might have been more definitely developed through the influence of Buddhism, with its Bauddha Stupa, or memorial topes, in which the relics, either of the Buddha himself, or of some great Buddhist Bhikshus, used to be deposited. It was quite probable that during the Buddhistic ascendancy the Hindus adopted this custom and used

---

[4] Monastic disciple and chief apostle of Sri Ramakrishna. He became famous in the West when he represented Hinduism at the Parliament of Religions in Chicago in 1893.

to erect memorials resembling their Skambha. The Shalagrama-Shilas were natural stones, resembling the artificially-cut stones of the Dhatu Garbha, or "metal-wombed" stone-relic-cases of the Bauddha Stupas, and thus being first worshipped by the Bauddhas gradually were adopted into Vaishnavism. The explanation of the Shalagrama-Shila as a phallic emblem was an imaginary invention. It had been a degenerate period following the downfall of Buddhism in India, which had brought on the association of sex with the Shiva-Linga. In reality, the Shiva-Linga and the Shalagrama-Shila had no more to do with Sex-worship than the Holy Communion in Christianity had in common with cannibalism."[5]

Aside from worshipping Shiva in the linga, Hindus also worship him in the form of a handsome man, bare-bodied except for a tiger skin around his waist. He has four arms. While in one hand he carries a trident and in another a damaru (a small drum), he uses the other two to bestow boons and fearlessness upon his devotees. In line with his responsibilities as God of Death, he frequents burial grounds and cremation sites. Shiva's favorite city is Varanasi, where he promises liberation to all who die there. Yet Shiva's main abode is the icy Mount Kailas in the Himalayas where he is seated in deep meditation. He is besmeared with ashes which have turned his body into a ghostly white, and, occasionally, he takes a puff or two from his pipe filled with hemp. He possesses nothing except a tiger skin to cover his body, a begging bowl, a hemp pipe, and an old bull by the name of Nandi who acts as his carrier.

---

[5] *The Life of Swami Vivekananda*, by His Eastern & Western Disciples (Calcutta: Advaita Ashrama, 1974) pp. 684-685.

Shiva is indrawn, constantly immersed in his own bliss. He is renunciation personified. On his forehead is the crescent of a waning moon, and his matted hair is piled up high on the crown of his head. When the river Ganga fell down from heaven and found no place to land on earth which wouldn't be immediately crushed by its force, Shiva let it fall on his head. It took the river many years to find its way through Shiva's matted locks and finally land on earth.

Shiva is a kind God. He gives refuge to all who would otherwise walk forlorn through this world. He denies none, not even ghosts and hobgoblins. The other Gods refused to accept the snakes, but Shiva gave them refuge and even allowed them to curl around his neck.

When the Gods churned the Ocean of Milk to obtain nectar, together with the nectar also rose terrible poison which threatened to destroy the three worlds with its leaping tongues of fire. All the Gods were terrified. Except Shiva. He gathered it in the palm of his hand and drank it, thus saving the worlds. Parvati, the Divine Mother, became alarmed, and in the form of Tara, fed Shiva milk from her breast. The milk curdled the poison and prevented it from going down into Shiva's stomach. It remained in Shiva's throat, turning it permanently bright blue.

Shiva's power is Shakti, the dynamic creative mother aspect of the Godhead. It is she who creates, and at the time of dissolution, it is she who swallows her own creation. Shakti cannot exist without Shiva, and Shiva cannot personify without Shakti. Therefore, the Tantras proclaim the highest personification of God, the supreme energy, to be feminine. They say that she should be contemplated as a Goddess under the names of Kali, Tara, Durga, Devi, Annapurna, Lakshmi, Sati, Uma, Parvati and countless others.

Grateful for not being forced into a particular religious mode, one stands in the courtyard of the Dakshineswar Kali Temple compound and looks all around at the beautiful temples. Who built this holy place? What was it like when it all started?

Questioning people who know, one discovers that construction of the Dakshineswar Kali Temple started in 1847 and was completed in eight years at a cost of 900,000 rupees. The temple was built by an extremely liberal woman—Rani Rasmani—whose life was dedicated to Kali. The Rani's life story is mysterious, and so is the story behind the building of the Kali Temple.

Rani Rasmani

The Rani[6] was born in Kona, a village located about thirty miles north of Calcutta. Her deep devotion—from an early age—to Mother Kali sustained her and her family for they were very poor. Although she was born into an indigent farmer's family of the lowest Hindu caste, destiny had singled out Rani Rasmani to become one of the richest, most influential women in Calcutta.

She was exceptionally beautiful. One day, when she was bathing in the Ganges, a wealthy landlord from Calcutta observed her from his luxury boat. Silently, the boat passed the girl, but the rich man could not get her out of his mind. He was so stunned by her beauty that the thought of her remained in his heart and he returned at a later date to ask the farmer for the hand of his daughter.

Rani Rasmani became the wife of Rajchandra Das, and, overnight, the poor girl became a multi-millionairess and lived in a mansion in Janbazar, Calcutta. But her years of marriage did not last long for Rajchandra suddenly fell ill and died. The Rani became a widow at age 44 and was left to manage single-handed four young daughters and a vast estate. See figure 23 on page 160.

Contrary to dire predictions by relatives, the Rani managed Rajchandra's properties with great skill. She ruled with

---

[6] The name Rani stands for queen.

Figure 23. Rani Rasmani, a liberal, devout and wealthy woman who built the Dakshineswar Kali Temple.

love, intelligence and wit. Her devotion to Kali made her fearless, and she became an outspoken champion of civil rights. When the British government imposed a tax on fishermen whose livelihood depended on fishing in the Ganges, the Rani took up their cause.

"I want to buy the fishing rights on the Ganga from Gushuri to Metiabruz," said the Rani. And as soon as the British sold her the rights for the then enormous sum of 10,000 rupees, she erected a barricade by putting chains across the river. No ship could pass.

When the British demanded that she remove the barricade at once, she replied, "Your ships disturb my fish which cost me 10,000 rupees. But if you return my money and abolish the fishing tax, I'll be happy to do as you want." The British government had to abolish the tax.

On another occasion, the Rani fought the British over the rights to perform religious services. She had started Durga worship at her mansion in Janbazar, and since the ritual calls for fresh water from the Ganges, a priest would go early in the morning to fetch the water. To the great chagrin of a certain British gentleman, a procession of musicians with drums and cymbals accompanied the priest through Janbazar, a noble section of Calcutta where many wealthy Europeans lived. Being awakened early in the morning by the religious music, he yelled and threatened and finally filed a formal complaint against the Rani at the police station. The Rani was summoned by the British and ordered to stop all devotional music in the morning.

She disobeyed and was fined 50 rupees. Rani Rasmani paid without a word of complaint, but on the same day, she erected a bamboo barricade across Babughat Road which she owned. No traffic could pass from South to North Calcutta and vice versa. The British government repeatedly asked her to remove the barricade, but the Rani did not give in until the British returned her 50 rupees and allowed her devotional procession to fetch water from the Ganges early in the morning.

The Rani's fearlessness and courage had a lot to do with her total dependence on Mother Kali. "My Mother Kali will protect me, and if she doesn't, none in this world can save me," the Rani often said. One day, a group of rowdy, drunken British soldiers forced their way into the Rani's mansion. Since all the men happened to be away at the time, the Rani, herself, took up arms and stood ready to confront the soldiers. Fortunately, an officer of higher rank passed by and stopped the soldiers from harming the Rani or her property.

Sri Ramakrishna said about the Rani that she was one of the eight companions of the Divine Mother. Among her many other noble qualities was a genuine sympathy for the poor. Many times, she distributed gifts and fed poor people. But today, when people think of her, they probably remember her most for her devotion to Kali.

> In 1847 she decided to go on a pilgrimage to Kashi because she had an intense desire to offer special devotions to Vishwanath Shiva and to the Divine Mother in the form of Annapurna.

> In those days there was no railway line between Calcutta and Kashi and it was more comfortable for the rich to make the journey by boat. So the Rani planned to travel with her entourage by boat. We are told that her convoy of twenty-four boats was made ready with provisions for six months. There were seven boats for food and other supplies, one for herself, three for her three daughters and their families, two for the guards, two for the servants, four for the other relatives and friends, two for her estate officials, one for the washerman, one for four cows, and one for fodder. . . .

> The devout Rani Rasmani's mind had reached a climax of fervor and delight at the prospect of the holy pilgrimage. But the night before the journey, Mother

Kali intervened. (Another version of this story tells that the Rani started out on her pilgrimage, and her first stop over night was near Dakshineswar.) She appeared to the Rani in a dream and said, "There is no need to go to Kashi. Install my image in a beautiful spot on the bank of the Ganga and arrange for my daily worship and food offering; I shall manifest myself in the image and accept your worship daily."

The next morning the Rani gave orders to cancel the pilgrimage. All the piled up food and provisions were distributed among the poor and needy. All the money meant for the journey was now put aside for the holy undertaking of building a temple. The inscrutable way of destiny was accepted by the Rani with full devotion and humility, for had not the intervention come from her Chosen Ideal, Mother Kali? Through the engraving on the official seal of her estate did she not proclaim to the world that she was "Sri Rasmani Dasi who only longed to attain the feet of Kali?"[7]

After an intensive search for a suitable place to build a Kali temple, the Rani found a 20-acre plot of land in the village of Dakshineswar on the eastern bank of the Ganges. The ground had the shape of the back of a tortoise. Part of this land belonged to an Englishman. The remaining part consisted of an abandoned Muslim burial ground, associated with the memory of a Mohammedan holy man. Such a burial ground, according to the Tantras, is very suitable for the installation of Shakti and her sadhana.

The Rani began construction in 1847, and it took eight years at great expense to complete the Kali Temple com-

[7] Pravrajika Atmaprana, *Sri Ramakrishna's Dakshineswar* (New Delhi: Ramakrishna Sarada Mission, 1986), p. 3.

pound which also included a Vishnu Temple and 12 Shiva temples. She spent 50,000 rupees for land, 160,000 rupees for building an embankment along the river, 900,000 rupees for the Kali Temple complex, and 226,000 rupees for property used as an endowment for the maintenance of the temple.

When the temple construction neared completion, the Rani contracted a sculptor to make the Kali image. The sculptor carved a beautiful, black image of Kali in basalt and used white Italian marble for the form of Shiva. Once Kali was completed to the satisfaction of the Rani, the statue was safely packed into a box lest it should be damaged.

Since the day of the temple's consecration was to be a big day in the Rani's life, she began to prepare herself early by practicing severe austerities. She bathed three times a day, ate only simple food, and spent many hours in japam and meditation.

Time went by and, still, the Rani had not fixed a date for the temple consecration. One night, she had a dream wherein Ma Kali appeared and said, "How long will you keep me confined this way? I feel suffocated. Install me as soon as possible." When the box which stored the image was opened, workers found the statue of Kali moist with perspiration.

The Rani quickly fixed the installation ceremony of Ma Kali on the day of the snana-yatra[8]. All was ready—almost. While building the Kali Temple, the Rani had overcome many obstacles at great expense and energy, but the greatest came at the end. This obstacle threatened to bring the entire project to a halt. Its point was the subject of caste. Even though the Rani had gained the respect from Brahmins and many high-caste Hindus, she, in spite of all her wealth, was looked upon as a person of low birth. And as such, she could not possibly own a temple and hope to feed Brahmins with cooked food.

---

[8] Bathing ceremony of Sri Krishna.

The Rani consulted with many pandits, but none could come up with a solution to her problem until Ramkumar, Sri Ramakrishna's elder brother suggested consecrating the temple in the name of a Brahmin and thereby bypassing the strict caste rules prevailing at that time.

The temple was consecrated in the name of Rani's guru, and Ramkumar, officiating as priest, installed the image of Kali in the new temple with great pomp on Thursday, May 31, 1855. Many professors of the Shastras, Brahmin pandits, and famous scholars came from faraway places like Kashi, Orissa, and Navadvip.

The extremely liberal-minded Rani, who desired to bring all people—irrespective of caste and religion—to the Kali temple achieved her goal soon after Kali was installed. Monks and pilgrims on their way to Gangasagar or Puri, all stopped at the Dakshineswar temple for darshan and prasad. Sadhus liked Dakshineswar for its holy atmosphere, easily available food, and surrounding secluded places for meditation.

"At certain times," said Sri Ramakrishna, "particular kinds of sadhus gathered in large numbers in Dakshineswar. At one time, the sannyasins, at another the paramahamsas. Once a sadhu stayed here who had a beautiful glow on his face. He used to sit and smile. He came out of his room once in the morning and once in the evening, gazed on everything—the trees, the plants, the sky, the Ganga—and then beside himself with joy, he danced with both his arms raised. He sometimes rolled with laughter and said, 'How wonderful is Maya.' That was his worship. He had the realization of bliss.

"On another occasion, a sadhu came who was ine-
briated with divine knowledge. He looked like a
ghoul. He was nude, with dust all over his body
and head, and he had longs nails and long hair. On
the upper part of his body he wore a wrapper of
shreds that looked like he had picked them up
where dead bodies are burnt. Standing before the
Kali temple, he looked at the image and then recited
a hymn with such power that the whole temple
seemed to shake. Mother Kali looked pleased and
smiled"[9]

The 19-year-old Sri Ramakrishna was also present at
this auspicious occasion. Noticing him as the brother of
Ramkumar, the Rani and her son-in-law Mathur Mohan
Biswas[10] asked him to become a priest in the Vishnu Temple.
At first Sri Ramakrishna did not want to accept any kind of
binding engagement but, later on, he had to yield.

Ramkumar, who served as priest in the Kali Temple,
died within a year after the dedication ceremony, and Sri
Ramakrishna took over his duties. Sri Ramakrishna's worship was unique. Whenever the Rani got a chance, she tried
to listen to Ramakrishna's songs of devotion to Kali.

One day, the Rani sat inside the Kali shrine while Sri
Ramakrishna sang a song full of longing for the Divine
Mother Kali. Suddenly he stopped, turned and slapped the
Rani's face. "What," he shouted. "You are thinking worldly
thoughts even in this holy place."

The temple guards rushed forward to protect the Rani
and drag Sri Ramakrishna out of the temple. "No, don't disturb him," ordered the Rani. "The Divine Mother herself
punished me and illumined my heart." She wondered how
Sri Ramakrishna could have known that she was thinking
about a lawsuit.

---

[9] *Sri Ramakrishna, the Great Master*, pp. 524-525.
[10] He is better known as Mathur Babu.

The Rani fell seriously ill in 1861.

The best doctors of Calcutta tried their utmost to cure her but, at last, gave up hope. They then suggested that she be moved to a healthier place. It was Rasmani's desire to go to her garden house at Kalighat, in South Calcutta, which was on the bank of the Adi Ganga, a small stream flowing into the Ganga.

Rasmani knew that her death was imminent and there was one task which she had left unfinished. The property which she had bought in Dinajput (now in Bangladesh) as an endowment for the maintenance of the Dakshineswar temple was still not transferred to the temple trust. She executed the deed of endowment on February 18, 1861 and died the next day.

Shortly before her passing away, she was brought to the bank of the Ganga. Seeing some lamps lighted in front of her, she exclaimed: "Remove, remove these lights. I don't care for this artificial illumination anymore. Now my Mother has come and the brilliance of her form has illumined the whole place." After a short pause she passed away, saying "Mother, you have come!"[11]

Although the Rani was a farsighted woman and had purchased a huge property for 226,000 rupees to assure proper temple maintenance after her death, she could not foresee the 1947 partition of India. Her land was located in a zone that became Bangladesh, and all her property was

---

[11] Swami Chetanananda, *They Lived with God* (St. Louis, MO: Vedanta Society of St. Louis, 1989), pp. 15-16.

confiscated by the government. From then on, the Dakshineswar Kali Temple had to be maintained without income from this property.

Mathur Nath Biswas

After the Rani's death, Mathur Babu, the Rani's favorite son-in-law, took over the temple management. He was also very devoted to Kali and to Sri Ramakrishna, whom he protected and served for fourteen years. See figure 24 on page 170. Without Mathur's help and protection, Sri Ramakrishna would have been in trouble with the temple guards on various occasions.

Sri Ramakrishna's supreme devotion to God made him do things that other people—and especially the guards—referred to as crazy and blasphemous. During the Kali worship in the temple, Sri Ramakrishna would lose himself in ecstasy, and instead of offering the specially prepared food to the Goddess Kali, he sometimes offered it to a cat and sometimes ate it himself. He put the flowers meant for Kali on his own head, and sometimes, filled with exuberant joy, he climbed on Shiva and embraced him.

Mathur was a great soul and, therefore, was able to understand the greatness and divine ecstasy of Sri Ramakrishna. When the guards complained about Sri Ramakrishna, Mathur asked them not to disturb him. "Let him worship in his own way," said Mathur Babu. Although lots of complaints against Sri Ramakrishna reached the temple office, Mathur ignored them all.

The only time he doubted Sri Ramakrishna's sanity was when the latter slapped the Rani's face inside the Kali Temple. Mathur employed a famous doctor to examine Sri Ramakrishna, but the doctor could not find anything wrong with him. Then Mathur thought that Sri Ramakrishna's mind

may be disturbed from too many years of absolute conti-
nence, and he engaged a courtesan from Calcutta.

When Sri Ramakrishna entered his room and saw a
beautiful woman sitting on his bed, he clapped his hands
and shouted with joy, "Ma, oh Ma, how beautiful you are."
Then he rushed outside and called all temple priests to come
to his room and see the beautiful Mother. The courtesan was
extremely embarrassed and quickly left through a side
entrance!

It was written in Mathur's horoscope that his Ishta (chosen deity), assuming a human form, would always be gracious to him, accompany him and protect him. One day,
Mathur Babu watched Sri Ramakrishna pacing back and
forth on the veranda in front of his room. When he walked in
one direction, he took on the form of Kali, when in another,
he became Shiva. Filled with extreme devotion, Mathur fell
at Sri Ramakrishna's feet.

"Get up, get up," cried Sri Ramakrishna. "Be calm. What
will people say if they see you at my feet. You are an aristo-
crat, and I am a poor temple priest."

As Mathur Babu protected Sri Ramakrishna, so Sri
Ramakrishna protected Mathur. When Mathur's first wife—
the Rani's third daughter Karuna—died, the Rani asked him
to marry her fourth daughter, Jagadamba. The Rani was very
fond of Mathur and didn't want to lose her favorite son-in-
law. When Jagadamba also became very sick and the doctors gave up hope for her recovery, Mathur approached Sri
Ramakrishna.

"Father, I won't be able to serve you anymore," said
Mathur. "If Jagadamba dies, the other sons-in-law of the Rani
will take over the temple management."

Sri Ramakrishna said, "Don't worry, your wife will
recover." Through yogic powers, Sri Ramakrishna took
Jagadamba's disease upon his own body and had to endure
great suffering from blood dysentery for the following six
months.

Figure 24. Mathur Nath Biswas, devout son-in-law of the Rani and Dakshineswar Kali Temple manager. He devotedly served Sri Ramakrishna.

One day, Mathur Babu asked Sri Ramakrishna, "Father, why don't you give me bhava!" Bhava is an intense spiritual mood.

"You are all right," said Sri Ramakrishna. "You are serving Ma Kali; you don't need bhava."

"No, no, Father you must give me bhava," said Mathur adamantly.

A few days later, Mathur Babu sat in his mansion in Janbazar when, all of a sudden, he felt an onrush of exuberant devotion. His personality changed completely. Whenever he spoke of God or heard God's name, Mathur cried profusely. His eyes were red, and his heart was pounding. And when he couldn't stand the strain of his religious passion any longer, Mathur sent for Sri Ramakrishna.

"Father, I've been in this state for three days and haven't been able to attend to my duties," said Mathur Babu. "Everything in my estate is going wrong. Please take back the ecstasy. It's a blissful state, but what's the use of bliss when my worldly affairs are going to pieces? This ecstasy suits you. The rest of us don't really want it."

Sri Ramakrishna rubbed his hand over Mathur's chest, and he returned to his normal self.

Mathur Babu worshipped Sri Ramakrishna as God, yet Sri Ramakrishna remained unaffected and never felt proud or treated Mathur as special because of it. When Mathur was suffering from an abscess in Calcutta, he asked for Sri Ramakrishna. He sent messenger after messenger, but Sri Ramakrishna did not visit him in Janbazar. At last, he came to see him.

Mathur said, "Father, give me the dust of your feet."

"What good will it do," said Sri Ramakrishna. "Will it cure your abscess?"

Mathur replied with folded hands, "Father, do you think I'm so mean and want your blessing to cure my abscess? Doctors are here for this purpose. I only want your blessings so that I can safely cross the ocean of Maya."

Highly pleased with Mathur's devotion, Sri Ramakrishna said, "Mathur, as long as you are alive, so long shall I remain in Dakshineswar."

Mathur became afraid. "My wife and my son Dwaraka love you, father. Please don't leave them."

"All right," said Sri Ramakrishna. "I shall not leave as long as they are alive."

Sri Ramakrishna kept his word and did not leave the Dakshineswar Kali Temple until 1885, after Mathur Babu, his wife Jagadamba, and his son Dwaraka had died.

Sri Ramakrishna's Room

Though Ma Kali is the main attraction at the Dakshineswar Temple, it was perhaps her great devotee, Sri Ramakrishna, who made this particular Kali Temple as famous as it is today. Sri Ramakrishna's room is northwest of the Kali Temple and adjacent to the most northern Shiva Temple. It has four entrances: one to the east which leads to the inner courtyard, one to the west, leading into a semi-circular porch, another to the north which leads to the kuthi and the Panchavati[12], and one which is blocked today but, if open, would lead to the long northern veranda. See figure 25 on page 173.

As one enters Sri Ramakrishna's room, one feels awed by the spiritual intensity of the place. The mere fact that Sri Ramakrishna lived in this very room in a God-intoxicated state for fourteen years is overwhelming. The ambience here is quite different from the Kali Temple. Sri Ramakrishna's room is much quieter although it, too, is crowded with devotees.

---

[12] An area where five specific trees were planted: banyan, peepul, ashoka, amlaki and bel. It is considered an excellent place for meditation and spiritual practices.

Figure 25. Beggars line up in front of the entrance to the inner courtyard of the Kali Temple. The building on the far left is the northern entrance to Sri Ramakrishna's room. The temple to the right is Rani Rasmani's temple.

Maintaining a respectful silence, devotees are standing, sitting, meditating, walking, and bowing to the pictures on the wall. Some people quietly read from *The Gospel of Sri Ramakrishna*, written by M., a householder disciple of the Master. Not even children shout, awed into tranquility by their parents' murmured prayers. The only distinctive noise one hears is produced by pilgrims tossing coins into the collection box. See figure 26 on page 174.

The warm air is sweet with perfume, and one's senses are open and closed at the same time. For instance, one is more aware of a soft breeze coming in from the Ganges and brushing against one's skin than of the many people all around. Alone, one gazes at eternity. A wall is not a wall any longer, and the room is no longer a room—mystically, all has

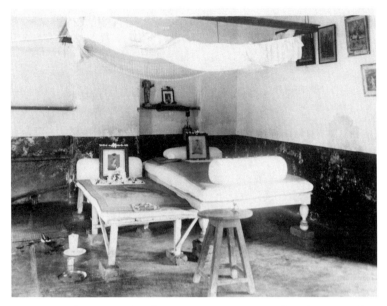

Figure 26. Sri Ramakrishna's room as it used to look. Today, a railing protects the beds from the hands of eager pilgrims, trying to take home a chip. The red cement floor of the room has since been replaced by a marble floor.

transformed itself into consciousness although the shapes remain exactly as they were before.

There are two beds standing next to each other in the southwestern corner of the room. The one next to the wall is a little higher. Sri Ramakrishna slept on this one and used the lower one as a seat when entertaining visitors and talking to them about God. Today, priests have put on each bed a picture of Sri Ramakrishna which they worship daily. A constant flow of devotees brings fresh garlands and flowers throughout the day, and priests use these offerings to decorate the pictures and beds. People also bring incense which they light and offer in a vessel filled with sand in front of Sri Ramakrishna's lower bed. See figure 27 on page 175.

Figure 27. This old painting of Sri Ramakrishna is kept on his lower bed. The picture is decorated daily with sandal-wood, tulsi leaves (favorite leaves of Vishnu) and flowers.

Most people bring some kind of offering. They hand a flower, a garland, some sweets to the officiating priest who sits next to the lower bed behind a railing that prevents ardent devotees from touching or chipping the beds. The priest takes the offered garland or flower and places it before the picture of Sri Ramakrishna on one of the beds. Then he takes a few flowers from the bed and hands them to the devotee as prasad. Sometimes, the priest also hands out a piece of sandesh or other sweet. With a tiny silver spoon, the priest pours a few drops of charanamrita into the right hand of the pilgrim who drinks it with devotion and wipes the remaining drops on the crown of his head. It is customary to pay "dakshina," a fee ranging from 2 to 50 rupees, to the priest for this service. People also toss a few coins for the upkeep of the temple into the iron box standing next to the railing.

For those who like to observe the behavior of others, it is interesting to watch the various people who enter Sri Ramakrishna's room. Some come quietly, unobtrusively. They sit down for a while and then leave quietly. Others enter the room with a self-assured air. Although they do this silently, their body language is bold and boisterous. Then there are the truly humble devotees. They bow down to the Master's beds with such reverence that the onlooker feels ashamed of his eyes' crude intrusion into someone else's sweet, delicate intimacy. There are monks and householders, women and children, beggars and rich men who wear diamond rings. They all sit side-by-side in adoration and, for the moment, they forget their differences.

Many old pictures hang on the wall of the fairly large room; some are from Sri Ramakrishna's time and others were added later. There are pictures of Ma Kali, Sri Krishna, Sri Ramakrishna, Sri Sarada Ma, Rani Rasmani, Mathur Babu, and many more—some so old, one can hardly tell what they represent. Low hanging pictures, within the reach of devotees bear signs of worship. A loving hand has put a flower on top of one and garlanded another. Many devotees like to walk from picture to picture, saluting each one with reverence. M., the recorder of *The Gospel*, left this vivid description:

> Sri Ramakrishna was walking up and down, now in his room, now on the south veranda. Occasionally pausing on the semicircular porch west of his room, he would look at the Ganges.
>
> After a little while he returned to his room and sat on the small couch. It was past three in the afternoon. The devotees took their seats on the floor. The Master sat in silence before them, now and then casting a glance at the walls, where many pictures were hanging. To Sri Ramakrishna's left was a picture of Sarasvati, and beyond it, a picture of Gaur and Nitai singing kirtan with their devotees. In front of the Master hung pictures of Dhruva, Prahlada, and Mother Kali. On the wall to his right was another picture of the Divine Mother, Rajarajesvari. Behind him was a picture of Jesus Christ raising the drowning Peter. Suddenly Sri Ramakrishna turned to M. and said, "You see, it is good to keep pictures of sannyasis and holy men in one's room. When you get up in the morning you should see the faces of holy persons rather than the faces of other men. People with rajasic qualities keep `English' pictures on their walls—pictures of rich men, the King, the Queen, the Prince of Wales, and white men and women walking together. That shows their rajasic temperament.
>
> "You acquire the nature of the people whose company you keep. Therefore even pictures may prove

harmful. Again, a man seeks the company that agrees with his own nature."[13]

There is a story to tell about almost every spot in this room. Sitting near the northern entrance, Sri Ramakrishna had worshipped his wife as the Divine Mother personified—an act previously unheard of in the orthodox Hindu community.[14] But Sri Ramakrishna, the bliss-intoxicated God-man, did not care. He followed higher rules, the rules of his Mother Kali.

Swami Saradananda wrote an account of this incident in *Sri Ramakrishna, the Great Master*:

It was the new-moon day, the holy occasion for the worship of the Phalaharini Kalika Devi. It was the day of a special festival at the Dakshineswar temple. The Master had made special preparations on that day with a view to worshipping the Mother of the universe. These preparations, however, had not been made in the temple, but privately in his own room. A wooden seat painted with Alimpana, the pigment of rice powder, for the Devi to sit on at the time of worship was placed to the right of the worshipper.

The sun had set. The new-moon night had veiled the earth in deep darkness. Hriday, the Master's nephew, had to perform a special worship of the Devi in the temple. He helped as much as possible in the preparations of the Master's worship and then went to the temple. Having finished the evening service and worship of Radha-Govinda,

---

[13] *The Gospel of Sri Ramakrishna*, p. 606.
[14] Although Hindu custom prescribes worship of little girls, they are worshipped only before puberty, never after.

Dinu, the first priest, came to help the Master in the preparations. It was 9 p.m. when all arrangements for the mystic worship of the Devi were complete. The Master had sent word to the Holy Mother to be present during the worship. She came to the room and the Master started the worship.

When the articles of worship were purified by mantras and all the rites preliminary to the worship were finished, the Master beckoned to the Holy Mother to sit on the wooden seat decorated with Alimpana. While witnessing the worship, the Holy Mother had already entered into a divine semi-conscious state. Not clearly conscious of what she was doing like one under the spell of a mantra, she sat facing north to the right of the Master, who was seated with his face to the east. According to scriptural injunctions, the Master sprinkled the Holy Mother repeatedly with the water purified by mantras from a pitcher before him. Then he uttered a Mantra and recited a prayer.

"O Lady, O Mother Tripurasundari, who art the Controller of all powers, open the door to perfection; purify her (the Holy Mother) body and mind, manifest Thyself in her and be beneficent."

Afterward the Master performed the nyasa of the mantras on the Holy Mother's body according to the injunctions of the Shastras and worshipped her with sixteen articles as the Devi Herself. He then offered food and put a portion of it into her mouth. The Holy Mother lost normal consciousness and went into samadhi. The Master, too, uttering mantras in a semi-conscious state entered into complete samadhi. In samadhi, the worshipper became perfectly identified and united with the Devi.

A long time passed. The second quarter of the night had long gone. Returning to the semi-conscious state again, the Master offered himself to the Devi. At the lotus feet of the Devi, he now gave away his all—the results of his sadhanas, his rosary, etc.— along with his ego. He saluted her, uttering mantras.

"O Thou, auspiciousness of all auspicious things, O doer of all actions, O refuge, O three-eyed One, O Thou fair-complexioned spouse of Shiva, O Narayani, I bow down to Thee, I bow down to Thee."[15]

Wherever one gets a chance to sit for meditation in Sri Ramakrishna's room, one can safely assume that on this very spot Sri Ramakrishna sang, danced, stood, walked, sat in ecstasy, or simply merged into samadhi. See figure 28 on page 182. Here is M.'s description of Sri Ramakrishna's divine moods:

Sri Ramakrishna was standing still, surrounded by a few devotees, and Narendra (later he became Swami Vivekananda) was singing. M. had never heard anyone except the Master sing so sweetly. When he looked at Sri Ramakrishna he was struck with wonder; for the Master stood motionless, with eyes transfixed. He seemed not even to breathe. A devotee told M. that the Master was in samadhi. M. had never before seen or heard of such a thing. Silent with wonder, he thought: "Is it possible for a man to be so oblivious of the outer world in the

[15] *Sri Ramakrishna, the Great Master*, pp. 291-292.

consciousness of God? How deep his faith and devotion must be to bring about such a state!"

Narendra was singing:

Meditate, O my mind, on the Lord Hari,
The Stainless One, Pure Spirit through and through.
How peerless is the Light that in Him shines!
How soul-bewitching is His wondrous form!
How dear is He to all His devotees!

Ever more beauteous in fresh-blossoming love
That shames the splendor of a million moons,
Like lightning gleams the glory of His form,
Raising erect the hair for very joy.

The Master shuddered when this last line was sung. His hair stood on end, and tears of joy streamed down his cheeks. Now and then his lips parted in a smile. Was he seeing the peerless beauty of God, "that shames the splendor of a million moons?" Was this the vision of God, the Essence of Spirit? How much austerity and discipline, how much faith and devotion must be necessary for such a vision!

The song went on:

Worship His feet in the lotus of your heart;
With mind serene and eyes made radiant
With heavenly love, behold that matchless sight.

Again that bewitching smile. The body motionless as before, the eyes half shut, as if beholding a strange inner vision.[16]

---

[16] *The Gospel of Sri Ramakrishna*, p. 89.

Figure 28. When Sri Ramakrishna looked out of his room, he may have had a view close to this one. Today, in front of Sri Ramakrishna's circular porch is a fence and little shops. This photo was taken from the Trustees' room, which is located on the opposite side of the 12 Shiva temples and looks similar to Sri Ramakrishna's room.

The Kuthi and the Nahabat

As one leaves Sri Ramakrishna's room through the northern entrance, one finds a two-storied villa on the right. This building is called the Kuthi. When the Rani bought the property in order to build the Kali Temple, this villa was already there. It had previously belonged to an Englishman. The Rani and her family used to stay in the Kuthi whenever they visited Dakshineswar. Sri Ramakrishna also lived there and spent sixteen years in a room on the ground floor before he moved to the room that is now known as "Sri Ramakrishna's room."

West of the Kuthi and opposite Sri Ramakrishna's room is another two-storied building, called the Nahabat, or concert tower. The upstairs compartment of this ornate building was built to function as a music room. Musicians would perform there and broadcast sweet devotional music on special occasions and during arati time. Yet from the two concert towers at the Dakshineswar Kali Temple compound, the one next to the Kuthi was rarely used for the purpose intended.

Sri Ramakrishna's mother, Sri Chandramani Devi, lived in the upstairs room until her death, and Sri Ramakrishna's wife, Sri Sarada Devi, lived for many years in a tiny chamber on the Nahabat's ground floor. Sarada Devi, lovingly referred to as the "Holy Mother" by her devotees, managed remarkably well in this small area. The floor space across the room is little more than seven feet, yet it served as her bedroom, storage room and guest room. She slept there, stored all groceries and cooking vessels there, and also entertained women devotees whenever they came to visit the Master.

Today, visiting devotees, especially Westerners, are shocked when they see this tiny room in which Sri Sarada Devi lived for so long. "How could the Holy Mother live so poorly in such small quarters? How could she be treated so badly?" they ask. On the one hand, Holy Mother's life was full of physical hardships, but on the other, her lot was not so bad when one considers the daily dose of bliss she must have received from close association with her God-intoxicated husband.

The love of this divine couple was unique. Though their marriage was never consummated, they were united in spirit. Sri Ramakrishna worshipped Sarada Devi as the Divine Mother and offered all the fruit of his actions at her feet. And she, in turn, worshipped Sri Ramakrishna as the embodiment of Kali.

Sri Sarada Devi was very shy, and to avoid being seen, she only came out of her room in the early morning hours.

Before anybody else was awake, she bathed in the nearby
Ganges and then quickly returned to her tiny room. Holy
Mother gained a bit more space when a bamboo screen was
erected around the Nahabat. Although she could freely move
on the veranda outside her room without being seen by
passers-by, she could no longer look out and watch Sri
Ramakrishna, who lived across the courtyard no farther than
a stone's throw away. She did not complain, but it greatly
distressed her that she could not witness Sri Ramakrishna's
divine play, his ecstasies and holy interaction with the
devotees.

Weeks went by. One day, visiting devotees reported to
Sri Ramakrishna that they had noticed little holes in the
screen in front of the Nahabat—too high for mice to have
bitten through. Sri Ramakrishna smiled. As time went on,
the holes increased in size, and passers-by could even detect
a shy hand pulling apart the bamboo.

Adjacent to the Nahabat runs a straight path along the
Ganges. When one turns south on it, this path leads directly
to the Panchavati and then to the Pine Grove. During Sri
Ramakrishna's time, very few people took this path because
it was surrounded by dense jungle which concealed fero-
cious animals. Today, the jungle is gone, and this area is no
longer secluded. Visitors crowd along this path which is lined
with beggars, especially near the Nahabat. Two lady devotees
in silk saris walk from beggar to beggar. One carries a cloth
bag and distributes handfuls of rice onto white sheets and
into aluminum bowls in front of the beggars. The other lady
drops coins in front of the beggars who return the favor by
mumbling a thanks and blessings. "May you and your family live long."

People in India consider it auspicious to give to beggars. Who knows who may be hidden in a beggar's garb?
This old man in rags may be the God Shiva in disguise.

A few beggar children run after a wealthy-looking
woman. Their thin arms stretched toward her, almost

clinging to her sari, they shout, "Ma, oh Ma, Ma go Ma, bak-shish, bakshish!" As young as they are, many of these children are already professional beggars. They have learned the trade from their parents who watch from a distance.

Some of the thin people seated on the path near the Nahabat are beggars not because they are too lazy to work but because life has dealt them a raw deal. One man has no arms, another no legs, and still another is blind, deaf, and dumb. In the West, people hear numerous stories about Indian beggars deliberately mutilating themselves in order to evoke pity in others to receive more money. Does it really matter if these stories are true or not? The fact remains, these people live in unbelievably poor conditions. They are a painful sight to the observer, and one asks, "Where do these people get strength to tolerate their pitiful existence?"

Contrary to Western conclusions about Indian attitudes, life is precious in India—even a beggar's life. Hindus believe that human life is a treasure because it is so difficult to be born as man. One of the ancient Hindu scriptures describes what happens when a person dies and what the soul has to undergo before it can take on another human body.

According to the Chandogya Upanishad, there are two paths through which souls depart from this life. The virtuous, who have done only good, take the path of light, the path of illumination. Those, who have performed both good and bad actions, must take the path of smoke, the path of darkness, the lunar path. They travel to the world of the Manes, from there to space, and from there to the moon.

> ...water, or the liquid libation, called "faith," when offered in the fire of heaven, creates an aqueous body through which one can experience pleasures in the world of the Moon. Householders (both ritualists and philanthropists) acquire such bodies. When their bodies are offered on the funeral pyre, the offering rises to heaven in an aqueous form,

enclosing the soul, and gradually reaches the world of the Moon where it creates the aqueous body. In their aqueous body, they experience the fruit of their past actions. When this fruit is consumed, like an oil lamp, they return to earth for a new round of pleasure and pain.[17]

After they have dwelled in the lunar world until their good works are consumed, they return the same way they came. First they reach the akasha (space), then air. Then they become smoke, then mist—which eventually forms a cloud—and then they fall to earth as rainwater. They are born as edibles, such as rice, barley, herbs, trees, sesamum or beans.

The exit from this state is most difficult, writes Shankara in his commentary on this Upanishad. Difficult, indeed, is the passage of the embodied soul through the relative universe. Unpredictable is the process of rebirth. There is no certainty where souls will land when they fall to the earth with rainwater. Unfortunates may be carried away by water currents from the mountains. They reach rivers and then the sea where they are swallowed by alligators or sea creatures. These, in turn, are swallowed by others, and then together with the latter, some disintegrate into the sea. With the seawater, these souls are again drawn up by the clouds to fall as rain upon deserts or inaccessible stony ground. While there, they are swallowed by serpents, deer, or other animals. These again are swallowed by others and the food chain goes on and on.

Thus, souls wanting to be born as human beings wander in an endless round. At times, they may enter inanimate objects that cannot be eaten. There, they linger for a while and then dry up. Even when they enter into edible inanimate

[17] Translation by Swami Nikhilananda, *The Upanishads*, Volume 4 (New York: Ramakrishna-Vivekananda Center, 1959), p. 268.

objects, their chance of being eaten by persons capable of procreation is one in a million because the number of inanimate objects is so vast. For this reason, says Shankara, an exit from this state is extremely difficult.

It is equally difficult to find exit from a man. If the food happens to be eaten by monks, children, impotent or old men, the souls attached to the food do not easily find release. When the food is eaten by a man capable of procreation, the soul enters that man and goes into the semen. When the semen is poured into the womb at the right time, the latent soul becomes a fetus and lies in the mother's womb in the shape of the father. Here it is that the soul is born as man, says the Chandogya Upanishad.

There are other souls that do not go to the lunar world at all but are born directly as wheat or barley on account of their past sinful actions. After those actions have been atoned by bearing their fruits, according to Shankara, the souls assume their bodies, such as those of subhuman beings.

Why are souls trying so hard to be born as human beings? Because, say the scriptures, the soul can only attain liberation while dwelling within a human body. A beggar's life may not be a desirable one, but even the poorest beggar feels he possesses a treasure. He may not have a highly developed intellect or have studied the Vedas, but his faith tells him that during his lifetime he, too, has a chance to attain the supreme realization that his consciousness is the same as the one dwelling in the rich man, in the king, in the queen—in all and everything.

A few saffron-clad mendicants sit quietly among the noisy beggars. They have renounced everything in order to realize God. Therefore, they do not beg, and accept only what is given without asking—and what is absolutely necessary to survive. One of the mendicants has sharp, distinct features, and his long, matted hair is piled up on top of his head. He sits cross-legged in the lotus posture in front of an old wall that separates the path leading to the Panchavati from the river Ganges. His hands lie calmly on his knees, and his dark eyes look moist, deep, and kind. In a way, he seems detached but, at the same time, he looks as if he were marveling at everything that comes in front of his eyes—the crowds of people passing by, the cows, the ornate buildings, all. Hindus say that when one has lost one's ego on the path to God, one becomes a joyful witness of God's play.

India is one of the few countries where it is still possible for religious mendicants to survive, because no matter how poor, Indians will always support holy men and women who have given up their worldly life to attain God. They also give them the greatest respect. Even a person of high social rank will approach a holy man or woman barefoot with head bowed in humility.

Bakultala Ghat

North of the Nahabat is the Bakultala,[18] adjacent to which are steep steps leading to the river. The Bakultala ghat has its own special history. Holy Mother used to bathe at this ghat at 3 A.M. when it was still dark outside. One morning she almost stepped on a sleeping crocodile and, after this near mishap, she began to carry a lantern. Sri Ramakrishna's dying mother was brought to this ghat where she breathed her last while—following ancient Hindu traditions—the lower half of her body was immersed in the holy waters of the Ganges.

Today, the steps of the Bakultala ghat are old and worn, but many people, especially women, like to bathe there. Some of the women of the Dakshineswar neighborhood come here every day to bathe and chat just as local women must have

---

[18] The literal meaning of Bakultala is "Foot of the Bakul," the place under the bakul tree.

done during Holy Mother's time. They talk about so-and-so's new baby, a son's marriage, the rich fabric of a new sari, which vegetable seller has the best eggplants, and what movie is playing at a nearby movie house. They chat like the big black birds that sit on the bakul trees, yet all their noise doesn't disturb the sleep of a couple of boatmen who have stretched out in the cool shade under the trees.

During Sri Ramakrishna's times, even larger boats could land at the main ghat opposite the Kali Temple. Today, the Ganges has deposited so much silt that only small boats can pass over the shallow water in front of the Dakshineswar Kali Temple. They generally land and anchor their boats just north of the Bakultala so they won't disturb the numerous bathers at the ghats.

The Panchavati

Following the path along the Ganges a little farther north, one reaches the Panchavati which is basically a grove of five trees: the banyan, peepul, ashoka, amlaki and bel. The Dakshineswar Panchavati grove was planted at the desire of Sri Ramakrishna, who spent many nights there immersed in deep meditation. Hindus say that when one meditates in a place where these five trees grow side by side, one quickly attains the object of one's meditation. See figure 29 on page 191.

Next to the Panchavati, another peepul tree grows jointly with a second banyan tree, and a terraced seat, which is still there, was built around the tree's base. Pointing to the Panchavati, Sri Ramakrishna told his disciples:

"I used to sit there," said Sri Ramakrishna. "In course of time I became mad. That phase also passed away. Kala, Shiva, is Brahman. That which sports with Kala is Kali, the Primal Energy. Kali moves even the Immutable."

Saying this, the Master sang:

My mind is overwhelmed with wonder,
Pondering the Mother's mystery;
Her very name removes
The fear of Kala, Death himself;
Beneath Her feet lies Maha-Kala . . . .[19]

Sri Ramakrishna added much to create a holy atmosphere in the Panchavati grove. As if his presence, his countless visions of Gods and Goddesses, his deep meditation, and his extensive sadhana practiced there weren't enough to make this place holy, Sri Ramakrishna walked all over the grove, sprinkling holy dust he had gathered while on pilgrimage in Vrindaban.

Vaishnavas say that dust taken from a particular grove where Krishna sported with the Gopis[20] has the power to turn any place, anywhere in this world, into holy Vrindaban. One full-moon autumn night, Krishna, who had promised the Gopis that he would spend one night with them, made himself into many—as many Gopis, so many Krishnas. He danced and sported with them all night. Even today, Hindus worship the ground of a particular grove in Vrindaban believed to have been touched by his holy feet, touched by the ecstasy of love. People of all ages come and gather dust there, and sprinkling it on the ground of their own homes, they hope Krishna will come and dance as he did in Vrindaban.

When one walks through the Dakshineswar Panchavati grove today, one must exercise good concentration to feel

---

[19] *The Gospel of Sri Ramakrishna*, p. 380.
[20] Milkmaids of Vrindaban.

Figure 29. The banyan tree of the Panchavati. Under its expansive branches, Sri Ramakrishna practiced many different spiritual disciplines and had visions of God in many forms.

the intrinsic holy vibrations of the place. There are so many shouting people everywhere in the Panchavati, and the once deserted grove looks much more like a picnic ground than a place of pilgrimage. Noisy vendors sell their wares from makeshift stalls, and people, snacking on junk food, feel free to toss their garbage onto this holy ground. Many trees have died and were never replaced.

Renovation is expensive. In an effort to improve the condition of the Panchavati, the Dakshineswar Temple authorities are currently working with a government agency to rebuild the temple garden area.

In spite of all the commotion going on today, many birds and monkeys live in the hollows of the Panchavati's ancient trees. East of the Panchavati is a small brick building—once a thatched hut—where Sri Ramakrishna practiced Vedantic disciplines under the guidance of Totapuri, a naked monk.

Totapuri was an itinerant Vedanta teacher who came from northwestern India to Bengal to bathe at Gangasagar where the river Ganga merges into the Bay of Bengal. He went farther south to visit Sri Jagannath at Puri, and on his way back, he came to Dakshineswar. Totapuri had a habit of never staying more than three days in one place, and certainly had no intentions of spending any more time at the Kali Temple. But, the Divine Mother Kali willed differently. Totapuri did not leave Dakshineswar until he had taught Sri Ramakrishna all he knew about Vedanta. Therefore, Totapuri lived at the Kali Temple for eleven months.

> Arriving at the Kali temple, Totapuri came, first of all, to the big open portico of the Ghat. Wearing only one piece of cloth, the Master absentmindedly sat there in a corner. As soon as Tota's eyes fell on the Master's face, radiant with austerity and beaming with the surge of devotion, he felt attracted toward him. Filled with curiosity, Tota thought, "Ah, can there be such a fit aspirant for Vedantic discipline in Bengal which is saturated with Tantric practices?" Observing him carefully, he asked the Master, "You seem to be well qualified. Would you like to practice Vedantic disciplines?"

> The Master answered the tall, naked mendicant with matted hair. "I know nothing of what I should or shouldn't do. My Mother knows everything. I shall do as She commands." Tota replied, "Then go; ask your Mother and come back quickly for I shall not stay here long."

The Master went slowly to the divine Mother's temple. He was in ecstasy when he heard her words of advice. "Go and learn. It is in order to teach you that the monk has come here."[21]

Sri Ramakrishna agreed to be initiated into sannyas, provided Totapuri would perform the ceremony in secret. Sri Ramakrishna wanted to spare the feelings of his old mother who would be afraid that her son would leave her if he were a monk.

> In the small hours of the morning, a fire was lighted in the Panchavati. Totapuri and Sri Ramakrishna sat before it. The flames played on their faces while Totapuri performed the sacred initiation rites wherein the disciple gives up all worldly attachments. The ceremony completed, teacher and disciple repaired to the meditation hut next to the Panchavati. Totapuri began to impart to Sri Ramakrishna the great truths of Vedanta.

> "Brahman," he said, "is the only Reality, ever pure, ever illumined, ever free, beyond the limits of time, space, and causation. Though apparently divided by names and forms through the inscrutable power of maya, that enchantress who makes the impossible possible, Brahman is really One and undivided. Whatever is within the domain of maya is unreal. Give it up."

> Totapuri asked the disciple to withdraw his mind from all objects of the relative world, including the Gods and Goddesses, and to concentrate on the Absolute. But the task was not easy, even for Sri

---

[21] *Sri Ramakrishna, the Great Master*, pp. 246-247.

Ramakrishna. He found it impossible to take his mind beyond Kali, the Divine Mother of the Universe.

"It is hopeless. I cannot raise my mind to the unconditioned state and come face to face with the Atman," said Sri Ramakrishna.

Totapuri grew excited and sharply said, "What? You can't do it? But you have to." He cast his eyes around. Finding a piece of glass he took it up and stuck it between Sri Ramakrishna's eyebrows. "Concentrate the mind on this point," he thundered.

"Then with stern determination I again sat to meditate," said Sri Ramakrishna to his disciples at a much later time. "As soon as the gracious form of the Divine Mother appeared before me, I used my discrimination as a sword, and with it, clove Her in two. The last barrier fell. My spirit at once soared beyond the relative plane and I lost myself in samadhi."

Sri Ramakrishna remained completely absorbed in samadhi for three days in this hut. "Is it really true?" Totapuri cried out in astonishment. "Is it possible that he has attained in a single day what took me forty years of strenuous practice to achieve? Great God! It is nothing short of a miracle."[22]

Today, a priest performs daily worship in the hut where Sri Ramakrishna attained samadhi. On the southern side of the hut is a window with bars, and if one peeks through, one can see a seated image of Shiva. But any image looks crude

---

[22] *The Gospel of Sri Ramakrishna*, pp. 28-29.

compared to one's own imagination of Sri Ramakrishna and what happened that night when he attained nirvikalpa samadhi for the first time.

Following the path north along the Ganges, one passes a newly renovated tank on the right, called the goose pond. And if one walks farther north, one reaches the Jhautala, a collection of a few trees known as the Bengali pine or singing tree. During Sri Ramakrishna's time this area was secluded, and he would go to the pine grove to answer calls of nature. Today, just as the Panchavati, the Jhautala is crowded with people. In an effort to restore some of the lost tranquility, temple officials erected a modern structure to serve as meditation hall amid the few pine trees that have survived. Beyond the Jhautala is the temple's boundary wall which separates the holy ground from a match factory which was previously the Government Magazine.

Sri Ramakrishna's Tantric Sadhana

East of the Jhautala is the Beltala (literally "foot of the bel tree") where Sri Ramakrishna practiced Tantra under the guidance of Bhairavi Brahmani. As discussed earlier in this book, Tantra bids people who are hopelessly attached to material objects to enjoy these but, at the same time, to discover the presence of God in them. Therefore, Tantric disciplines aim to spiritualize sense objects and transform one's sense attraction into love for God. The Tantric practices his sadhana mainly at night, meditating under a bel tree on a seat supported by three skulls: one of a man, one of a buffalo and one of a cat. Some Tantrics use five skulls to support their seat of meditation. In the four corners, they put the skulls of a jackal, a snake, a dog, and a bull, and in the middle, the skull of a man. See figure 30 on page 198.

Sri Ramakrishna's Tantric teacher was a woman, and he referred to her as the Brahmani. Like Totapuri, the Brahmani came to Dakshineswar as if sent by the Divine Mother Kali to teach Sri Ramakrishna.

Swami Saradananda wrote in *Sri Ramakrishna, the Great Master*:

> One day, the Master was plucking flowers in the garden when a boat anchored at the Bakul-ghat. A beautiful lady, wearing the ochre-colored cloth of a Bhairavi, alighted. Her hair was loose, and she carried a bundle of books in her arm. She proceeded toward the portico of the wide ghat to the south. Although the Brahmani was past her youth, she had retained her youthful grace and beauty. We cannot say how far the Master foresaw at first sight his close future relationship with her. But it is true that he felt that great attraction toward her which people feel when they see someone whose life is bound up with their own. For, as soon as the Master saw the Bhairavi from a distance, he returned to his room, called Hriday and asked him to invite the Sannyasini. Hriday hesitated and said, "The lady is a stranger. Why should she come at all?" The Master said, "Request her in my name and she will readily come."
>
> Hriday went to the portico, saw the Bhairavi sitting there and said to her that his maternal uncle, who was a devotee of God, requested her to meet him. Hriday was amazed to see the Bhairavi unhesitatingly stand up and accompany him without question.
>
> When the Bhairavi came to the Master's room and saw him, she was overwhelmed with joy and said,

"Ah, my child. You are here! I knew you were living somewhere on the bank of the Ganga, and I have been searching for you ever so long. At long last, I have found you." The Master said to her, "How could you know me, mother?" The Bhairavi answered, "I knew long ago, by the grace of the universal Mother, that I would have to meet three of you. I have already met two in eastern Bengal, and today I meet you here."[23]

The Brahmani was an adept in the Tantric and Vaishnava methods of worship. She wore the orange robes of renunciation and had little need for worldly goods. Her sole possessions were a few books and two pieces of wearing-cloth. Sri Ramakrishna often told his disciples about his attractive female guru:

"In the day time the Brahmani went to various places far away from the temple garden and collected and brought various rare articles prescribed by the Tantras. Placing them under the Vilva (Bel) tree or under the Panchavati at night, she called me, taught me how to make use of those things, and helped me in the performance of the worship of the Divine Mother according to the prescribed rules with their aid, asking me at last to merge in Japa and meditation. I acted accordingly. But I had to perform almost no Japa; for hardly did I turn the rosary once when I merged completely in Samadhi and realized the results proper to those rites. There was no limit to my visions and experiences, all very extraordinary."[24]

[23] *Sri Ramakrishna, the Great Master*, pp. 185-186.
[24] *Sri Ramakrishna, the Great Master*, p. 195.

Figure 30. A priest performs daily worship at the foot of the ancient Panchamundi—the tree under which Sri Ramakrishna practiced Tantra. Here, the Brahmani taught him many secret Tantric practices.

One day Sri Ramakrishna was meditating under the bel tree when he had a peculiar vision. He told his disciples, "I saw in front of me money, a shawl, a tray of sandesh, and two women. I asked my mind, `Mind, do you want any of these?' Then I saw the sandesh to be mere filth. One of the women had a big ring in her nose. I could see both their inside and outside—entrails, filth, bones, flesh and blood. The mind did not want any of these, neither money, shawl, sweets nor women. It remained fixed at the lotus feet of God."[25]

Sri Ramakrishna began to study Vedanta although the Brahmani forbade him to associate with Totapuri. "My child, do not mix with him," she said. "These people lack devotion. Your love and affection for God will vanish." But the Master did not pay heed to her advice and was absorbed day and night in the discussion of the Vedanta and its realization.[26]

Today, when one stands near the bel tree where Sri Ramakrishna practiced so many Tantric disciplines under the guidance of the Brahmani, one can overlook the entire area all the way to the Nahabat where the Holy Mother lived. The dense jungle of Sri Ramakrishna's time is gone and so is Rani Rasmani's beautiful flower garden. Very few of the trees and flowering bushes M. describes in *The Gospel of Sri Ramakrishna* are left.

M. described the temple garden of Dakshineswar as it was during Sri Ramakrishna's time as follows:

Just before the break of day, the sweet sound of bells comes from the temple to the ears of the devotee. They herald the morning service with the "Waving of Lights" which brings the tidings of Love and Joy

[25] *The Gospel of Sri Ramakrishna*, p. 745.
[26] *Sri Ramakrishna, the Great Master*, pp. 354-355.

to all of God's creatures; for the Mother of the Universe is up again and will continue to bless her own, her beloved children. From the Concert Room, the morning tunes are played on the flageolet (Rasunchouki) to the accompaniment of drums and cymbals. It is not as yet red in the East—for the sun, the day-star, is not up yet to give light and life to this world of ours. At such an early hour, they are plucking flowers in the temple garden to be offered during the morning service to God.

On the bank of the holy river and just to the west of the Panchavati are the bel tree and sweet-scented, milk-white gulchi flower tree. Close to them is the mango-creeper (Madhavi). Sri Ramakrishna was very fond of the flower plant mallika (a kind of jasmine), the mango-creeper so dear to Sri Radhika, and the gulchi flower. Sri Ramakrishna had brought the mango-creeper from Vrindaban.

The part of the temple garden to the east of the path running towards the cow-house contains many flower plants. Among others, there are the fragrant champak, the five-faced jaba (hibiscus), the jaba pendant that looks like ear rings, the rose, and the gold flower (kanchan). On the hedges grows the creeper amaranth, called aparajita or the "unvanquished." It has blue flowers and is used for the worship of the Divine Mother. Very close to these are the jui (jasmine) and the shefalika flower.

Alongside the long line of the 12 temples of Shiva and situated just to the west of them are also many flower plants—the white oleander (kirva), the red oleander, the rose, the jasmine (jui), the large double-petalled jasmine (bel). There is also the thorn apple (dhutura), which is used for the worship of

Shiva. At intervals there is the sacred basil plant growing on brick-built platforms.

To the south of the Concert Room are the double-petalled jasmine, the single jasmine—"the king of scents," and the rose—all sweet-scented flowers. Within a short distance of the southern river-ghat are two flower plants with beautiful fragrant flowers—one called the lotus oleander and the other the cuckoo-eyed. The color of the latter resembles that of the eyes of a cuckoo.

Near the Master's room and growing west of it are a couple of plants with flowers called the Krishna-crest (the cox-comb flower) resembling the crest adorning the head of Sri Krishna, the Incarnation of Divine Love; also the double jasmine, the jasmine, the rose, the tulip, the jaba, the white oleander, the red oleander, the five-faced jaba, the China-rose, etc.

Sri Ramakrishna was once plucking bel leaves off the bel tree near the Panchavati when a portion of the bark came off. It seemed to him as if the Divinity that was within him and manifest in all things without had received a severe wound. He felt this in his very soul and henceforward ceased plucking leaves off the bel tree. On another occasion, he was walking about, gathering flowers for the worship of the Mother. It occurred to him that all the flowering trees were worshipping too, and he couldn't pluck any more flowers.

The temple garden has become an abode of joy and gladness. The Deity is worshipped night and day in various aspects as the Father, as the Incarnation of Divine Love, and again, as the Mother of the Universe, Savior of the world. The offerings regularly made during the divine worship every day are many and various. The guest house which accords welcome to holy men and mendicants is an institution connected with the Temple, highly valued by those that resort to it. The view of the sacred river flowing past the temple garden calls up thoughts that appeal to the highest nature of man. No less inspiring is the garden within the temple compound, with flowers of variegated hues which charm the devout lovers of God with their fragrance, beauty and sanctity. What gives the finishing touch to this fascinating picture of the Temple garden is the saintly figure of the God-man intoxicated night and day with the joy of the Lord.[27]

Storage Rooms, Kitchens and Staff Rooms

On the western side, the Dakshineswar Kali Temple's rectangular courtyard is enclosed by twelve Shiva temples and, on the other sides, by long buildings with lengthy, covered verandas supported by pillars. Walking over the cool marble floor of a veranda, one strolls past numerous doors, some open, some closed.

Since the temple was built, the rooms along these verandas have served pretty much the same functions. The rooms which were used for storage one hundred years ago still serve the same purpose. Some rooms store vegetables and pulses, others store luchis[28] and sweetmeats, and still others

---

[27] M., *The Condensed Gospel of Sri Ramakrishna* (Mylapore: Madras: Sri Ramakrishna Math), pp. 21-23.
[28] Round bread which becomes very light and puffy when fried.

are used for cutting fruits and preparing offerings to Kali. There are two entirely separate kitchens. One for Kali where meat and fish are prepared and one for Vishnu where only vegetarian food is cooked.

A long veranda near the kitchens serves as a dining hall for pilgrims. After the noon-meal offering to Kali, people with "prasad tickets" obtained earlier line up here, then sit cross-legged on mats along the corridor walls. The food is very tasty at the Dakshineswar Kali Temple. In fact, it is a temple tradition dating back to Rani Rasmani's time to serve tasty meals to visiting devotees. Therefore, this veranda is generally packed during prasad time.

A typical meal served from the Kali kitchen consists of rice, fried vegetables, raw green chilies, dal (curried lentils), curried fish, two different kinds of curried vegetables, goat meat (on special occasions when a goat has been sacrificed to Kali), chutney, curds, rice pudding and rasagollas (sweet cheese balls).

Prasad from the Vishnu Temple is served on a different veranda. A typical meal from the Vishnu kitchen consists of khichuri (a mixture of rice and curried lentils), fried vegetables, raw green chilies, nuts, a few different vegetable preparations, chutney, curds, rice pudding and rasagollas.

East of the kitchens is a rather large tank called the Gazipukur. It has two ghats, one to the north and the other to the west of the tank. The western ghat is used for washing sacred utensils and is appropriately called the "Plate-Washing Ghat." Near the northern ghat is an old banyan tree called Gazitala. A long time ago, at the foot of this tree lived a Mohammedan saint who passed his days in the contemplation of God. His departed spirit is worshipped even today by both Hindus and Mohammedans living in the vicinity of the Dakshineswar Kali Temple.

Quoting from Swami Saradananda's writing on how Sri Ramakrishna practiced Islam:

Govinda [a sufi] came to the Kali Temple at Dakshineswar and spent his time with his "seat" spread under the peaceful shade of the Panchavati. Muslim Fakirs, as well as Hindu Sadhus, were welcome at Rasmani's Kali Temple, and her hospitality was equally accorded to both. Therefore, while staying there, Govinda had not to go around for alms. He spent his days joyfully meditating.

The Master was attracted to the devout Govinda and the Islamic religion. "This also is a path to the realization of God. The sportive Mother, the source of infinite Lila, has been blessing many people with the attainment of her lotus feet through this path also. I must see how she makes those who take refuge in her attain their desired end."

The Master expressed his desire to Govinda, became initiated and engaged himself in practicing Islam according to the prescribed rules. "I then devoutly repeated the holy syllable `Allah', wore my cloth like the Muslims, said Namaz thrice daily, and felt disinclined to see Hindu deities... I spent three days in that mood and had the full realization of the result of practices according to that faith."[29]

Sri Ramakrishna practiced many different sadhanas prescribed by many different cults and religions. Although the Brahmani taught him most Vaishnav sadhanas, Sri Ramakrishna practiced the affectionate attitude (of a mother toward her child) toward God after he was initiated by Jatadhari, a holy man who belonged to the Ramayat sect (followers of Ramachandra). Sri Ramakrishna became the mother and the God Rama his child.

---

[29] *Sri Ramakrishna, the Great Master*, pp. 259-260.

Swami Saradananda recorded:

> Urged by an irresistible inward devotional mood, the Master now regarded himself as a woman, both in body and mind and acted accordingly. So, when he had the vision of Rama as a sweet child, he assumed the attitude of maternal affection toward him. He had been, no doubt, initiated in the mantra of Rama long ago in order to perform the worship and service of his family deity, Raghuvir. But then, he was not attracted to him in any mood except that of a servant toward his master. Having the new mood toward the deity, he now became anxious to be initiated by a guru according to the scriptures and receive a mantra befitting the new mood and to reach the ultimate limit of realization in that discipline.[30]

Jatadhari initiated Sri Ramakrishna with the mantra of his own Chosen Ideal, namely that of Rama. Jatadhari's love for Ramachandra was extraordinary and, wherever he went, he carried an image of Ramlala, the child Rama, which he worshipped daily. Others observed Jatadhari worshipping a metal image, but Sri Ramakrishna, with his spiritual insight, knew about Jatadhari's many wonderful visions.

Jatadhari was a fit guru and taught Sri Ramakrishna the sadhana in accordance with his mantra. When Jatadhari left the Dakshineswar Kali Temple, he gave Sri Ramakrishna the image of Ramlala which he had worshipped so long.

Among the spiritual disciplines of major religions, Sri Ramakrishna practiced the Christian faith and listened to readings of the Bible. One day, looking at a picture of the Madonna and Child, Sri Ramakrishna had a vision of the Divine Child Jesus. On another occasion, he had a vision

---

[30] *Sri Ramakrishna, the Great Master*, p. 214.

of Lord Jesus near the Panchavati wherein Jesus merged into his body.

One after the other, Sri Ramakrishna practiced sadhanas prescribed by various faiths. He experienced that all lead to the same goal.

The long building which forms the northern boundary of the Kali Temple's inner courtyard houses Sri Ramakrishna's room on the western and priests' quarters on the eastern extremities. One reaches the long veranda in front of Sri Ramakrishna's room by climbing a few steep steps that run alongside the veranda. Just outside his room is a small book stall which displays religious books and pictures. It is the only shop allowed within the inner courtyard and is run by a member of Sri Ramakrishna's family. See figure 31 on page 208.

Just past the long veranda outside Sri Ramakrishna's room is the large, ornate main entrance to the inner courtyard. And next to the main entrance is a smaller one, used by priests, servants, and people who know about it. It is only a narrow passage between two columns that help support the covered veranda, but it is convenient to use when the main entrance is too crowded with people. A few steep steps lead up to the passage, followed by a few more leading down on the other side toward the Kuthi.

The rest of this northern building is occupied by the priests' quarters which are individually accessible from the inner courtyard. More priests' quarters are located within the long eastern building, just south of the kitchens and the "Plate-washing Ghat." Although very few priests actually live within the Kali Temple compound, they use their assigned rooms to rest, change, and take their meals. The rooms are furnished rather sparsely. Wooden cots covered by a thin mattress form their beds, and a clothesline suspended from the ceiling serves as their wardrobe. In spite of the austere furnishing, the priests' quarters are quite cozy. Most of the rooms are shared by a few priests, and visitors frequently stop by for a smoke and a chat. Cats, dogs, even goats come for a visit and look around—mostly in search of food.

The long building, enclosing the courtyard to the south, houses the temple office where one finds the temple manager seated behind an enormous wooden desk. Other office staff members, seated among piles of papers, dusty ledgers and dainty teacups, busy themselves with their various assigned duties. A continuous flow of storekeepers, servants, priests, Brahmin cooks, porters and visitors walk in and out of the office, ignoring a mother cat peacefully suckling her young next to the manager's desk.

"These are Ma Kali's cats," explains the temple manager with a grin as he watches one of the frisky kittens run off with a pencil. "Nobody will dare to harm them."

East of the temple office are storerooms which are locked because they contain sacred utensils, old furniture and carpets—all from a different era. One wonders whether the chandeliers Sri M. talks about in the *Gospel of Sri Ramakrishna* are kept here in one of these rooms. What a pleasure it would be to rummage through the Rani's attic and glimpse the Dakshineswar Kali Temple's royal history.

West of the temple office are the VIP/Trustee quarters. Whenever the trustees and descendants of Rani Rasmani visit the Kali Temple, they generally rest and take their meals in the VIP quarters. Passing through the most spacious of these rooms, one is vaguely reminded of a stateroom in a medieval castle. The various people depicted in the huge old paintings that cover the walls stare down as valiantly as the best of British knights. There are old paintings of members of the Rani Rasmani family and two large pictures depicting her family's genealogy. The room closest to the Ganges leads out onto a semicircular porch that resembles the one in front

Figure 31. Shankar Chatterjee, a distant relative of Sri Ramakrishna, displays his wares on the southern veranda outside Sri Ramakrishna's room.

of Sri Ramakrishna's room. A breeze from the river blows softly through one's hair as one stands on this ornately pillared porch overlooking the Ganges. It's quiet in this section of the Kali Temple. Since only a few people are allowed to come here, one gets a chance to feel what the temple must have been like during the time of Sri Ramakrishna.

A few steps lead down from the porch to a garden and then to a fairly high river embankment. A narrow path along the embankment is lined with flowering plants, and if one walks south, one reaches a Nahabat that looks like the one Holy Mother occupied. During Sri Ramakrishna's time, this Nahabat was used by musicians who produced hauntingly beautiful melodies during the early morning hours and at evening vespers. M., the recorder of *The Gospel of Sri Ramakrishna*, practiced sadhana here for one week. He described his experience as follows:

> The whole symbolic world is represented in the temple garden—the Trinity of the Nature Mother (Kali), the Absolute (Shiva), and Love (Vishnu), the Arch spanning heaven and earth. The terrific Goddess of the Tantra, the soul-enthralling Flute-Player of the Bhagavata, and the Self-absorbed Absolute of the Vedas live together, creating the greatest synthesis of religions. All aspects of Reality are represented there. But of this divine household, Kali is the pivot, the sovereign Mistress. She is Prakriti, the Procreatrix, Nature, the Destroyer, the Creator. Nay, She is something greater and deeper still for those who have eyes to see. She is the Universal Mother, "my Mother," as Ramakrishna would say, the All-powerful, who reveals Herself to Her children under different aspects and Divine Incarnations, the Visible God, who leads the elect

to the Invisible Reality, and if it so pleases Her, She takes away the last trace of ego from created beings and merges it in the consciousness of the Absolute, the undifferentiated God. Through Her grace, "the finite ego loses itself in the illimitable Ego-Atman-Brahman."[31]

One could explore the Dakshineswar Kali Temple compound for months at a time, and still, one would discover new things. "Everything there is in this world is right here in the Dakshineswar temple," said Dadu[32], a colorful devotee with a long, gray beard. Dadu comes to Dakshineswar almost every day and spends hours praying, talking, worshipping God. His eyes are full of joy, and when one inquires about his well-being, he points one arm toward the Kali Temple and says with utmost humility, "The kindness, the kindness. Oh, what kindness!"

---

[31] *The Gospel of Sri Ramakrishna*, pp. 9-10.
[32] "Dadu" is the Bengali expression for grandfather.

Chapter 5

MA KALI'S GOD-INTOXICATED MYSTICS

O Mother, make me mad with Thy love!
What need have I of knowledge or reason?
Make me drunk with Thy love's Wine;
O Thou who stealest Thy bhaktas'[1] hearts,
Drown me deep in the Sea of Thy love!

Here in this world, this madhouse of Thine,
Some laugh, some weep, some dance for joy:
Jesus, Buddha, Moses, Gauranga,
All are drunk with the Wine of Thy love.
O Mother, when shall I be blessed
By joining their blissful company?[2]

---

[1] Devotees.
[2] *The Gospel of Sri Ramakrishna*, p. 399.

The Quest for Bliss

The quest for bliss is universal. People drink alcohol, take drugs, spend most of their energy running after fame, wealth, a lover. Why? Because they think when they obtain these, they will have bliss. There is not one person alive who doesn't want bliss and doesn't actively pursue it.

"I wanted to live deep and suck out all the marrow of life," said the American naturalist and writer, Henry Thoreau. In our own way, we all want that fulfillment, the knowledge of living life to the fullest extent. But happiness in this world is, oh, so temporary. One moment bliss, the next sorrow.

We strive to enjoy, but instead, we end up being enjoyed. We desire, but we can't keep up with our desires. When one's face has become marred with wrinkles and one's hair has turned gray, it is no longer easy to run after one's ever young and vigorous desires. Nevertheless, tossed between hope and hopelessness, people continue to chase the fleeting bird of happiness.

This world is like a museum—full of signs that say "Do not touch." But we want to touch; we want to possess. Faced with endless social pressures and responsibilities, we realize that we cannot have all that we want. And then we become depressed. We watch TV or go to sleep so we won't have to deal with our depression. A third of our precious lives are spent in bed, sleeping.

People dream of love, of mad passion. But who dares to love? Who dares to live life to the fullest? Who dares to be mad with joy? This world is a wonderful place for the one who knows how to live.

Permanent bliss lies in the spirit which is subtle and difficult to grasp. And yet, although the road to attain this pinnacle of bliss is strewn with tremendous obstacles, it's certainly worth pursuing if one wants it all. We call people who have attained the highest—as we can understand it— saint, yogi, master, avatar.

The power of their influence on us lies partially in their conviction that God is the only thing worth pursuing in this world and that a passionate knowledge of God is the highest obtainable bliss here and hereafter. We worship these blissful souls. We accept them as our teachers because they can show us the way to the bliss we seek.

Ramprasad, the Minstrel of Kali

Ramprasad was a great Kali worshipper and is famous among all who worship the great Shakti. Although Ramprasad never physically went to the Dakshineswar Kali Temple—he lived long before the temple was built—his influence is most certainly there. In fact, it is everywhere the Divine Mother's name is being sung. Wherever Kali is being worshipped, Ramprasad, her melodious mystic, is present through his songs. Countless times, Sri Ramakrishna sat in the inner shrine before the image of Kali and sang Ramprasad's inspiring songs.

> *Come, let us go for a walk, O mind,*
> *to Kali, the Wish-fulfilling Tree,*
> *And there beneath It gather the four fruits of life.*
> *Of your two wives, Dispassion and Worldliness,*
> *Bring along Dispassion only, on your way to the Tree,*
> *And ask her son Discrimination about the Truth.*
>
> *When will you learn to lie, O mind,*
> *in the abode of Blessedness,*
> *With Cleanliness and Defilement on either side of you?*
> *Only when you have found the way*
> *To keep these wives contentedly under a single roof,*
> *Will you behold the matchless form of Mother Syama.*
>
> *Ego and Ignorance, your parents,*
> *instantly banish from your sight;*

And should Delusion seek to drag you to its hole,
Manfully cling to the pillar of Patience.
Tie to the post of Unconcern the goats of Vice and Virtue,
Killing them with the sword of Knowledge if they rebel.

With the children of Worldliness, your first wife,
plead from a goodly distance
And, if they will not listen,
drown them in Wisdom's sea.
Says Ramprasad: If you do as I say,
You can submit a good account,
O mind, to the King of Death,
And I shall be well pleased with you
and call you my darling.[3]

Ramprasad was born in a village named Halisahar (previously called Kamarhati) on the bank of the Ganges, about 34 miles north of Calcutta. His actual birth date is hard to determine because birth records during his time were not kept as they are today. It was most probably in the year 1723 when Ramprasad was born into an old Tantric Vaidya[4] family that can be traced back many generations.

One of his remote ancestors was Krittivasa, a generous and ardent devotee of the Divine Mother Kali—Ramprasad gives a vivid description of his ancestors in his poetical composition "Vidyasundara." Ramprasad's father, Ramram Sen, was an eminent Ayurvedic physician and Sanskrit scholar. He had two wives. Ramram Sen's first wife, Katyayani, bore him one son by the name of Nidhiram, and his second wife, Siddheswari, gave birth to two daughters, Ambika and Bhavani, and two sons, Ramprasad and Viswanath.

Ramprasad was a precocious child. When young Ramprasad was sent to the local village school, he amazed

---

[3] *The Gospel of Sri Ramakrishna*, p. 139.
[4] Family of mixed caste—Brahmin and Kshatria. Many physicians belong to this caste.

everyone with his extraordinary capability for learning. Pleased with his intelligent son, Ramram Sen sent him to a Sanskrit school (tol) where Ramprasad learned Sanskrit grammar, literature, and Bengali poetry. He had a special talent for writing poetry and learning new languages. Ramram Sen encouraged his son to learn Persian and Urdu, the languages of the Muslim rulers, since he was convinced that it would help him find a job later on. Bengal at this time was under Muslim rule.

Although Ramprasad mastered both languages in a relatively short time and would have been ready to look for a job, he showed no interest in entering the family's traditional profession to become an Ayurvedic physician. Instead, during adolescence he exhibited spiritual inclinations which he expressed by writing poetry. As time passed, Ramprasad's other-worldliness caused great anxiety to his parents. In an attempt to instill a sense of worldly responsibility in the boy, Ramram Sen arranged his marriage to a beautiful young girl by the name of Sarvani. Ramprasad was then 22.

According to family tradition, the newlywed couple was initiated by the family's spiritual teacher, Madhavacharya.[5] As the guru whispered the mantra of Kali—the family deity—into Ramprasad's ear, something deep inside him stirred and lifted its hood, as it were. Ramprasad felt consumed by an inner, painfully sweet longing for Kali. Though he loved his wife, the attraction for the Divine dominated his actions and prevented him from turning his attention toward worldly duties. Ramprasad was indifferent toward things others covet. He did not look for a job and even neglected his responsibility of maintaining the family. Instead, he devoted himself more and more to practicing spiritual disciplines.

One year after his initiation, his guru suddenly died. Ramprasad was grief-stricken. He yearned for the Divine

---

[5] Alias Srinath Bhattacharya.

Mother and, now that his guru was gone, who was going to teach him about the Divine Mother and how to worship her? Ramprasad did not have to worry for long. An earnest spiritual seeker will always get the needed guidance. As if brought by divine providence, a famous Tantric yogi and scholar by the name of Krishnananda Agamavagisha came from Navadwip to Halisahar. He was a famous devotee of Kali and had written the renowned book *Tantrasara*. As soon as Agamavagisha saw Ramprasad, he recognized the young man's spiritual potential and began to instruct him in the intricacies of Tantric sadhana. Ramprasad learned the secret of Kali worship from Agamavagisha, and it did not take him long to merge his thought into Kali and become absorbed in meditation and prayer.

Soon after, another calamity befell Ramprasad's life. His father suddenly died before he could make provisions for his family. He did not leave enough money or property for the family's maintenance. The family's burden fell upon Ramprasad's shoulders and, reluctantly, he left his seat of meditation to search for a job that would bring income. Even though Ramprasad had made up his mind to actively look for a job and though he was a learned scholar, it was difficult finding employment. Unaccustomed to the business world, Ramprasad appeared naive to many potential employers and, consequently, they would not hire him.

Finally, Lakshmi Narayana Das, one of Ramprasad's relatives, helped him secure a job in Calcutta. Ramprasad was appointed as an accounting clerk by Durga Charan Mitra of Garanhata and earned a monthly salary of thirty rupees. He sincerely and carefully performed his duties but, every so often, he could not prevent his mind from trailing off and thinking of the Divine Mother Kali. At such times he would feel so overwhelmed by his own thoughts that he could not help but write down the passionate songs that freely poured out of the inner recesses of his heart. In lieu of better paper, he wrote these songs onto blank pages in the back of the account book.

O my forgetful mind,
thou knowest not how to keep accounts.
When thou wast born,
thou wast credited[6] and began to be debited.[7]
O! Enter receipts and expenses aright;
if they are equal, there is no cash balance.
If receipts are greater than expenses,
thou art accountable for the balance.
If there is a cash balance,
there will be no end to thy writing to account for it.
Twice-born Ramprasad says,
"What is the use of writing credit[8] and debit[9]?
O! Meditate on Kali,
Tara, Durga in the mind."[10]

Some of Ramprasad's fellow employees did not understand him and, therefore, did not like him. As oil and water
do not mix, worldly-minded people and spiritual seekers do
not comprehend each other. When they observed that
Ramprasad was writing songs into the account book, they
were shocked and complained to the manager. Durga Charan
Mitra ordered Ramprasad into his office. But when he
opened his account book and read Ramprasad's soul-stir-
ring songs to Ma Kali, Durga Charan recognized the spiritual
greatness of his strange accountant. He embraced Ramprasad
and said with a voice choked with emotion, "Please, go home
and devote all your time to the worship of the Divine Mother.
I shall continue to pay your monthly salary. All you need to
do is keep composing these wonderful songs to Kali."

---

[6] Ramprasad looks upon birth as a credit.
[7] Life daily decreases.
[8] Merits, good works.
[9] Bad actions.
[10] Dr. Jadunath Sinha, *Ramaprasada's Devotional Songs*, p. 62.

Ramprasad went home in an ecstatic mood and, chanting Kali's name, he again immersed himself in sadhana, meditation, and prayer. Ramprasad practiced many esoteric spiritual disciplines. For instance, he had a peculiar habit of standing neck-deep in the Ganga, deeply absorbed in the thought of the Divine Mother. And then, with tears rolling down his cheeks, he'd sing one fervent song after another. While his powerful voice echoed over the Ganga, Ramprasad lost himself in Kali. And, in awe, people and animals would stand still to listen.

Mother, this is the grief that sorely grieves my heart,
That even with Thee for Mother,
and though I am wide awake,
There should be robbery in my house.
Many and many a time I vow to call on Thee,
Yet when the time for prayer comes round,
I have forgotten.
Now I see it is all Thy trick.

As Thou hast never given,
so Thou receivest naught;
Am I to blame for this, O Mother?
Hadst Thou but given,
Surely then Thou hadst received;
Out of Thine own gifts I should have given to Thee.
Glory and shame, bitter and sweet, are Thine alone;
This world is nothing but Thy play.
Then why, O Blissful One,
dost Thou cause a rift in it?

Says Ramprasad:
Thou hast bestowed on me this mind,
And with a knowing wink of Thine eye
Bidden it, at the same time, to go and enjoy the world.
And so I wander here forlorn through Thy creation,

Blasted, as it were, by someone's evil glance,
Taking the bitter for the sweet,
Taking the unreal for the Real.[11]

One day, the Maharaja Krishna Chandra of Nadia, a landlord under Nawab Sirajuddaula of Bengal, was traveling in his boat on the Ganges when he heard Ramprasad's enchanting song. The song seemed to come straight from Ramprasad's heart and delighted the Maharaja so much that he called him to his court in Krishnanagar. Being a great devotee of Kali and desiring inspiration from Ramprasad's songs on a regular basis, the Maharaja appointed him to be his court poet.

But, can one put a free spirit like Ramprasad in any kind of binding situation? Although Ramprasad rarely attended the Maharaja's court, the Maharaja was very kind to him and offered him a gift of thirty-three acres of rent-free land for the maintenance of his family. Happy like a child because his earthly obligations were removed, Ramprasad immersed himself in sadhana and the worship of the Divine Mother Kali.

Taking the name of Kali, dive deep down, O mind,
Into the heart's fathomless depths,
Where many a precious gem lies hid.
But never believe the bed of the ocean bare of gems
If in the first few dives you fail;
With firm resolve and self-control
Dive deep and make your way to Mother Kali's realm.

Down in the ocean depths of heavenly Wisdom lie
The wondrous pearls of Peace, O mind;
And you yourself can gather them,
If you but have pure love and follow the scriptures' rule,

---

[11] *The Gospel of Sri Ramakrishna*, p. 137.

Within those ocean depths, as well,
Six alligators[12] lurk—lust, anger, and the rest—
Swimming about in search of prey.
Smear yourself with the turmeric of discrimination;
The very smell of it will shield you from their jaws.

Upon the ocean bed lie strewn
Unnumbered pearls and precious gems;
Plunge in, says Ramprasad, and gather up handfuls there![13]

In a garden near Ramprasad's house was a Panchavati grove where the five holy trees—banyan, bel, amalaki, ashoka and peepul—grew side by side. According to the Tantrics, this type of grove is an ideal place to practice Tantric sadhana. Ramprasad spent hours there, forgetful of the world and meditating on a panchamundi asana. This asana is a seat made up of five skulls—the skull of a snake, a frog, a rabbit, a fox and a man. On special days, such as ekadasi,[14] purnima (full moon) and amavasya, he fasted all day and remained in the Panchavati instead of going home. Immersed in the thought of the Divine Mother, he felt intoxicated with a mad surge of love.

I drink no ordinary wine,
but Wine of Everlasting Bliss,
As I repeat my Mother Kali's name;
It so intoxicates my mind that people take me to be drunk!
First my guru gives molasses for the making of the Wine;
My longing is the ferment to transform it.
Knowledge, the maker of the Wine,
prepares it for me then;

---

[12] The six passions—lust, anger, avarice, delusion, pride, and envy.
[13] *The Gospel of Sri Ramakrishna*, p. 124.
[14] The eleventh day after the full and new moon. Devotees spend this day fasting, praying and worshipping the Lord.

And when it is done,
my mind imbibes it from the bottle of the mantra,
Taking the Mother's name to make it pure.
Drink of this Wine, says Ramprasad,[15]
and the four fruits[16] of life are yours.[17]

The realization of God is very difficult to attain, indeed. In the beginning, the spiritual aspirant has to work hard to overcome desires of the flesh, and desires for fame and fortune. As if this isn't hard enough, the seeker of God needs a lot more strength and endurance even when he or she has overcome all base desires. The stamina to endure one's own spiritual restlessness, one's spiritual emotions, is essential to success. What agony of separation, what longing—the soul mad for God has no rest. Sri Ramakrishna used to say that longing is a prerequisite for the vision of God. He said:

One must have for God the yearning of a child. The child sees nothing but confusion when his mother is away. You may try to cajole him by putting sweetmeat in his hand; but he will not be fooled. He only says, "No, I want to go to my mother." One must feel such yearning for God. Ah, what yearning! How restless a child feels for his mother! Nothing can make him forget his mother. He to whom the enjoyment of worldly happiness appears tasteless, he who takes no delight in anything of the world—money, name, creature comforts, sense pleasure—becomes sincerely grief-stricken for the vision of the Mother. And to him alone the Mother comes running, leaving all Her other duties.

---

[15] It is customary for writers of devotional songs in India to mention their names at the end of their songs.
[16] Dharma, artha, kama, and moksha—righteous conduct, wealth, desire and liberation.
[17] *The Gospel of Sri Ramakrishna*, p. 95.

Ah, that restlessness is the whole thing. Whatever path you follow—whether you are a Hindu, a Mussalman, a Christian, a Sakta, a Vaishnava, or a Brahmo—the vital point is restlessness. God is our Inner Guide. It doesn't matter if you take a wrong path—only you must be restless for Him. He Himself will put you on the right path.

Besides there are errors in all paths. Everyone thinks his watch is right; but as a matter of fact, no watch is absolutely right. But that doesn't hamper one's work. If a man is restless for God, he gains the company of sadhus and as far as possible corrects his own watch with the sadhus' help."[18]

In his songs, Ramprasad left us a record of his agony of longing for a vision of the Divine Mother Kali. His constant dialogue with the Divine Mother sets an example of how one should approach her. How long can a mother stay away when her child cries as pitifully as Ramprasad in his songs?

Mother, am I Thine eight-months child?[19]
Thy red eyes cannot frighten me!
My riches are Thy Lotus Feet,
which Shiva holds upon His breast;
Yet, when I seek my heritage,
I meet with excuses and delays.
A deed of gift I hold in my heart,
attested by Thy Husband Shiva;
I shall sue Thee, if I must,
and with a single point shall win.

If Thou dost oppose me,
Thou wilt learn what sort of mother's son I am.

---

[18] The Gospel of Sri Ramakrishna, p. 673.
[19] A premature child is generally weak and fearful.

This bitterly contested suit between the Mother and Her son—
What sport it is! says Ramprasad.
I shall not cease tormenting Thee
Till Thou Thyself shalt yield the fight
and take me in Thine arms at last.[20]

Ramprasad had the first vision of Mother Kali in a garden near his house—most probably in the Panchavati. People noticed a transformation in Ramprasad but they did not know the cause. For instance, Ramprasad's body began to glow. He emanated a certain bewitching beauty that attracted people in hordes.

Many wonderful things began to happen in Ramprasad's life. One day, he needed to repair a fence and asked his daughter Jagadiswari to help him pass the cord back and forth.

"My dear father, I have to finish some other work first," said Jagadiswari. "I'll come when I am done."

But to Ramprasad's surprise, Jagadiswari appeared as soon as he sat down next to the fence. She must have had a change of mind, he thought. Ramprasad began to work, weaving the cord, pushing it through the fence to the other side. Jagadiswari returned the cord quite skillfully, and the work was finished in no time.

The fence repaired, Ramprasad leisurely went inside the house and sat down on the veranda. Jagadiswari came after a little while and said, "Father, I see the work is done. Who helped you pass the cord back and forth?"

"Well, who else but you, my child," replied the surprised Ramprasad.

"No, father, I haven't been near the fence," said Jagadiswari. "I just returned from my other work and was looking for you to help with the fence."

---

[20] *The Gospel of Sri Ramakrishna*, pp. 263-264.

Ramprasad was dumbfounded. The Divine Mother in the form of Jagadiswari had come and helped him in his daughter's absence. As was his habit, he immediately began to compose a song to the Divine Mother.

O mind, why do you keep away from the Mother's feet?
O mind, meditate on the Mother; you will then get mukti.
Tie then (the Mother's feet) with the cord of devotion.
So bad is your luck that though having eyes,
You did not see that the Mother came as your daughter
And tied the fence with the devotee. . . .[21]

One day when Ramprasad was about to go to the river for a bath, a beautiful young woman stopped him and asked him to sing a devotional song to the Divine Mother.

"Please wait. It is getting late for the noon worship," said Ramprasad. "Let me bathe and finish the worship first. Then I'll be happy to sing a few songs."

But when he returned, he couldn't find the woman anywhere. He thought that this may have been the play of the Divine Mother. He sat down and closed his eyes. After meditating for a while, Ramprasad began to see a glow of light all around him and heard a female voice. "I am Annapurna,"[22] said the divine voice. "I came all the way from Varanasi to hear your songs but, alas, I had to leave disappointed."

Ramprasad was extremely angry with himself. He decided to leave at once and go to Varanasi and sing for Mother Annapurna there. After walking many miles, he reached Triveni where, exhausted and sleepy, he took rest under a tree that stood on the bank of the Ganges.

[21] Swami Budhananda, *Ramprasad, the Melodious Mystic* (New Delhi: Ramakrishna Mission, 1982), p. 27.
[22] A name of the Divine Mother as the giver of food. Her temple is in Benares next to her divine husband Shiva's temple—the famed Viswanath Temple.

No sooner had he closed his eyes, than he saw the mysterious light again and heard the Mother's voice, "Stay here and sing for me. You will not have to walk any further. Varanasi is not the only place where I live; I pervade the whole universe."

Ramprasad forgot that he was tired. Full of joy, he lost himself in the Divine Mother. Song after song echoed over the Ganges. And nature stood still to listen to the saint.

> *Of what use is my going to Kasi[23] any more?*
> *At Mother's feet lie Gaya, Ganga and Kasi.*
> *I swim in the ocean of bliss*
> *while I meditate on Her in my heart lotus.[24]*
> *O Kali's feet are red lotuses*
> *wherein lie heaps of holy places.[25]*
> *All sins are destroyed by Kali's name*
> *as heaps of cotton are burnt by fire.*
> *How can a headless[26] man have a headache[27]?*
> *People think, they will discharge their debts*
> *to forefathers by offering them pinda[28]at Gaya!*
> *But, O! I laugh at him who meditates on Kali*
> *and still goes to Gaya!*
> *Shiva assures: Death at Kasi leads to salvation.*
> *But devotion is the root of all;*
> *O mind! Salvation is its maid.[29]*
> *Of what use is nirvana?*
> *Water mingles in water.*

---

[23] Another name for Varanasi.
[24] Anahata chakra.
[25] Constant meditation on God makes pilgrimage to holy places unnecessary.
[26] Sinless.
[27] Sin.
[28] Cakes made of rice or flour to be offered to ancestral spirits.
[29] According to Ramprasad, devotion, desirelessness and undivided supreme love for God are superior to salvation.

O mind! becoming sugar[30] is not desirable;
I am fond of eating sugar.[31]

Bemused Ramprasad says, "By the strength of gracious
Mother, O! Meditation on Her, the wearer of dishevelled
hair, puts four goods[32] into the palm of our hands."[33]

There is no end to the intimate, blissful experience of a lover of God. Just when the lover thinks he or she has reached a certain point, a plateau, as it were, another door opens and the lover goes deeper and deeper—toward more and more joy. As Ramprasad's passionate love for the Divine Mother Kali increased further and further, the language of his songs became more mystical.

This time I shall devour Thee utterly, Mother Kali!
For I was born under an evil star,
And one so born becomes, they say, the eater of his mother.
Thou must devour me first, or I myself shall eat Thee up;
One or the other it must be.

I shall besmear my hands with black[34]
and with black my face;
With black I shall besmear the whole of my body.
And when Death seizes me,
with black I shall besmear his face.

O Mother, I shall eat Thee up
but not digest Thee;
I shall install Thee in my heart
And make Thee offerings with my mind.

---

[30] Becoming identified with God.
[31] Enjoying the supreme delight of devotion to God.
[32] Wealth, happiness, virtue, and salvation.
[33] *Ramaprasada's Devotional Songs*, pp. 12-13.
[34] Black is the color of Kali's complexion.

You may say that by eating Kali
I shall embroil myself
With Kala,[35] Her Husband,
but I am not afraid;
Braving His anger,
I shall chant my Mother's name.
Come what may, I shall eat Thee up—
Thee and Thy retinue—
Or lose my life attempting it.[36]

Ramprasad and his wife Sarvani had four children—two daughters named Paramesvari and Jagadisvari and two sons named Ramdulal and Rammohan. Ramprasad's mother was in charge of the daily household, and when she suddenly died, the family was left in great despair. Ramprasad's land did not yield adequate crops for want of supervision and portions of it were eroded and engulfed by the Ganges. The rent remained uncollected from the tenants, and the family's affairs were in a state of neglect. Yet, Ramprasad could not tear his mind away from the Divine Mother.

During this period, Ramprasad began to practice the severest kind of Tantric sadhana and went where most people are afraid to go. Ramprasad started to spend nights in a cremation ground and even sat on a corpse while meditating on the Divine Mother. His sincere devotion was rewarded and Ramprasad had the vision of the Adyashakti Mahamaya. She blessed him and his family. And after that, Ramprasad and his family always had all they needed though they never enjoyed affluence.

O Mother Kali with a necklace of human heads!
What magic hast Thou shown me!
O Mother! Thou didst teach me how to call Thee 'mother,'

---

[35] Shiva, the Absolute; Kala also stands for Time.
[36] *The Gospel of Sri Ramakrishna*, pp. 564-565.

and make me mad by calling Thee 'mother' constantly.
Tell me, O Mother Tara,
where Thou didst get such a name full of nectar[37]
Worldly people call me mad Prasad
whenever they meet me.
Even the members of my family call me names.
But do I deviate from my path,
O Mother Kali, being misled by their abuses?
Let them say whatever they like;
I will always mutter 'Kali,' 'Kali.'
Honor and dishonor are all alike to me;
I have cast aside maya,
And made Thy rosy feet the be-all-and-end-all of my life;
shall I be misguided by worldly people anymore?[38]

Very little is known about Ramprasad's wife. Like a typical Hindu wife, Sarvani always remained in the background, but her share in Ramprasad's sainthood cannot be discounted. She served her God-intoxicated husband untiringly and took over the household after his mother passed away. By relieving Ramprasad of the burden of worldly responsibilities, she enabled him to remain absorbed in the thought of God and attain these remarkable spiritual heights.

The Maharaja Krishna Chandra, who had been Ramprasad's benefactor for many years, suddenly became gravely ill. Ramprasad rushed to his bedside and stayed with him. Listening to the songs of Ramprasad, the inspired son of Kali, the Maharaja passed away with the Mother's name on his lips.

The death of Krishna Chandra greatly affected Ramprasad. He detached himself even further from the world and immersed himself in the consciousness of the Divine Mother. Ramprasad's mind was so absorbed that it was

---

[37] Kali's name is very sweet.
[38] *Ramaprasada's Devotional Songs*, p. 88.

difficult for him even to perform the formal worship of Ma
Kali. He constantly experienced the Mother, formless and
with form, within and without. Who shall worship whom
when one sees nothing but "Oneness."

> *Once for all, this time,*
> *I have thoroughly understood;*
> *From One[39] who knows it well,*
> *I have learnt the secret of bhava.*
> *A man has come to me from a country*
> *where there is no night,*
> *And now I cannot distinguish*
> *day from night any longer;*
> *Rituals and devotions have all grown profitless for me.*
>
> *My sleep is broken;*
> *how can I slumber any more?*
> *For now I am wide awake*
> *in the sleeplessness of yoga.*
> *O Divine Mother,*
> *made one with Thee in yoga-sleep[40] at last,*
> *My slumber I have lulled asleep for evermore.*
>
> *I bow my head, says Prasad,*
> *before desire and liberation;*
> *Knowing the secret that Kali*
> *is one with the highest Brahman,*
> *I have discarded, once for all,*
> *both righteousness and sin.[41]*

---

[39] God, whom the poet worshipped as the Divine Mother.
[40] Samadhi, which makes one appear asleep.
[41] *The Gospel of Sri Ramakrishna*, pp. 474-475.

Though he realized Brahman and merged with the eternal Oneness, Ramprasad never fully gave up ritual and formal worship. Ramprasad preferred "tasting sugar" to "becoming sugar" and liked to keep a sense of separateness in order to worship the Divine Mother and offer his exuberant love at her lotus feet.

All creation is the sport of my mad Mother Kali;
By Her maya the three worlds are bewitched.
Mad is She and mad is Her Husband;
mad are Her two disciples!
None can describe Her loveliness,
Her glories, gestures, moods;
Shiva, with the agony of the poison in His throat,
Chants Her name again and again.
The Personal does She oppose to the Impersonal,
Breaking one stone with another;
Though to all else She is agreeable,
Where duties are concerned She will not yield.
Keep your raft, says Ramprasad,
afloat on the sea of life,
Drifting up with the flood-tide,
drifting down with the ebb.[42]

Time passed on and Ramprasad became old. Sarvani died and their son Ramdulal and daughter-in-law Bhagavati looked after Ramprasad. Although his limbs had become feeble, Ramprasad's mind was ever active and continued to worship the Divine Mother with vigor and intensity.

Throughout his life, Ramprasad had always been fond of Kali Puja on the night of Diwali, the festival of lights. He

[42] *The Gospel of Sri Ramakrishna*, p. 619.

liked to stay up all night and worship Kali. In fact, his exuberant worship had become so famous among the people of
the locality that they turned it into a tradition to watch
Ramprasad perform Kali worship. His infectious spirit, his
ecstatic singing inspired them and enticed them to lose their
inhibitions and give themselves to the madness of divine
love.

One particular Kali Puja night, people noticed a difference in the old saint. He did not greet them jovially as usual,
nor did he invite them to watch the worship. Instead, he sat
on the worshipper's seat, aloof from the world and absorbed
within his inner self. He sang one song after another throughout the night—sometimes glorifying Kali, sometimes crying
piteously, and sometimes shouting with joy.

In the morning Ramprasad carried the jar of Mother's
sanctified water on his head to the Ganges. He was still
singing. The devotees followed, carrying the clay image of
Kali that was to be immersed in the Ganges after the nightly
worship. Ramprasad slowly waded into the holy river until
the water came up to his neck, all the while singing his soul-
enthralling songs.

> O Death! Get away; what canst thou do?
> I have imprisoned Mother Kali.
> I have bound Her feet with my mind
> and imprisoned Her in my heart
> I have unfolded my heart lotus
> and fixed my mind at the sahasrara.[43]
> I have entrusted my heart to Kulakundalini.
> Such contraption have I made that She can't escape!
> Devotion guards Her always as a watchman;

---

[43] The highest chakra, a thousand-petaled lotus at the top of the head.

my two eyes have I made gatekeepers.
I predicted: fateful fever[44] would attack me;
So I have taken my Master's drug[45]
—remedy for all diseases.
"Death! I have humbled thy pride,"
says Ramprasad,
"I am ready to start on my journey, uttering "Kali, Kali!"[46]

As Kali's image was immersed in the warm water of the Ganges, Ramprasad breathed his last. He was about 80 years old. Though his mortal frame was burnt to ashes on the funeral pyre, he continues to live on. Ramprasad's spirit comes to life whenever and wherever a lover of the Divine Mother Kali sings his songs.

Kamalakanta

Can everyone have the vision of Shyama?
Is Kali's treasure for everyone?
Oh, what a pity my foolish mind
will not see what is true!
Even with all His penances,
rarely does Shiva Himself behold
The mind-bewitching sight
of Mother Shyama's crimson feet.

To him who meditates on Her,
the riches of heaven are poor indeed;

---

[44] Causing death.

[45] A mantra given by the spiritual guide.

[46] *Ramaprasada's Devotional Songs*, p. 19.

If Shyama casts Her glance on him,
he swims in Eternal Bliss.
The prince of yogis, the king of the Gods,
meditate on Her feet in vain;
Yet worthless Kamalakanta
yearns for the Mother's blessed feet![47]

After Ramprasad, Kamalakanta is perhaps the next best-known writer of songs that glorify the Divine Mother Kali. Kamalakanta was born roughly fifty years after Ramprasad's birth, but it is unrecorded and doubtful that these two great Shakti worshippers ever met.

Historians estimate that Kamalakanta was born in 1773 in the village of Ambika Kalna in the district of Burdwan. Kamalakanta's father, Maheshwar Bhattacharya, was a poor Brahmin priest who died when Kamalakanta was still a young boy. His mother, Mayadevi, was a strong woman who had great dreams for her son. Although the income derived from the family land was so little that she ran the household with great difficulty, she still managed to save and send Kamalakanta to the village school. When she discovered she had too little money for Kamalakanta's higher education, she tried to save money by moving back to her father's home.

Kamalakanta studied Sanskrit under a learned pundit. He was an excellent student and especially talented in writing poetry. He also had a special talent for music and composed many songs during this period. Kamalakanta's heart opened to the love of God when he was instated with the sacred thread and began to take spiritual instructions from Chandra Shekhar Goswami.

When Kamalakanta's ambitious mother noticed in her son a certain indifference toward the world, she quickly

---

[47] *The Gospel of Sri Ramakrishna*, p. 474.

looked for a beautiful bride. But, her happiness about the extended family did not last long. Soon after marriage, the young woman died and Mayadevi had to look for another suitable girl. Kamalakanta married again and started a Sanskrit tol (school) to maintain his family.

Kamalakanta wanted to practice Tantric sadhana and took initiation from Kenaram Bhattacharya, a famous Tantric yogi. As his taste for spiritual experience increased, a tempest arose in Kamalakanta's heart. Many times he was found in Vishalakshi's[48] temple, worshipping the Mother with love and sincerity.

> *O Kali, my Mother full of Bliss!*
> *Enchantress of the almighty Shiva!*
> *In Thy delirious joy Thou dancest,*
> *clapping Thy hands together!*
> *Eternal One! Thou great First Cause,*
> *clothed in the form of the Void!*
> *Thou wearest the moon upon Thy brow.*
> *Where didst Thou find Thy garland of heads*
> *before the universe was made?*
> *Thou art the Mover of all that move,*
> *and we are but Thy helpless toys;*
> *We move alone as Thou movest us*
> *and speak as through us Thou speakest.*
> *But worthless Kamalakanta says,*
> *fondly berating Thee:*
> *Confoundress! With Thy flashing sword*
> *Thoughtlessly Thou hast put to death*
> *my virtue and my sin alike!*[49]

---

[48] A name of the Divine Mother.

[49] *The Gospel of Sri Ramakrishna*, p. 223.

Kamalakanta earned exceedingly little money. Neither his services as a priest nor as a Sanskrit teacher brought him enough earnings to maintain his family. When things were especially bad one day, and he didn't have enough money to buy articles for the worship of Kali or food for his family, Kamalakanta went to the Mother's temple and prayed with an earnest heart. "Mother, I have given up my life for you; and you can't even give me a little food so that I can worship you and maintain my family?" Upon return to his home, he heard from his wife that a beautiful girl she had never seen before had brought food for the family and all the accessories necessary for the worship of Kali.

Kamalakanta's songs came out of the fullness of his heart. They sprung up spontaneously from the joy he got glorifying the Divine Mother.

> *The black bee of my mind is drawn in sheer delight*
> *To the blue lotus flower of Mother Shyama's feet,*
> *The blue flower of the feet of Kali, Shiva's Consort;*
> *Tasteless, to the bee, are the blossoms of desire.*
> *My Mother's feet are black, and black, too, is the bee;*
> *Black is made one with black! This much of the mystery*
> *My mortal eyes behold, then hastily retreat.*
> *But Kamalakanta's hopes are answered in the end;*
> *He swims in the Sea of Bliss, unmoved by joy or pain.*[50]

Just as she had done for her son Ramprasad, the Divine Mother Kali also took care of her son Kamalakanta's worldly needs. She sent him a rich man to take care of him. Tej Chandra, the king of Burdwan, asked Kamalakanta to initiate him and become his guru. Highly pleased with Kamalakanta's instructions, Tej Chandra built a house for

---

[50] *The Gospel of Sri Ramakrishna*, p. 193.

him in Kotalpat, a village close to Burdwan. He also appointed Kamalakanta as one of his court pundits.

Now that his worldly anxieties were gone, Kamalakanta could devote more time to the worship of Mother Kali. He built a shrine room in his house and spent hours singing songs in glorification of Kali. Kamalakanta's singing had a special effect on all who listened. Villagers still say that Kamalakanta's Kali songs provoked such a rare fascination that wild animals became tame, children stopped crying, and venomous snakes lifted their hoods and danced.

One day, as Kamalakanta returned late from a neighboring village, he found himself surrounded by dacoits (robbers). It was a deserted area, and there was no one to help him. After the dacoits stripped him and took everything he had, they threatened to kill him. "Please, allow me to prepare for death," said Kamalakanta and began to sing a song to Ma Kali, his only refuge. The dacoits listened and were so moved that they begged Kamalakanta's pardon, returning all they had stolen.

Years passed, and when Kamalakanta lay on his deathbed, expressing his last wish, he asked the Maharaja Tej Chandra to take him to the Ganges. As the dying saint was laid on the embankment, a sudden flood came and swept Kamalakanta into the river. The Mother Ganges, herself, carried his holy body to the abode of Kali.

Raja Ramkrishna

Raja Ramkrishna, not to be confused with Sri Ramakrishna who lived at the Dakshineswar Kali Temple, was born sometime during the mid-18th century. He was the youngest son of Harihar Roy of Atgram in the district of Rajshahi. Rather than allowing him to live a quiet life with his family, fate singled him out and elevated him to the throne of Natore.

As it so happened, the queen of the Natore royal family was without children and, in order to properly administer her estate and continue the family line, she decided to adopt a son. Rani Bhavani held a festival at the Natore palace and, among the assembled Brahmin boys, each desirous of becoming her son, she chose one boy who exhibited particular auspicious signs. The boy was Ramkrishna.

The Maharani personally trained Ramkrishna in the administration of her estate. She was a pious woman and thought the sooner her adopted son could take care of things, the sooner she would be free to go to Varanasi and live a holy life. In order to get Ramkrishna settled, she arranged his marriage when he was still very young.

Although young Ramkrishna had everything—a royal throne, wealth, a beautiful wife—his heart was not satisfied. He longed for the vision of the Divine Mother Kali and spent long hours in meditation on her. He created a panchamundi asana (seat made of five skulls) and practiced sava sadhana[51] according to Tantric rites. Ramkrishna also dedicated a zamindari exclusively for the worship of the Mother at the Bhavanipur pith.

People observing the young prince's devotional activities called him a saint, a great Mother worshipper. But, from a spiritual standpoint, it wasn't enough. When God's call comes, the person chosen cannot give up things partially. His or her whole being is consumed with a flame that sees nothing but God. When one dark night of the new moon Ramkrishna was meditating on Ma Kali, a sannyasin (monk) appeared and accused him of being bound by worldly ties. And then he vanished.

---

[51] Spiritual disciplines in a cremation ground—generally performed at night while seated on a corpse.

After that, Ramkrishna's mind was so preoccupied with thoughts of Kali that he could not devote himself to worldly matters. The estate the Rani had entrusted to him suffered greatly. A corrupt local government official snatched away a good portion of it through unfair means, and the treachery of a so-called friend whom Ramkrishna had tried to help cost him another chunk of his estate. In spite of these heavy losses, Ramkrishna remained generous toward the poor and never denied anyone who sought his help. When he saved one poor Brahmin's life by giving him money, the mysterious sadhu who had previously warned him about worldly attachments appeared and looked as if he were approving of Ramkrishna's actions. And, again, he vanished.

Raja Ramkrishna's kindness and preoccupation with spiritual things had disastrous effects and, in order to save the zamindari from bankruptcy, the aged Rani returned from Varanasi. She tried to persuade Raja Ramkrishna to pay more attention to his worldly affairs—to no avail. Instead, Ramkrishna spent even longer hours in meditation on his panchamundi asana at the Bhavanipur pith.

One day, Raja Ramkrishna had a vision of the Divine Mother. It happened during a festival which had attracted not only thousands of devotees but also a gang of dacoits (robbers). When the robbers tried to attack the pious assembly, the Universal Mother appeared to Raja Ramkrishna in her terrible aspect, and he drove the robbers away. Repentant, the robbers later came back and begged pardon of the royal sadhu.

The mysterious sadhu that had so influenced Raja Ramkrishna's life appeared to him again as he was riding on his elephant one day. The moment Raja Ramkrishna saw the sadhu, he alighted and confronted him. "Who are you?" he asked. The strange sadhu revealed to Ramkrishna that he was Sriji, a descendant of the royal family of Bundi. He had left his palace long ago, and after practicing austerities for a number of years, he had become a mahayogi (great yogi) by the grace of God.

Suddenly, Sriji held out his hand and put it on Raja Ramkrishna's back. The moment Sriji's hand touched his body, Raja Ramkrishna felt something like an electric shock passing through his entire being. In an instant, he remembered his previous life. He remembered that Sriji was his brother disciple, studying under the same great guru. They both practiced tapasya (austerities) in a cave in Hardwar at the foothills of the Himalayas where the holy river Ganges meets the lowland. He remembered taking birth in this life for the sole purpose of fulfilling his quest for perfection. As soon as Raja Ramkrishna had regained the knowledge of who he really was, Sriji, the mysterious sadhu, vanished again.

Raja Ramkrishna could no longer stay in the palace. He took leave of his wife and entrusted his minor children to her care. Ramkrishna wanted to withdraw from all worldly activities and devote himself fully to the realization of the Great Mother. But before he could do so, he had to obtain the pardon and blessings of his foster mother, the Rani Bhavani, whose hopes he had greatly disappointed. Though he was physically seated on his panchamundi asana, through his yogic powers, he appeared before the Maharani.

And with her blessing Ramkrishna renounced the world and spent the rest of his life in constant communion with the Divine Mother. The great royal yogi died in 1795.

Sri Ramakrishna

It is difficult to refute someone who doubts that Christ, Buddha, Krishna or Mohammed ever lived since the only evidence that they ever existed is artists' renditions of their likeness and scriptures written long ago. We have plenty of evidence that Sri Ramakrishna was not just a myth. There are photographs taken of him and first-hand accounts of his life from people who lived with him and knew him intimately. See figure 32 on page 242.

Sri Ramakrishna lived a simple life that was centered in God. Yet, someone trying to explain to another who Sri Ramakrishna really was will find it difficult to define him. One could say that Sri Ramakrishna was a great saint of Kali who lived at the Dakshineswar Kali Temple. But, that's not all he was. So many people from different religions see Sri Ramakrishna as their very own chosen deity. Sri Ramakrishna's mystic aura is all-inclusive.

Who can fathom Sri Ramakrishna's depth? Even the great Swami Vivekananda[52] recoiled when someone asked him to write the life of Sri Ramakrishna. "Ask me to dry up the ocean, I shall do that," said Swamiji. "Ask me to crush mountains into grains of sand, I shall do that. But, please, do not ask me to write the life of Sri Ramakrishna."

Some people see Sri Ramakrishna as an embodiment of Kali while others call him an Incarnation of God. People who were fortunate enough to come in contact with Sri Ramakrishna during his lifetime saw him as their very own beloved God, be it Kali, Shiva, Krishna, Buddha, or Christ. How can one find the real Sri Ramakrishna? Swami Bhajanananda, a monk of the Ramakrishna Order, wrote:

For a devotee of Sri Ramakrishna the most important problem of his life is the quest for the real Sri Ramakrishna. A true devotee of his does not remain

---

[52] Monastic disciple and chief apostle of Sri Ramakrishna.

Figure 32. Sri Ramakrishna, Kali's God-intoxicated saint of Dakshineswar.

satisfied with reading or hearing about his life and teachings. Making use of the knowledge thus gained, he tries to seek the Reality of which this knowledge is only a shadow. He soon finds that this mystic quest is leading him on to the depth of his soul which is the gateway to the world of the Spirit. It is there that the real Ramakrishna is to be sought.[53]

Sri Ramakrishna was born on February 18, 1836, in Kamarpukur, a small village in West Bengal. An atmosphere of peace pervades this agricultural village surrounded by extensive rice fields. Before harvest, when the tender green blades in the fields sway softly in the gentle breeze, Kamarpukur looks like an island floating in a vast green sea. Cows graze along narrow ridges between the rice fields and long, skinny palm trees, add dark-green silhouettes along the pale blue horizon.

Besides cultivating fields, the Kamarpukur villagers engage themselves in various small industries. There is the sweet maker—Kamarpukur is still famous for its excellent quality of jilipis[54]—and then there is the manufacturer of ebony hookah pipes which sell very well in Calcutta. There are cloth merchants and people who produce anything from yarn to saris, dhotis and towels and other handicrafts. Every Tuesday and Saturday, a market is held in Kamarpukur, and people from the surrounding villages bring their wares for sale. Along with the produce for one's daily use, one can buy cooking pots, yarn, baskets, coarse mats, and cotton saris.

Although most villagers are fairly poor, they know how to celebrate and, with great zeal, they observe numerous religious festivals throughout the year. These are grand parties

---

[53] *A Bridge to Eternity* (Calcutta: Advaita Ashrama, 1986) p. 104.
[54] A sweet that looks like a golden spiral. It is made of gram flour, first fried, then soaked in syrup.

in the name of God, and the Brahmin, the weaver, the milk-
man, blacksmith, potter, fisherman and the dom[55], all—high
and low castes—celebrate together in harmony.

Sri Ramakrishna's father, Khudiram Chattopadhyaya,
was a pious man of the Brahmin caste. He was greatly
devoted to God and daily performed ritual and meditation.
One day when he was sleeping under a tree, Khudiram had
a dream of Bhagavan Sri Rama. God, appearing as a divine
boy, asked Khudiram to take him to his house and take care
of him. "O Lord, I am very poor," said Khudiram alarmed. "I
cannot give you the proper service." But the Lord was
adamant. Khudiram awoke and saw a Shalagrama[56] stone
nearby. A snake with extended hood was guarding it. When
the snake slid away, Khudiram picked up the Shalagrama
stone, took it home and worshipped it. This same stone is
still in Kamarpukur and is worshipped daily by members
of Sri Ramakrishna's family.

Sri Ramakrishna's mother, Chandradevi, was a loving
and guileless woman. The poor in the vicinity not only
received food from Chandradevi but also respect, a genuine
welcome and affection. Her door was always open to holy
men, living on alms. They liked to come to Khudiram's house
and looked upon Chandradevi as their own mother.

One day, when Khudiram was in Gaya[57] on pilgrimage,
Chandradevi had a vision while standing with her friend
Dhani outside a Shiva temple near her home. As soon as her
husband returned, she guilelessly told him about her vision:

All of a sudden, I saw that the holy image of Lord
Shiva inside the shrine was alive! It began to send

---

[55] The traditional profession of doms is the cremation of dead bodies.
[56] A round black stone which bears certain marks, identifying it as a symbol of Vishnu.
[57] Famous Hindu place of pilgrimage—the abode of Vishnu where his
holy feet are worshipped. A pilgrimage to Gaya marked the turning point
in Sri Chaitanya's life.

forth waves of the most beautiful light. Slowly at first, then quicker and quicker. They filled up the inside of the temple, and then they came pouring out—it was like one of those huge flood-waves in the river—right towards me! I was going to tell Dhani—but then the waves washed over me and swallowed me up, and I felt that marvelous light enter into my body. I fell down on the ground, unconscious. When I came to myself, I told Dhani what had happened. But she didn't believe me; she said I'd had an epileptic fit. That can't be so, because, since then, I've been full of joy and my health is better than ever. Only—I feel that light is still inside me; and I believe that I'm with child."[58]

Khudiram listened to his wife's story, and remembered a dream he had in Gaya. He said, "During my stay in Gaya, Gadadhar[59] revealed to me that a son would be born to us."

Chandradevi had many visions of Gods and Goddesses during her time of pregnancy. One spring morning, a few minutes before dawn, Chandradevi gave birth to a beautiful baby boy while the sacred sound of the conch filled the humble thatched-roof cottage. In remembrance of Khudiram's dream in Gaya, they called him Gadadhar. It's not certain when people began to refer to Gadadhar as Sri Ramakrishna. Thus, for the sake of clarity, we'll call him Sri Ramakrishna throughout this biography.

Sri Ramakrishna was a curious, intelligent child. Sitting on his father's lap, he could easily learn whole passages of the Ramayana and repeat them from memory. Since Khudiram was convinced of his extraordinary intelligence, he sent Sri Ramakrishna to the local village school when he was

[58] Christopher Isherwood, *Ramakrishna and His Disciples* (Hollywood, CA: Vedanta Press, 1965), p. 21.
[59] Another name for Vishnu.

only 5 years old. Sri Ramakrishna did well in all subjects except one. He hated arithmetic. Nothing could persuade him to learn arithmetic, and whenever forced, he would run off and play.

Whenever Sri Ramakrishna's mind, which was naturally one-pointed, became fascinated with a particular object, he would become forgetful of himself and completely identify with the object of interest.

> The enchanting view of the vast green fields fanned by the gentle breeze, the incessant flow of the river, the melodious songs of birds, and above all, the magic of ever-changing clouds in the deep blue sky would, at times, unfold their mystery and glory to the boy's inner vision and hold him spell-bound. He would then lose himself completely and enter the unknown, distant, and solitary domain of the spirit.

> One day, while roaming carefree in the fields, Sri Ramakrishna looked up at the sky and saw a newly formed dark cloud, and against it, the rhythmic movement of a flock of cranes in full flight, with their snowwhite wings outspread. The boy became so completely absorbed in the beauty of it all that awareness of his own body and of all other earthly things vanished altogether, and he fell down unconscious.[60]

Although young Sri Ramakrishna was a naughty boy, he was charmingly so and, therefore, loved by all villagers. He lived his life in undisturbed merriment until a calamity befell the peaceful household. Khudiram suddenly died, leaving the not yet 8-year-old Sri Ramakrishna to deal with

---

[60] *Sri Ramakrishna, the Great Master*, p. 48.

growing up without a father. Outwardly, Sri Ramakrishna did not exhibit grief, but inwardly, his carefree nature changed. He began to wander off by himself and spent hours in solitary places such as the Bhutir Khal, Kamarpukur's cremation ground. He also spent much time in the company of wandering holy men in a hut next the road that leads to Puri.[61]

From early childhood on, Sri Ramakrishna was very truthful. He had promised his nurse, Dhani, that she would be his "Godmother" during his sacred-thread ceremony. When Sri Ramakrishna was 9 years old, Ramkumar, his elder brother and head of the family after Khudiram's death, arranged to hold this rite. There was one problem. Sri Ramakrishna belonged to the highest Brahmin caste and the woman he had chosen to be his Godmother belonged to the low blacksmith caste. "This has never been done before in a Brahmin family," said Ramkumar, trying to persuade Sri Ramakrishna to change his mind. "If I break my promise, I will be an untruthful person, unfit to wear the sacred thread," said Sri Ramakrishna. Ramkumar had to yield. Much later when little Ramakrishna had grown into Sri Ramakrishna, the spiritual phenomenon, he said to his disciples, "Truthfulness is the tapasya[62] of the Kali yuga."[63]

Throughout his entire life, Sri Ramakrishna stuck to the truth in the most minute detail. When he offered his everything to the Divine Mother Kali, there was one thing he could not give up, and that was truth. "O Mother, take Thy good and Thy bad, Thy virtue and Thy vice, and grant me only pure love for Thee." But Sri Ramakrishna could not offer up truth and untruth.

---

[61] Famous place of pilgrimage. The presiding deity in the Puri Temple is Jagannath, another name for Krishna.

[62] Austerities.

[63] The Kali yuga is the last age of the Hindu time cycle—a time of conflict, loss of virtue, and endurance.

Sri Ramakrishna loved the theater. In Indian villages, dramatic performances are called yatra and held outdoors. One day one of the actors fell ill, and the people in charge of the performance asked Sri Ramakrishna to act in the role of the great God Shiva. It was not a large speaking part, and the theater manager was sure that the boy could manage quite well. He was wrong. As soon as Sri Ramakrishna appeared on stage as Shiva—besmeared with ashes, rudraksha beads, and matted hair—he was so overwhelmed with spiritual emotion that he lost external consciousness and stood like a log. When Sri Ramakrishna could not be brought back to his senses for a long time, the performance had to be canceled.

Khudiram's demise caused poverty to knock on the door of the small family. In order to earn some money, Ramkumar took a job as a Sanskrit teacher in Calcutta, and the next brother in line, Rameswar, took over the responsibility of looking after the Kamarpukur household. Rameswar was not a fatherly authority figure like Ramkumar and did not keep a sharp eye on his 13-year-old brother's education. Without a guardian who would prod him on, Sri Ramakrishna was free to do whatever he wanted.

Although Sri Ramakrishna enjoyed studying the scriptures, he did not like the fact that school education was almost exclusively geared toward teaching children how to earn a living. Sri Ramakrishna began to stay home and devote his time to the worship of the family deity Raghuvir. When he sang devotional songs before the image, people from all around would stop their work and listen. All villagers, and especially the women, loved Sri Ramakrishna. They would neglect their household duties in order to be near him. No one had a sweet voice like Sri Ramakrishna or could dance and make merry like him. Wherever Sri Ramakrishna went, there was festivity.

His little friends, who continued to attend the village school, missed their favorite companion. In order to be with

Sri Ramakrishna, they asked him to form a theater group, knowing very well that his love for drama would not let him say no. The boys met with Sri Ramakrishna in the secluded mango grove of Manikraja where, undisturbed and hidden by the majestic trees, they could rehearse scenes from various religious plays. Sri Ramakrishna's keen imagination directed their efforts and inspired them while they acted out the roles of Sri Ramachandra or Sri Krishna. Often, while frolicking in the woods, the boys noticed how Sri Ramakrishna entered into a strange kind of ecstatic mood. But, being young boys, they paid no attention to his moods.

Sri Ramakrishna was very creative and had an exceptional sense for beauty. When he and his friends skipped down a narrow lane one day, they noticed that the village potter was in the process of making a clay image of Mother Durga. Sri Ramakrishna suddenly stopped and said to the potter, "What kind of image is this? The eyes of a Goddess do not look like that!" Saying so, he showed the amazed potter how to draw the eyes of God. The image immediately began to look divine and alive.

One day, very unexpectedly, Sri Ramakrishna's eldest brother came home to Kamarpukur to check on the welfare of his family. Ramkumar noticed Sri Ramakrishna's indifference toward study and his absence from school. His younger brother's attitude toward education worried him, and after consulting with their mother, Ramkumar decided to take Sri Ramakrishna to Calcutta with him. There, he thought, he could keep a better eye on Sri Ramakrishna's education and, at the same time, use him in his Sanskrit school as an assistant.

Although Sri Ramakrishna was only a teenage village boy when he arrived in Calcutta, the big city did not intimidate him. On the contrary, he carried on with his boyish light-heartedness and made merry with people he met in Calcutta. And much to the dismay of Ramkumar, his study, of course, suffered. Whenever Ramkumar would take him to task, Sri Ramakrishna said, "Brother, what shall I do with a mere bread-winning education? I want to acquire that wisdom which will illumine my heart and give me satisfaction forever."

No matter how brightly Ramkumar described the happy and easy life of a scholar in Calcutta, Sri Ramakrishna found no attraction in worldly security and insisted that all he wanted was the knowledge of God. Sri Ramakrishna liked to worship. He was Ramkumar's competent assistant and performed numerous religious ceremonies at people's houses, which fetched a few additional rupees. Although Sri Ramakrishna was extremely popular, his non-materialistic attitude stopped him from building a career as a religious scholar.

Ramkumar's Sanskrit school in Jhamapukur flourished, and his opinion on religious matters was highly respected among people in Calcutta. When the wealthy Rani Rasmani was in a dilemma because she, being of low caste, could not get the high-caste Brahmins to worship and eat at the Kali Temple she had built in Dakshineswar, Ramkumar solved her problem. He advised her to make a gift of the temple property to a Brahmin and let him install the Goddess and then worship and make an offering of cooked food. Through a series of circumstances, the Rani was able to persuade Ramkumar to install the image of Kali in the Dakshineswar Temple.

Sri Ramakrishna accompanied Ramkumar to Dakshineswar on that day and observed the lavish festivities. But, conscious of caste restrictions, he refused to stay at the temple overnight and returned to Jhamapukur. When Ramkumar did not return to the school for over a week, Sri Ramakrishna came to Dakshineswar in search of his elder brother. To his surprise, he discovered that Ramkumar had agreed to leave the Sanskrit school and assume fulltime charge of the Divine Mother Kali's worship in the temple. Mindful of his orthodox father's example, Sri Ramakrishna did not approve of his elder brother working for a low-caste woman. What was Sri Ramakrishna to do?

Facing an uncertain future, Sri Ramakrishna went to the Ganges to think quietly about things. He watched the majestic river flow peacefully past the Kali Temple and decided to live next to the Ganges for a while. He cooked his own food and spent much time in prayer. The beautiful, wide river, the holy atmosphere of the temple garden, the solitude of the Panchavati, the sweet songs of the birds, the loving care of his elder brother, the faith and devotion of Rani Rasmani and her son-in-law Mathur Babu—all made a deep impression on Sri Ramakrishna.

He liked the holy atmosphere of the Kali Temple, yet he could not bring himself to become "bound" by entering the temple service. But when his nephew Hriday arrived in Dakshineswar and agreed to be responsible for Kali's costly ornaments, Sri Ramakrishna reconsidered and became a priest of Kali. His brother Ramkumar switched to the Radha-Govinda Temple and became a priest of Vishnu.

Sri Ramakrishna was approximately 20 years old when he became a Kali priest and Hriday, who was about three years younger, became his assistant. Hriday was extremely devoted to Sri Ramakrishna and followed him like a shadow. He served him, fed him, and looked after him as a mother would.

One year after the Kali temple consecration, Ramkumar suddenly died. The loss of his beloved brother kindled a fire of renunciation in Sri Ramakrishna. He developed a strong inner conviction of the transitory nature of the world. Whenever he finished the daily worship, he began to spend a lot of time sitting before the Divine Mother Kali inside the temple. He wooed her, he praised her, he sang song after song. With his sweet voice, he sang songs by Ramprasad and songs by Kamalakanta. He sang songs made up by his own heart and, deeply in love with Kali, he cried for her vision. And when the temple doors closed at midday or at night,

Sri Ramakrishna avoided human company and entered the jungle around the Panchavati to meditate on his Beloved, the Great Mother of the universe.

Hriday became worried about his uncle. One day, he followed him to the Panchavati and observed that Sri Ramakrishna had taken off his clothes and the sacred thread Brahmins wear. Hriday approached his stark naked uncle sitting in a pose of meditation under a tree. "What are you doing?" shouted Hriday. "Have you gone mad? If you want to meditate, do so by all means. But why must you take off the only cloth you are wearing?"

Sri Ramakrishna slowly opened his eyes and said, "One should practice meditation freed from all ties. When one calls on the Mother, one should discard the eight bondages— hatred, fear, shame, aversion, egoism, vanity, pride of noble descent and obsession with formal good conduct—so that one can cry to her with a concentrated mind."

In order to destroy vanity born of noble descent and acquire true humility, Sri Ramakrishna made himself clean the dirty toilets outside the temple. And to teach his mind to regard money and lumps of earth as one and the same, he took a few coins in one hand and some earth into the other. Throwing both into the Ganges, he said over and over again, "Rupee is clay; clay is rupee." In order to develop the knowledge that Shiva (God) is Jiva (man), Sri Ramakrishna picked up the leavings of the poor, ate, and put them on his head as prasad.

As Sri Ramakrishna's love for Ma Kali deepened, he became forgetful of the formalities during regular worship. He was caught in an agony of longing for the vision of the Divine Mother. "Thou hast shown Thyself to Ramprasad, O Mother," cried Sri Ramakrishna. "Why, then, dost Thou not reveal Thyself to me?" Watching a sunset at the bathing ghat next to the Ganges, Sri Ramakrishna would cry in agony, "Another day has gone and, still, Thou hast not revealed Thyself to me!"

He felt the pangs of a child separated from its mother. Sometimes, in agony, he would rub his face against the ground and weep so bitterly that people, thinking he had lost his earthly mother, would sympathize with him in his grief. Sometimes, in moments of skepticism, he would cry: "Art Thou true, Mother, or is it all fiction—mere poetry without any reality? If Thou dost exist, why do I not see Thee? Is religion a mere fantasy and art Thou only a figment of man's imagination?" Sometimes he would sit on the prayer carpet for two hours like an inert object. He began to behave in an abnormal manner, most of the time unconscious of the world. He almost gave up food; and sleep left him altogether.[64]

Sri Ramakrishna felt intolerable anguish. It seemed to him as if someone had caught hold of his heart and was forcibly twisting and squeezing it as one twists and squeezes the water out of a towel. "I was dying of despair," said Sri Ramakrishna. "Living in such agony, I thought there was no use to continue with this life."

Sri Ramakrishna's eyes fell on the sword that hangs behind the altar of Kali. Determined to put an end to his life, he rushed toward it. And then a wonderful thing happened. Ma Kali revealed herself to Sri Ramakrishna.

It was as if houses, doors, temples, and all other things vanished altogether; as if there was nothing anywhere. And what I saw was a boundless, infinite conscious sea of light. However far and in whatever direction I looked, I found a continuous succession of effulgent waves coming forward,

---

[64] *The Gospel of Sri Ramakrishna*, p. 13.

raging and storming from all sides with great speed. Very soon, they fell on me and made me sink to the unknown bottom. I panted, struggled and fell unconscious."[65]

This was the first time that Sri Ramakrishna had a vision of Ma Kali, and when he regained consciousness, the only word that was on his lips was "Mother." The sight overwhelmed Sri Ramakrishna and gave him so much bliss that he was intoxicated and unable to perform any kind of work. He could not perform the daily worship, and Hriday somehow managed with the help of another Brahmin.

Yet this was only a foretaste of the intense experiences to come. The first glimpse of the Divine Mother made him the more eager for Her uninterrupted vision. He wanted to see Her both in meditation and with eyes open. But the Mother began to play a teasing game of hide and seek with him, intensifying both his joy and his suffering. Weeping bitterly during the moments of separation from Her, he would pass into a trance and then find Her standing before him, smiling, talking, consoling, bidding him be of good cheer, and instructing him. During this period of spiritual practice he had many uncommon experiences. When he sat to meditate, he would hear strange clicking sounds in the joints of his legs, as if someone were locking them up, one after the other, to keep him motionless; and at the conclusion of his meditation, he would again hear the same sounds, this time unlocking them and leaving him free to move about. He would see flashes like a swarm of fire flies floating before his eyes, or a sea of deep mist around him, with

---

[65] *Sri Ramakrishna, the Great Master*, p. 141.

luminous waves of molten silver. Again, from a sea of translucent mist he would behold the Mother rising, first Her feet, then Her waist, body, face, and head, finally Her whole person; he would feel Her breath and hear Her voice. Worshipping in the temple, sometimes he would become exalted, sometimes he would remain motionless as stone, sometimes he would almost collapse from excessive emotion. Many of his actions, contrary to all tradition, seemed sacrilegious to the people. He would take a flower and touch it to his own head, body, and feet, and then offer it to the Goddess. Or, like a drunkard, he would reel to the throne of the Mother, touch Her chin by way of showing his affection for Her, and sing, talk, joke, laugh, and dance. Or he would take a morsel of food from the plate and hold it to Her mouth, begging Her to eat it, and would not be satisfied till he was convinced that She had really eaten. After the Mother had been put to sleep at night, from his own room he would hear Her ascending to the upper story of the temple with the light steps of a happy girl, Her anklets jingling. Then he would discover Her standing with flowing hair, Her black form silhouetted against the sky of the night, looking at the Ganges or at the distant lights of Calcutta.

Naturally the temple officials took him for an insane person. His worldly well-wishers brought him to a skilled physician; but no medicine could cure his malady. Many a time he doubted his sanity himself. For he had been sailing across an uncharted sea, with no earthly guide to direct him. His only haven of security was the Divine Mother Herself. To Her he would pray: "I do not know what these things are. I am ignorant of mantras and the scriptures. Teach me, Mother, how to realize Thee. Who else can help me? Art Thou not my only refuge and guide?" And the sustaining presence of the Mother never failed him in his distress or doubt.[66]

Sri Ramakrishna surrendered himself totally to the will of Ma Kali and spent day and night in constant communion with her. At this time, a spiritual tempest was blowing at the Dakshineswar Kali Temple. All people felt it. Hriday was not quite sure what to think of his uncle. Sometimes he was convinced that Sri Ramakrishna had gone mad and, at other times, he was in awe of him.

"One now felt awe-struck when one entered the Kali temple even when the Master was not there, let alone when he was," said Hriday. "Yet I could not give up the temptation of seeing how the Master behaved during the time of worship. What I saw there when I entered suddenly filled my heart with awe and devotion. But doubt arose when I came out. I thought, 'Has uncle really gone mad? Otherwise why does he do such forbidden acts at the time of worship?' I felt apprehensive about what the Rani and Mathur Babu would think and say when they came to know of it. But such thoughts never crossed uncle's mind, nor did he give ear to what I told him.

"I saw uncle prepare an Arghya consisting of china roses and Vilva leaves, touch his head, his bosom, all his limbs, and even his own feet with it and at last offer it at the lotus feet of the Mother of the universe.

"I saw that he, while offering cooked food to the Divine Mother, got up suddenly, took in his hand a

---

[66] *The Gospel of Sri Ramakrishna*, pp. 14-15.

morsel of rice and curry from the plate, touched the Divine Mother's mouth with it and said, 'Mother, eat it; do eat it, Mother.' Then he said, 'Dost Thou ask me to take it? Wilt Thou take it afterward? Very well, I am taking it now.' Saying this, he took a part of it himself and put the rest to Her mouth again.

"I saw him on some occasions at night put the Mother to bed and himself lie on Her silver bed-stead for some time, saying, 'Dost Thou ask me to lie down? All right, I am doing so.'"[67]

Sri Ramakrishna's unconventional ways of worshipping Ma Kali could, of course, not be hidden for long. Temple garden officials, considering themselves responsible for the proper conduct of the worship, reported the young Kali priest's sacrilegious behavior to Mathur Babu. In order to see things with his own eyes, Mathur Babu took a horse carriage from the Rani's mansion in Janbazar to Dakshineswar. He silently entered the Kali Temple, observed Sri Ramakrishna's worship, and left without a word. The next day the chief temple officer received this order from Mathur Babu: "Do not obstruct the Bhattacharya[68] in his worship in whatever manner he might perform it." The liberal Rani also accepted Sri Ramakrishna's behavior as divinely inspired and was convinced that his fervent devotion had awakened the Goddess.

Sri Ramakrishna's ecstatic love for Ma Kali became more and more intimate. And when his exaltation over the Divine Mother's constant company overwhelmed him to a degree that he could no longer serve the Goddess, Hriday took over

---

[67] *Sri Ramakrishna, the Great Master*, pp. 144-145.
[68] A surname added to the name of some Brahmins; Bhatta = title of a learned Brahmin; acarya = guru, or teacher.

the responsibility of the Kali worship. News of Sri Rama-krishna's "madness" traveled all the way to Kamarpukur.

> A garbled report of Sri Ramakrishna's failing health, indifference to worldly life, and various abnormal activities reached Kamarpukur and filled the heart of his poor mother with anguish. At her repeated request he returned to his village for a change of air. But his boyhood friends did not interest him anymore. A divine fever was consuming him. He spent a great part of the day and night in one of the cremation grounds in meditation. The place reminded him of the impermanence of the human body, of human hopes and achievements. It also reminded him of Kali, the Goddess of destruction.[69]

Sri Ramakrishna was approximately 23 years old when he returned to Kamarpukur. His mother thought that marriage might cure her son's malady and looked for a suitable bride. She searched everywhere but could not find a bride for her son. All the while, Sri Ramakrishna acted with complete indifference toward his mother's efforts but, when he noticed her extreme concern, he said, "It is useless to search here and there. Go to the family of Ram Chandra Muk-hopadhyaya in the village of Jayrambati. The bride has been marked with a straw[70] and kept there reserved for me."

The bride Sri Ramakrishna had selected was a 5-year-old girl by the name of Sarada—child marriage was a custom during this time in India, and after marriage, the children would live at home with their parents until they were of age. When all details were settled among the parents, the marriage ceremony between Sri Ramakrishna and Sarada was

---

[69] *The Gospel of Sri Ramakrishna*, p. 17.
[70] Farmers marked their best fruit and vegetables with a straw, which indicated to others to stay away because this fruit was reserved for God.

duly performed. Afterward, little Sarada went back to her parents' house in Jayrambati, and Sri Ramakrishna remained in Kamarpukur for almost two years. After that he returned to Calcutta and the Dakshineswar Kali Temple.

> Scarcely had he performed the worship for a few days when he became so much absorbed in it that everything about Kamarpukur—mother, brother, wife, worldly affairs, want, etc.—got shut up in a dark secluded corner of his heart. The only idea that occupied the whole of his mind was how he could see the Divine Mother in all beings at all times.[71]

Sri Ramakrishna was not satisfied with the vision of the Divine Mother Kali. He wanted more. He wanted to see the Divine Mother in all beings, in all things and taste her bliss in a variety of ways by means of a variety of rites.

His first vision of Kali, Sri Ramakrishna had attained without following traditional ways or a particular guru. His intense longing for the Mother was enough to prompt him in the right direction. But now, he wanted someone to explain his own visions to him, someone who could teach him the ancient religious traditions. Following his call, one by one, various teachers came to the Dakshineswar Kali Temple to instruct Sri Ramakrishna according to established rites and traditions.

The first teacher to come was Bhairavi Brahmani. She was a learned Tantric and the first to assure Sri Ramakrishna that his visions were true.

> Sri Ramakrishna described to her his experiences and visions and told her of people's belief that these were symptoms of madness. She listened to him

---

[71] *Sri Ramakrishna, the Great Master*, p. 179.

attentively and said: "My son, everyone in this world is mad. Some are mad for money, some for creature comforts, some for name and fame; and you are mad for God." She assured him that he was passing through the almost unknown spiritual experience described in the scriptures as mahab-hava, the most exalted rapture of divine love. She told him that this extreme exaltation had been described as manifesting itself through nineteen physical symptoms, including the shedding of tears, a tremor of the body, horripilation, perspiration, and a burning sensation. The Bhakti scriptures, she declared, had recorded only two instances of the experience, namely those of Sri Radha and Sri Chaitanya.[72]

The Brahmani continued to stay at the temple garden, and being a Sadhika[73], temple officials gave her rice, flour, and vegetables from the temple stores. She cooked her own food in the Panchavati, and before eating, she always sat in meditation, offering the cooked food to the stone symbol of Raghuvir which she worshipped and carried with her hanging from her neck.

One day she entered into a deep ecstasy and had an extraordinary vision of Sri Raghuvir, who physically came to eat the offered food. Meanwhile, Sri Ramakrishna, also in an ecstatic mood, came out of his room, entered the Panchavati, and began to eat the food offered to Sri Raghuvir. As the Brahmani opened her eyes, she saw Sri Ramakrishna eating the food meant for the Deity. Feeling a bit uneasy about his action, Sri Ramakrishna later said, "Mother, who knows why I lose control over myself and do these things?"

---

[72] *The Gospel of Sri Ramakrishna*, pp. 18-19.
[73] Woman who practices austerities.

The Brahmani said reassuringly: "You have done well, my child. It is not you who has eaten the food but the One within you. Now, I feel, I don't have to perform ceremonial ritual any longer. My worship has, at last, borne fruit." Saying so, she walked to the Ganges and tenderly immersed the stone image of Raghuvir she had worshipped for so many years.

Observing Sri Ramakrishna's actions minutely, the Brahmani became convinced that he was an incarnation of God. And she didn't mind proclaiming her belief in public. With the help of Mathur Babu, she invited many prominent scholars to the Dakshineswar Kali Temple for a debate. The scholars came and debated at great length whether Sri Ramakrishna was an incarnation of God or not. All the while, Sri Ramakrishna listened, smiled, and kept quiet. At a much later point in his life, Sri Ramakrishna told devotees about his thoughts on a Divine Incarnation:

> That which is Brahman is verily Shakti. I address That, again, as the Mother. I call It Brahman when It is inactive, and Shakti when It creates, preserves, and destroys. It is like water, sometimes still and sometimes covered with waves. The Incarnation of God is a part of the lila[74] of Shakti. The purpose of the Divine Incarnation is to teach man ecstatic love for God. The Incarnation is like the udder of the cow, the only place milk is to be got. God incarnates Himself as man. There is a great accumulation of divinity in an Incarnation, like the accumulation of fish in a deep hollow in a lake."[75]

Sri Ramakrishna began to practice the prescribed rules of the heroic mode of Tantric worship. Although he did so under the guidance of the Brahmani who was an attractive

---

[74] Play.
[75] *The Gospel of Sri Ramakrishna*, p. 285.

woman, he never deviated from his filial attitude toward her. Not even once did lust arise though he went through all kinds of esoteric disciplines involving women, some naked. To him, all women were part of his Divine Mother.

> Following the heroic mode the aspirants have all along been taking a woman companion at the time of sadhana. As they do not see any aspirant of the heroic mode deviate from that practice, people have got a firm conviction that the realization of the desired end of the discipline, the attainment of the grace of the Divine Mother, is quite impossible if that practice is not followed. It is doubtless that, under the influence of this conviction, people condemn the Tantra scriptures.

> It is only the Master, the incarnation for this epoch, who told us repeatedly that he never in his life kept the company of a woman even in a dream.[76]

When Sri Ramakrishna had become perfect in practicing the major Tantric disciplines, the Brahmani began to teach him Vaishnav sadhana. According to the Vaishnava tradition, bhakti (intense love for God) is the only thing needed to realize God. In order to increase love, a Vaishnava establishes a particular intimate attitude toward God: God is my master, my friend, my child, my husband, my sweetheart. During his Vaishnav sadhana, Sri Ramakrishna regarded himself for some time as a female friend of the Divine Mother. He completely immersed himself in this role and actually looked like a woman. Dressed in a sari and surrounded by other ladies, not even Mathur Babu recognized Sri Ramakrishna during one Durga Puja festival in his house.

Sri Ramakrishna still looked upon God from a female point of view when his next teacher, the Vaishnava monk

---

[76] *Sri Ramakrishna, the Great Master*, pp. 198-199.

Jatadhari, arrived in Dakshineswar. As soon as he saw Jatadhari's metal image of God as the child Rama, Sri Ramakrishna cherished it with motherly love. He had many visions of Ramlala, and baby Rama became his constant companion. When Jatadhari left Dakshineswar, he gave Ramlala's image to Sri Ramakrishna and said, "I don't need the image anymore. Ramlala has fulfilled my innermost prayer."

The next teacher to arrive in Dakshineswar was Totapuri, who was to teach Vedanta to Sri Ramakrishna. Totapuri was a naked monk who had practiced severe austerities on the bank of the sacred river Narmada for many years before he realized his identity with the Absolute. After realizing God, he began to roam, living on alms and staying nowhere longer than a few days. When Totapuri met Sri Ramakrishna, his insight immediately told him that Sri Ramakrishna would be a fit student of Vedanta. But Totapuri was stunned when Sri Ramakrishna, following his instructions, attained nirvikalpa samadhi.[77] "Is it possible that he attained in a single day what took me forty years of strenuous practice to achieve?" cried Totapuri. "Great God! It is nothing short of a miracle."

Totapuri looked upon the world as maya[78] and the worship of Gods and Goddesses as the fantasies of a deluded mind. He only believed in the formless Brahman. Sri Ramakrishna also saw the world as an illusion, but instead of negating it like Totapuri, he acknowledged the power of maya on a relative plane. Maya is none else than Kali, the Divine Mother of creation and destruction.

> After nirvikalpa samadhi, Sri Ramakrishna realized maya in an altogether new role. The binding aspect of Kali vanished from before his vision. She no

---

[77] The highest Vedantic experience: the knower, knowledge and the knowable become one.
[78] Illusion.

longer obscured his understanding. The world
became the glorious manifestation of the Divine
Mother. Maya became Brahman. The Transcendental
Itself broke through the Immanent. Sri Ramakrishna
discovered that maya operates in the relative world
in two ways, and he termed these "avidyamaya"
and "vidyamaya." Avidyamaya represents the dark
forces of creation: sensuous desires, evil passions,
greed, lust, cruelty, and so on. It sustains the world
system on the lower planes. It is responsible for the
round of man's birth and death. It must be fought
and vanquished. But vidyamaya is the higher force
of creation: the spiritual virtues, the enlightening
qualities, kindness, purity, love, devotion.
Vidyamaya elevates man to the higher planes of
consciousness. With the help of vidyamaya the
devotee rids himself of avidyamaya; he then
becomes mayatita, free of maya. The two aspects
of maya are the two forces of creation, the two powers of Kali; and She stands beyond them both. She is
like the effulgent sun, bringing into existence and
shining through and standing behind the clouds of
different colors and shapes, conjuring up wonderful
forms in the blue autumn heaven.[79]

The "Naked One," as Sri Ramakrishna called Totapuri,
remained at the Dakshineswar Kali Temple for eleven
months. He did not believe in Kali when he arrived but,
when he left, he did. This change of attitude happened as
follows. Totapuri, one day, began to suffer from acute dysentery. Excruciating pain did not allow him to rest or meditate
on Brahman. And, one night, when the pain was especially
bad, Totapuri felt he should give up his body. Chanting "Hari
Om," he walked into the Ganges. Although he walked

[79] The Gospel of Sri Ramakrishna, p. 30.

farther and farther into the river and almost reached the other shore, the water never got higher than his ankles. "Is there not enough water in the Ganges to drown myself?" cried Totapuri.

> Suddenly, in one dazzling moment, he sees on all sides the presence of the Divine Mother. She is in everything; She is in everything. She is in the water; She is on land. She is the body; She is the mind. She is pain; She is comfort. She is knowledge; She is ignorance. She is life; She is death. She is everything that one sees, hears, or imagines. She turns "yea" into "nay," and "nay" into "yea." Without Her grace no embodied being can go beyond Her realm. Man has no free will. He is not even free to die. Yet, again, beyond the body and mind She resides in Her Transcendental, Absolute aspect. She is the Brahman that Totapuri had been worshipping all his life.[80]

Toward the end of 1866, Sri Ramakrishna began to practice the disciplines of Islam under the direction of the Sufi Govinda and attained God. Some years later, Sri Ramakrishna desired to know the truth of the Christian religion. He listened to readings from the Bible and became fascinated by the life and teachings of Jesus Christ. One day in the Panchavati, Sri Ramakrishna had a vision of Christ, who merged into his body.

Sri Ramakrishna's attitude toward religion was one of harmony. He did not like fanatic sectarianism and expressed his feelings on the subject to members of the Brahmo Samaj[81]:

---

[80] *The Gospel of Sri Ramakrishna*, p. 31.

[81] A 19th century religious and social reform movement. Its members did not believe in idol worship.

I was told that you had put up a "signboard" here that people belonging to other faiths are not allowed to come in.

But I say that we are all calling on the same God. Jealousy and malice need not be. Some say that God is formless, and some that God has form. I say, let one man meditate on God with form if he believes in form, and let another meditate on the formless Deity if he does not believe in form. What I mean is that dogmatism is not good. It is not good to feel that my religion alone is true and other religions are false. The correct attitude is this: My religion is right, but I do not know whether other religions are right or wrong. I say this because one cannot know the true nature of God unless one realizes Him. Kabir used to say: "God with form is my Mother, the Formless is my Father. Which shall I blame? Which shall I praise? The two pans of the scales are equally heavy."

Hindus, Mussalmans, Christians, Shaktas, Shaivas, Vaishnavas, the Brahmajnanis of the time of the rishis, and you, the Brahmajnanis of modern times, all seek the same object. A mother prepares dishes to suit the stomachs of her children. Suppose a mother has five children and a fish is bought for the family. She doesn't cook pilau or kalia for all of them. All have not the same power of digestion; so she prepares a simple stew for some. But she loves all her children equally.

Do you know my attitude? I love all the preparations of fish. I have a womanly nature. I feel myself at home with every dish—fried fish, fish cooked with turmeric powder, pickled fish. And further, I equally relish rich preparations like fish-head, kalia, and pilau.

Do you know what the truth is? God has made different religions to suit different aspirants, times, and countries. All doctrines are only so many paths; but a path is by no means God Himself. Indeed, one can reach God if one follows any of the paths with whole-hearted devotion. Suppose there are errors in the religion that one has accepted; if one is sincere and earnest, then God Himself will correct those errors."[82]

Sri Ramakrishna went on pilgrimage with Mathur Babu in 1868. They visited Varanasi and Vrindaban but, aware of his father's vision at Gaya before his birth, Sri Ramakrishna refused to go to Gaya. He believed that if he visited the temple of Vishnu in Gaya, his mind would become permanently absorbed in God and he wouldn't be able to come back. In fact, he almost didn't return from Vrindaban because he loved the spiritual atmosphere of Krishna's birthplace so much. But, the thought of his old mother who was then living alone at the Dakshineswar Kali Temple made him return.

Years had passed since Sri Ramakrishna's wife who lived in Jayrambati had seen her husband. Sarada Devi heard many rumors that Sri Ramakrishna had gone mad and, concerned, she paid her first visit to Dakshineswar in 1872. The child Sarada had now turned 18, a young maiden—gentle, shy and lovingly unselfish.

Sri Ramakrishna had always lived a life of unbroken chastity and, with the arrival of his young wife, he was confronted with the final test. Would he remain celibate or could the mad saint of Dakshineswar become a householder and live a life with wife and children? As Sri Ramakrishna watched Sarada Devi sleeping by his side one night, he searched his mind.

---

[82] *The Gospel of Sri Ramakrishna*, pp. 558-559.

"This is, O mind, a female body. People look upon it as an object of great enjoyment, a thing highly prized, and they die for enjoying it. But if one goes for it, one has to remain confined in the body and cannot realize God who is Existence-Knowledge-Bliss. Do not, O mind, harbor one thought within and a contrary attitude without. Say in truth whether you want to have it or God. If you want it, it is here before you, have it."

He discriminated thus; but scarcely had he entertained in his mind the idea of touching the body of the Holy Mother when his mind shrank and at once lost itself so deeply in samadhi that it did not regain its normal consciousness that night.[83]

While she massaged Sri Ramakrishna's feet one day, Sri Sarada Devi asked him, "How do you look upon me?" Quickly, Sri Ramakrishna replied, "The Mother who is in the temple, the Mother who has given birth to this body and is now living in the Nahabat, the same Mother is now massaging my feet. Truly, I always look upon you as a form of the blissful Divine Mother." See figure 33 on page 270.

Sri Ramakrishna cared for his young wife and instructed her in spiritual matters. One of her first lessons was: "Just as all children love the moon, God is everybody's Beloved. Everyone has the same right to pray to Him. Out of His grace He reveals Himself to all who call upon Him. You, too, will see Him if you but pray to Him."

The marriage of this divine couple was unique: never consummated but with a love between them that was so intense that people around caught its fire and felt divinely inspired. The union of Sri Ramakrishna and Sri Sarada Devi was in the spirit. "I felt as if he [Sri Ramakrishna] had put a pitcher of bliss into my heart," Sri Sarada Devi told devotees long after Sri Ramakrishna had passed on.

---

[83] *Sri Ramakrishna, the Great Master*, p. 290.

The word slowly got around Calcutta that a mysterious holy man who had countless visions of Gods and Goddesses was living at the Dakshineswar Kali Temple. Many distinguished people came to see Sri Ramakrishna, sat at his feet and listened to his holy words. Keshab Chandra Sen, the leader of the Brahmo Samaj, was the one who was mainly responsible for telling a large audience about Sri Ramakrishna. He wrote various articles on Sri Ramakrishna in Brahmo journals. Many of Sri Ramakrishna's disciples came to Dakshineswar after reading Keshab's articles.

Compared to Sri Ramakrishna, Keshab was an extremely famous man. He was a sophisticated, well-traveled, well-known orator and writer. Sri Ramakrishna, on the other hand, was a guileless man who expressed himself in simple village colloquialism. He had an absolute horror of lecturing and barely knew how to write his name. What did it matter? Sri Ramakrishna was a spiritual phenomenon and Keshab its admirer. Keshab was, indeed, a great man, for it takes a great person to recognize another. Whenever Keshab visited Sri Ramakrishna, he humbly approached him with offerings of flowers and fruits.

Many of society's leaders came to Sri Ramakrishna but he was bored with their attention. Sri Ramakrishna had not the slightest interest in fame. Instead, he longed for sincere devotees who would take the same delight as he in talking about God. As the sun was setting across the Ganges, Sri Ramakrishna would climb up on the roof of the kuthi (mansion) and cry out, "Come, my children! O where are you? My tongue is parched from talking to the worldly-minded. O come, I long to talk to you!"

Sri Ramakrishna did not employ orthodox ways to teach others. Although he was a hard taskmaster and uncompromising when it came to purity, he often taught the most profound truths while joking and having fun with his disciples. Merriment and roars of laughter were often heard coming from Sri Ramakrishna's room whenever his beloved boys came to visit him.

Figure 33. As the sun turns golden in the evening hours, the bells of the Vishnu, Kali and Shiva temples call devotees to evening arati. Sri Ramakrishna used to stand here on the roof of the Kuthi and call out for his devotees with longing: "Where are you, oh my children? Where are you? I am waiting for you!" (Photograph by Pranab Ghosal.)

Among Sri Ramakrishna's lay disciples were medical practitioners, wealthy men, students, a chemist, an actor and playwright, a schoolmaster and many others. Among Sri Ramakrishna's young disciples were boys who came from all kinds of families. While one boy was illiterate and of obscure parents, another came from a wealthy family. One thing they all had in common: an intense love for Sri Ramakrishna, a love that later made them renounce the world and become monks, forming the Ramakrishna Order. Some of Sri Ramakrishna's disciples were women and first and foremost among them was his wife, Sri Sarada Devi.

Sri Ramakrishna's British-educated disciples could not use the logic they had learned in school to help them understand their Master. Instead, they often had to relearn what they had previously learned and change their attitudes. Being very young, some of the boys thought of themselves as modern while looking upon Sri Ramakrishna as backward and superstitious. Sri Ramakrishna respected all religious and social systems and abided by them. Although he totally depended on the Divine Mother Kali, he lived as prescribed by the almanac. Much to the chagrin of the modern young boys from the Brahmo Samaj, where image worship was not allowed, Sri Ramakrishna humbly bowed down and worshipped clay or stone images of Gods and Goddesses. Nevertheless, they flocked to him like bees to honey and sucked up every word he said.

Joseph Campbell, American orientalist and authority on mythology, wrote:

> The Europeans who protested against the empire of mediocrity, themselves failed to attain to the springs of power. So their world of ideals went down before the steamroller. But in Dakshineswar, only a few miles outside the Victorian metropolis of Calcutta, practicing his sadhana, not according to enlightened, modern methods, but after the most ancient, most superstitious, most idolatrous traditions of timeless India: now hanging to a tree like a monkey; now posturing and dressing as a girl; now weeping before an image; now sitting night and day like a stump; six years unable to close his eyes, himself terrified at what was happening to him; swooning in the ocean of the Mother's love; stunned by the experience of Brahman—Sri Ramakrishna cut the hinges of the heavens and released the fountains of divine bliss.[84]

---

[84] *A Bridge to Eternity*, pp. 410-411.

Sri Ramakrishna's throat became inflamed in April 1885, and doctors diagnosed his illness as "clergyman's sore throat." They asked him to stop talking for a while and advised him to refrain from going into ecstasy. Though Sri Ramakrishna followed doctor's orders regarding diet, he could not control entering into samadhi or stop talking to devotees who came to him for spiritual advice. Sometimes he talked twenty hours out of twenty-four. His door was always open. All sincere seekers were welcome—city magistrates, famous writers, office workers, housewives, yogis, hemp smokers, actors, drunkards, singers, and prostitutes. To Sri Ramakrishna, all were his beloved Divine Mother Kali, playing hide and seek, acting in so many different forms.

Sri Ramakrishna's illness got worse and, to the great distress of all who loved him, it was diagnosed as cancer. His disciples brought Sri Ramakrishna to Calcutta where he could receive better care and treatment, and some of the young boys began to live with him. As Kali Puja approached, Sri Ramakrishna asked them to procure all items necessary for the Kali worship.

All the articles were gradually brought. Incense was burnt and lamps were lighted, and the room became illumined and filled with fragrance. Seeing that the Master was still sitting quietly, the devotees sat beside him. Some among them awaited his command and looked at him with a concentrated mind while others meditated on the Divine Mother of the universe. The room was thus completely silent; and although there were thirty or more persons in it, the room seemed to be vacant altogether. Some time passed this way. The Master continued to sit quietly without making any effort to perform the worship or ask any one of us to do it.

The elderly devotees, Mahendranath, Ramchandra, Devendranath, Girish Chandra and others as well as the young devotees were present. Of them all,

Girish Chandra—the Master often had said—had the most amount of faith. Many of them were surprised to see the Master take that attitude regarding the worship. But Girish had a different sentiment surging in his heart. It struck him that the Master had no need to worship Kali for his own sake. If it was suggested that he had a desire to perform the worship under the impulse of selfless devotion, why was he sitting thus quietly without doing so? It did not seem so. Might it not be then that these preparations were meant for the devotees so that they might be blessed by worshipping the Mother of the universe in the living image of the Master? It was certainly that. Thinking so, he was beside himself with joy and, suddenly taking the flowers and sandal-paste meant for the worship, he offered handfuls of them at the lotus feet of the Master, uttering, "Victory to Mother."

At this all the hair of the Master's body stood on end, and he entered into a profound ecstasy. His face radiating effulgence, his lips adorned with a divine smile and both his hands assuming the attitude of granting boons and freedom of fear—all indicated the manifestation of the Divine Mother in him.[85]

"Jai Kali, Jai Kali. Victory to the Mother," shouted the devotees, each one offering flowers, leaves, sweets and fruit to the Divine Mother Kali in the form of Sri Ramakrishna. All felt intoxicated with bliss with the exception of one person. Sri Sarada Devi's heart was pounding with fear because she witnessed in front of her eyes all the signs Sri Ramakrishna had prophesied would be an indication of his near departure from this world. A long time ago he had told her, "When you see me spend nights in Calcutta and see

---

[85] *Sri Ramakrishna, the Great Master*, p. 857.

devotees worshipping me as an incarnation of God, know that I shall depart from this world very soon."

Sri Ramakrishna was transferred from Shyampukur to Cossipore in December, 1885. Although his illness took a turn for the worse and he could no longer talk, Sri Ramakrishna did not desist from communicating and teaching his disciples. When Naren, his chief disciple, stood beside his bed and, seeing the terrible condition of his body, doubted his divinity, Sri Ramakrishna knew and said in sign language, "He who was Rama, He who was Krishna, verily, in this body is Ramakrishna."

Crying out three times the name of Kali in a loud, ringing voice, Sri Ramakrishna left his body on August 16, 1886. Heartbroken, Sri Sarada went to his room and cried: "Mother! O Kali! What have I done that you have departed, leaving me alone in the world?"

When the cremation of Sri Ramakrishna's body was over, Sarada Devi was about to remove her jewelry and put on the garb of a Hindu widow. Suddenly, she heard Sri Ramakrishna's voice, "What are you doing? Have I gone? I have only passed from one room to another."

Bamakhepa

Although Bamakhepa is not particularly known for worshipping Kali, he was such a great Mother worshipper and contemporary of Sri Ramakrishna that he should be mentioned in this book. Bamakhepa worshipped Mother in the form of Tara and became a famous Tantric saint practicing sadhana at the Tarapith cremation ground. Tarapith in West Bengal is difficult to get to and, therefore, only a few Westerners have visited this ancient spiritual center. Tarapith is situated in the district of Birbhum, home of the Bauls and birthplace of famous Vaishnava and Shakta saints. See figure 34 .

Bamakhepa was born in 1837—one year after Sri Ramakrishna—near Tarapith in the village of Atla. Although his parents were poor Brahmins, Bamakhepa's father, Sarvananda Chatterjee, was well-known and respected for his piety and so was Bamakhepa's mother, Rajkumari. His name was actually Bama, but since he showed absolutely no interest in worldly matters even from early youth on, people called him mad and added "khepa" (mad) to his name. Khepa is a term used mostly by Tantrics and Bauls and is

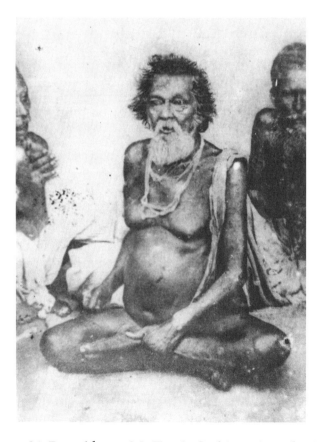

Figure 34. Bamakhepa, Ma Tara's God-intoxicated saint.

Figure 35. The holy feet of Ma Tara in Tarapith, an ancient place of Shakti worship in rural Bengal.

not an ordinary madness. One who is called khepa is generally considered a great soul.

As a young boy, Bamakhepa had a peculiar habit. At the dead of night, he liked to steal into his neighbors' houses, take their images of Gods and Goddesses and carry them to a river bank some distance away. There he worshipped the images all night long. When, in the morning, the villagers couldn't find their family deities, they would make a big scene. Bamakhepa was discovered as the culprit but, no matter how severely his parents scolded him, they could not prevent him from taking the images.

Bamakhepa's education never went beyond the simple village school he attended. There was not enough money in the family to send the boy away for higher education and study of the scriptures. His father died when Bamakhepa was very young, and, therefore, his mother and widowed elder sister were the first ones who gave him any kind of spiritual instructions. They told the boy ancient Hindu stories from the Ramayana and Mahabharata, and it was due to their efforts that Bamakhepa developed a spiritual sentiment early in life. He enjoyed singing devotional songs which he became rather good at it, to the delight of his mother and elder sister.

Financial troubles worsened, and Bamakhepa's mother had to send him and his brother to live at an uncle's house. The uncle made an effort to make the boys active parts of his family and dispatched them to look after his cows. But when he found Bamakhepa unfit to take care of even this simple task, he sent him back home to his mother.

Bamakhepa proved incompetent to perform any kind of work. All he wanted to do was worship Mother Tara. When he saw a red hibiscus flower, he thought of Ma Tara. When he uttered "Ma Tara," he became unconscious of his surroundings. Even his mother was convinced her son was mad and, in order to keep him out of harm's way, she put him under house arrest. But at an opportune moment, Bamakhepa broke out, swam across the river Dwaraka and walked all the way to holy Tarapith. See figure 35 on page 276.

He had heard about Kailaspati Baba, the well-known Tantric who was believed to be a realized soul. Bamakhepa went straight to his cottage. Recognizing Bamakhepa's potential for spiritual realization, the Baba accepted him as his disciple. Bamakhepa began to practice serious Tantric sadhana under the guidance of Kailaspati Baba.

Meanwhile, Bamakhepa's mother was worried about her son and, after a long search, found him in Kailaspati Baba's cottage. When she realized that she couldn't persuade him to come with her, she asked one of her family members who was a prominent man in town to help him. This uncle, by the name of Durga Charan Sarkar, was an agent of the Maharaja of Natore and, using his influence in Tarapith, he procured Bamakhepa a job of collecting flowers for the service at the Tarapith Temple.

But Bamakhepa was not meant for work, and couldn't perform this task. Instead of picking flowers, he sat absorbed in thoughts of the Divine Mother. Forgetful of his physical comforts, he was unaware if it was day or night, hot or cold, rain or sunshine. Smoking hemp, he lived in the Tarapith cremation ground surrounded by snakes, dogs, cats, and jackals.

Although Bamakhepa seemed to have caused nothing but trouble to his mother, and he had not contacted her for a long time, he had great love and reverence for her. When news reached Tarapith that she had died and that her body could not be brought to the Tarapith cremation ground due to excessive flooding, Bamakhepa swam across the flood-swollen river. With his mother's dead body in his arms, he returned to Tarapith and asked his brother Ramcharan to perform the funeral rites. How could this poor family afford to pay for the funeral? By divine providence, as it were, money and food came to feed all the guests. People in Tarapith still tell the story about the dark clouds that appeared in the sky as the body of Bamakhepa's mother was burnt. Though all of Tarapith was flooded by a sudden heavy downpour, not a single drop fell on the funeral gathering.

Bamakhepa was in the habit of moving around completely naked. One day someone asked him, "Why are you naked?" Bamakhepa replied, "My father (Shiva) is naked; my mother (Tara) is also naked. So, I am practicing that. Moreover, I don't live in society. I live in the cremation ground with my mother. So I have no shame or fear!"

Under the guidance of his guru Kailaspati Baba and the Tantric master Mokshananda, Bamakhepa completed all the major Tantric rites and sadhana in accordance with the Shastras. It is interesting that Bamakhepa, like Sri Ramakrishna, practiced Tantra while remaining absolutely celibate. Just as Sri Ramakrishna, Bamakhepa also looked upon women as mother. One day a beautiful, young woman tried to tempt Bamakhepa by offering herself to him as his Bhairavi. No matter how much she tried, she could find no "male sign" in him. Suddenly, Bamakhepa cried out "Ma Tara" and bit the woman's breast. Blood oozed from her breast and she fell down, unconscious.

When Bamakhepa's spiritual guides saw that their disciple had attained perfection, Kailaspati Baba and Mokshananda installed him as the spiritual leader of Tarapith and left. Yet nothing, not even this high honor, could bind Bamakhepa. He neglected to follow temple regulations and did not obey social rules. Sometimes he sat with stray dogs, sharing his food with them, and sometimes he answered calls of nature within the holy temple terrain. He was not concerned, and the thought of purity or impurity did not enter his mind. He had practiced same-sightedness for so long.

One day the temple priests caught Bamakhepa eating the temple food before it was offered to Ma Tara. They were so angry with him that they stopped supplying him with food. Four days after this incident, the Maharani of Natore had a strange dream. Ma Tara appeared to her and said: "I am thinking of leaving this place. I asked my favorite son Bamakhepa to eat, and the priests have beaten him and taken away his food. If my son does not eat first, how can I, his mother?" When she woke up, the Maharani ordered that, henceforth, Bamakhepa should be fed before Ma Tara. After that, nobody dared to obstruct Bamakhepa.

The mad saint of Tarapith became famous for his yogic powers and even people from far away came to see him. Some sought nothing but his blessings while others asked to be healed or helped in distress.

Bamakhepa healed many sick people with his psychic powers. Once a dying man came to Tarapith and asked Bamakhepa for prasad. Bamakhepa took pity on him and fed him with his own hand. Soon after, the man miraculously recovered and walked home. There was a leper in Tarapith by the name of Nanda Handi, who belonged to the untouchable caste. Nanda often brought Bamakhepa food and, although he was a Brahmin of the highest caste, Bamakhepa accepted Nanda's food. In return for the favor, he gave Nanda some mud one day and asked him to rub it on his sores. Nanda did as told and the terrible leprosy left his body.

A man from Belagram by the name of Nimai suffered terribly from hernia problems. He had so much pain that he was unable to maintain his family. Thinking he was of no use to anybody, not even to himself, he resolved to commit suicide. Rope in hand, he came to Tarapith one dark night with the intention to hang himself. Suddenly, he heard a terrible voice. It was Bamakhepa calling upon Ma Tara. Nimai was too scared to commit suicide and, not knowing what to do with himself, he remained in Tarapith near Bamakhepa. One day Nimai enraged Bamakhepa because he lit his pipe on Bamakhepa's holy dhuni fire. The angry saint kicked the hernia patient in the lower part of his abdomen and Nimai fell down unconscious. But to his great surprise, when Nimai got up some time later, he was completely cured of his hernia afflictions.

Another story about Bamakhepa tells of a dying tuberculosis patient who was brought to the saint on a stretcher for final blessings. Instead of blessing the man, Bamakhepa caught him by the neck. Furiously choking and shaking the man, Bamakhepa shouted, "Now, will you commit any more sin?" Strangely enough, after Bamakhepa's rough treatment, the man got off the stretcher, asked for some food and drink and then walked home, healthier and wiser.

But not all people who approached Bamakhepa were so lucky. When a couple of snobbish young men made fun of Bamakhepa because he shared his food with stray dogs, Bamakhepa suddenly touched them. To their horror, they saw that Bamakhepa and the dogs had turned into Gods while they had turned into hideous bats.

Having heard about Bamakhepa's healing powers, a priest by the name of Nagen Panda brought a dying man to Tarapith. The sick man was very rich, and Nagen Panda thought that he would be richly rewarded if he could get Bamakhepa to cure him. But contrary to Nagen Panda's expectation, Bamakhepa did nothing of the sort. He just uttered the word "phat,"[86] and the man died immediately. Furious, Nagen Panda accused Bamakhepa of killing the man. "I am not responsible," said Bamakhepa, "for it was the Mother who spoke through me."

Bamakhepa was not learned but the Mother revealed everything to him, as he used to say. The saint of Tarapith lived a long life and through his holy presence sanctified the place and the people who came in contact with him. He entered Mahasamadhi in 1911.

Sri Sarada Devi

She was so quiet, so dignified. People do not think of the quiet consort of Sri Ramakrishna as a mad, God-intoxicated saint. Outwardly Sri Sarada Devi, or the Holy Mother as she is called by her devotees, rarely showed any signs of the mad, passionate love Sri Ramakrishna and other Kali saints exhibited in their lives. On the contrary, Holy Mother liked to hide herself and her sweet divinity.

> When anybody spoke of her, in her presence, as a divine being, she would at once stop such flattering words and say with the utmost sincerity that she was what she was only because the Master had given her shelter at his feet. The veil with which she always hid her face in public seemed to be symbolic of this more profound veil of modesty with

---

[86] The word also means "gone" in Bengali.

which she loved to hide her own towering greatness. It was for this reason that Sri Ramakrishna,
in fun, likened her to a cat that loved to hide its real
color with ashes.[87]

The Holy Mother lived her early life simply and joyously in the small village of Jayrambati. Being a child bride,
she quietly prepared herself for the time when she was going
to leave her parents' house and move in with her husband.
When nasty gossip about Sri Ramakrishna's madness
reached remote Jayrambati, the Holy Mother often overheard
women at the well discussing her husband's state of mind. It
hurt her deeply. She wanted to go to Sri Ramakrishna and see
for herself what was the matter. See figure 36.

An opportunity to go to Dakshineswar presented itself
when a few villagers planned a trip to Calcutta to take a bath
in the Ganges on a particularly auspicious day. Sri Sarada's
father agreed to accompany the girl. It was a long journey
along a dusty road, across rice fields and open meadows.
The Holy Mother, unaccustomed to walking such a distance,
fell ill with high fever after a couple of days and had to take
shelter in a rest house. There seemed to be no way that she
could continue her journey.

A divine vision came to her in this hour of dejec-
tion and cheered her up. As the Mother lay on the
bed, she saw a dark woman of peerless beauty sitting by her caressing the Mother's head and body
with her soft, cool hands. It seemed to remove all
her pain. The Mother asked, "Where do you come
from, my dear?" The stranger replied, " I come from
Dakshineswar." The Mother wondered at this and
said, "From Dakshineswar! I thought I would go

---

[87] Swami Tapasyananda, *Sri Sarada Devi the Holy Mother*, (Mylapore:
Madras: Sri Ramakrishna Math, 1969), p. 160.

Figure 36. Sri Sarada Devi, Sri Ramakrishna's spiritual consort. She hid her divinity but some fortunate ones saw her in the form of Kali.

there, see him, and serve him. But as I am laid down
with fever on the way, I fear this may never come to
pass." The dark woman said, "Don't you worry!
You will certainly go to Dakshineswar; you will
recover soon and see him. It is for you that I have
been keeping him there."[88]

The Holy Mother had visions of Kali throughout her
life, and it is safe to infer that she was aware of her own
divinity at all times. Although she lived like any other Indian
woman—taking care of cooking, cleaning, and family
affairs—yet whoever came in contact with her felt something
special. People felt her extraordinarily sweet love—she gave
more than their own mother at home could give them. It was
a subtle divinity people felt, and it was truly rare that Sri
Sarada Devi was provoked enough to reveal her true nature.
Once she showed herself as Kali to a robber and his wife.

It so happened that the Holy Mother traveled one day
from Jayrambati to Calcutta on foot. She was accompanied by
a few village women. The small party halted in Arambagh,
about eight miles from Kamarpukur, because before them
lay the uninhabited, notorious fields of Telo-bhelo. People
hesitated to cross these fields alone even during the day for
they were infested with robbers. Deep in the heart of Telo-
bhelo there is, to this day, the terrible image of the Goddess
Kali which the dacoits used to invoke before roaming the
fields in search of people to rob. This particular image of Kali
is appropriately called "Robbers' Kali."

It was still early in the day, and Holy Mother's party
decided that there was plenty of time, even for a moderate
walker, to pass the dangerous area and reach Tarakeshwar
before dark. Holy Mother's feet already hurt and were tired
but, by nature unobtrusive, she didn't want to delay the

---

[88] Swami Gamhirananda, *Holy Mother Sri Sarada Devi* (Mylapore, Madras:
Sri Ramakrishna Math, 1969), p. 42.

others on her account. Soon she lagged behind her companions who had to halt and wait for her to catch up. It was getting late, and rather than exposing the whole group to danger, the Holy Mother asked them not to worry about her and keep going. She did not have to press them much. They gladly quickened their steps and soon were out of sight. The Holy Mother slowly walked on alone.

The sun set. Night turned the solitary fields dark, and bushes and trees loomed as ominous black shadows. Frightened, the Holy Mother tried to walk faster when, all of a sudden, she saw a tall figure emerge from behind a bush. It was a fierce looking man who carried a lengthy staff. His thick, long hair hung down unkempt, and he wore heavy silver bangles around his wrists. She instinctively knew he was a robber. Obviously enjoying her terror, the robber shouted with a throaty, harsh voice, "Hello! Who is this standing here at this time?"

He was about to grab the Holy Mother when, suddenly, he stopped as if stunned by a gun. Much later on he told people that at this very moment he saw the full manifestation of Kali standing in front of him. The Holy Mother had turned into Kali and stunned the robber. He was still in a daze when the Holy Mother began talking to him:

> Father, my companions have left me behind and I have lost my way. Will you kindly take me to them? Your son-in-law lives in the Kali temple of Rani Rasmani at Dakshineswar. I am on my way to him. If you take me to that place, he will treat you cordially.[89]

The robber was too startled to do or say anything. His wife came out of the shadows to help him but before she could do anything, the Holy Mother had taken hold of her hand.

---

[89] *Holy Mother Sri Sarada Devi*, p. 70.

Full of confidence and affection she said, "Mother, I am your daughter Sarada; I was in a terrible plight having been left behind by my companions. Fortunately you and father appeared; otherwise I can't say what I would have done." This simple behavior, extreme confidence, and sweet disposition conquered the hearts of the robber couple who belonged to the lowly Bagdi caste. As a result they forgot the gulf of social difference that separated them from a Brahmin woman and consoling her as though she was truly a daughter of theirs, they did not allow her to proceed further because she was tired.[90]

The next morning, the Bagdi couple took the Holy Mother safely to Tarakeshwar and delivered her to her worried companions. What started out as a potential disaster, turned into an intimate experience, one that the Bagdi couple was not to forget for the rest of their lives. Under the influence of Holy Mother's love, the robber gave up his evil ways and took on a regular job. Love made all the difference. They looked upon the Holy Mother as their sweet daughter Sarada and even came to visit her in Dakshineswar.

The Holy Mother served Sri Ramakrishna and looked upon him as a personification of Ma Kali. As Sri Ramakrishna entered Mahasamadhi, Holy Mother cried out, "O Mother Kali, why have you left me?"

The Holy Mother lived for the good of society. Shortly before Sri Ramakrishna died, he said to her, "Well, my dear, won't you do anything? Should this [body] do everything single-handedly?"

The Master seemed to have returned from some far-off land and while still in that mood of aloofness, he said, "See, the people of Calcutta appear

[91] *Holy Mother Sri Sarada Devi*, p. 71.

to be crawling about like worms in the dark. Do look after them." The Mother pleaded, "I am a woman. How can that be?" The Master pointed towards his body and continued in the same strain, "What, after all this one has done? You'll have to do much more."[91]

Sri Sarada Devi's ministry continued thirty-four years after the passing of Sri Ramakrishna.

Swami Vivekananda

In dense darkness, O Mother,
Thy formless beauty sparkles;
Therefore the yogis meditate in a dark mountain cave.
In the lap of boundless dark,
on Mahanirvana's waves upborne,
Peace flows serene and inexhaustible.
Taking the form of the Void,
in the robe of darkness wrapped,
Who art Thou, Mother,
seated alone in the shrine of samadhi?
From the Lotus of Thy fear-scattering Feet
flash Thy love's lightnings;
Thy Spirit-Face shines forth
with laughter terrible and loud!

As Narendra sang the line, "Who art Thou, Mother, seated alone in the shrine of samadhi?", Sri Ramakrishna went into deep samadhi and lost all outer consciousness.[92]

Narendranath Datta, who later became the famous Swami Vivekananda, was Sri Ramakrishna's chief disciple.

---

[91] *Holy Mother Sri Sarada Devi*, pp. 120-121.
[92] *The Gospel of Sri Ramakrishna*, p. 692.

Figure 37. Swami Vivekananda, Sri Ramakrishna's foremost
disciple and Indian national hero. Swami Vivekananda
brought the ancient teachings of Vedanta to the West when he
attended the Parliament of Religions in Chicago in 1893.
Outwardly, he taught non-dual Vedanta but, in his heart, he
was the son of Ma Kali.

He was the one destined to carry the message of Vedanta to the West and represent Hinduism in 1893 at the Parliament of Religion in Chicago. See figure 37 on page 288. Sri Ramakrishna had a vision of Narendra long before he actually met him.

One day I found that my mind was soaring high in samadhi along a luminous path. It soon transcended the stellar universe and entered the subtler region of ideas. As it ascended higher and higher, I found on both sides of the way ideal forms of Gods and Goddesses. The mind then reached the outer limits of that region, where a luminous barrier separated the sphere of relative existence from that of the Absolute. Crossing that barrier, the mind entered the transcendental realm, where no corporeal being was visible. Even the Gods dared not glance into that sublime realm and were content to keep their seats far below. But the next moment I saw seven venerable sages seated there in samadhi. It occurred to me that these sages must have surpassed not only men but even the Gods in knowledge and holiness, in renunciation and love. Lost in admiration, I was reflecting on their greatness when I saw a portion of that undifferentiated luminous region condense into the form of a divine child. The child came to one of the sages, tenderly clasped his neck with his lovely arms and, addressing him in a sweet voice, tried to drag his mind down from the state of samadhi. That magic touch roused the sage from the superconscious state, and he fixed his half-opened eyes upon the wonderful child. His beaming countenance showed that the child must have been the treasure of his heart. In great joy the strange child spoke to him, "I am going down. You too must go with me." The sage remained mute but his tender look expressed his assent. As he kept gazing at the child, he was again immersed in samadhi. I was surprised to find that a fragment of his body and mind was descending to earth in the form of a bright light. No sooner had I seen Narendra than I recognized him to be that sage."[93]

Narendra was a brilliant student, free-thinker and advocate of the poor and handicapped. His Western education did not leave room for idols or people who worshipped them. Yet, he felt immensely drawn to Sri Ramakrishna, who worshipped so many Gods and Goddesses. Narendra often said to him, "Sir, I don't believe in your Gods and Goddesses. I come to you because I love you."

When Narendra's father suddenly died, his family was so poor that they almost faced starvation. Desperate, Narendra went in search of a job. But no matter how hard he tried, he could not find a job. His heart full of anguish, he turned to Sri Ramakrishna for help.

One day the idea struck me that God listened to Sri Ramakrishna's prayers. So why should I not ask him to pray for me for the removal of my pecuniary wants, a favor the Master would never deny me. I hurried to Dakshineswar and insisted on his making an appeal on behalf of my starving family. He said, "My boy, I can't make such demands. But why don't you go and ask the Mother yourself? All your sufferings are due to your disregard of Her." I said, "I do not know the Mother; you speak to Her on my behalf. You must." He replied tenderly, "My

---

[93] *The Life of Swami Vivekananda*, quotes by *Eastern and Western Disciples*, (Calcutta: Advaita Ashrama, 1974), p. 50.

dear boy, I have done so again and again. But you do not accept Her, so she does not grant my prayer. All right, it is Tuesday—go to the Kali Temple tonight, prostrate yourself before the Mother and ask her any boon you like. It shall be granted; She is Knowledge Absolute, the Inscrutable Power of Brahman and by Her mere will She has given birth to this world. Everything is in Her power to give." I believed every word and eagerly waited for the night.

About nine o'clock, the Master commanded me to go to the temple. As I went I was filled with a divine intoxication. My feet were unsteady. My heart was leaping in anticipation of the joy of beholding the living Goddess and hearing Her words. I was full of the idea. Reaching the temple, as I cast my eyes upon the image, I actually found that the Divine Mother was living and conscious, full of divine love and beauty. I was caught in a surging wave of devotion and love. In an ecstasy of joy I prostrated myself again before the Mother and prayed, "Mother, give me discrimination! Give me renunciation; give me knowledge and devotion; grant that I may have an uninterrupted vision of Thee!" A serene peace reigned in my soul. The world was forgotten. Only the Divine Mother shone within my heart.

As soon as I returned, Sri Ramakrishna asked me if I had prayed to the Mother for the removal of my worldly wants. I was startled at this question and said, "No sir, I forgot all about it. But is there any remedy now?" "Go again," said he, "and tell Her about your wants." I again set out for the temple, but at the sight of the Mother forgot my mission, bowed to Her repeatedly and prayed only for knowledge and devotion. The Master asked if I had done it the second time. I told him what had happened. He said, "How thoughtless! Couldn't you restrain yourself enough to say those few words? Well, try once more and make that prayer to Her. Quick!" I went for the third time, but on entering the temple a terrible shame overpowered me. I thought, "What a trifle have I come to pray to the Mother for! It is like asking a gracious king for a few vegetables! What a fool I am!" In shame and remorse I bowed to Her respectfully and said, "Mother, I want nothing but knowledge and devotion!" Coming out of the temple I understood that all this was due to Sri Ramakrishna's will. Otherwise how could I fail in my object three times? I came to him and said, "Sir, it is you who have cast a charm over my mind and made me forgetful. Now please grant me the boon that my people at home may no longer suffer the pinch of poverty!" He said, "Such a prayer never comes from my lips. I asked you to pray for yourself, but you couldn't do it. It appears that you are not destined to enjoy worldly happiness. Well, I can't help it." But I wouldn't let him go. I insisted on his granting that prayer. At last he said, "All right, your people at home will never be in want of plain food and clothing."[94]

This was a major turning point in Narendra's life. He fully began to accept Ma Kali though he kept his love for her mostly to himself and preached Vedanta instead. Yet, on a few occasions, he could not hide his feelings and, out of the fullness of his heart, he sat down one day and wrote the poem, "Kali the Mother."

---

[94] *The Life of Swami Vivekananda*, pp. 94-96.

Kali the Mother

The stars are blotted out,
       The clouds are covering clouds
It is darkness vibrant, sonant.
          In the roaring, whirling wind
Are the souls of a million lunatics
          Just loosed from the prison-house,
Wrenching trees by the roots,
          Sweeping all from the path.

The sea has joined the fray,
          And swirls up mountain-waves,
To reach the pitchy sky.
          The flash of lurid light
Reveals on every side
          A thousand, thousand shades
Of Death begrimed and black —
          Scattering plagues and sorrows,
Dancing mad with joy,
          Come, Mother, come!

For Terror is Thy name,
          Death is in Thy breath,
And every shaking step
          Destroys a world for e'er.
Thou `Time', the All-destroyer!
          Come, O Mother, come!

Who dares misery love,
          And hug the form of Death,
Dance in Destruction's dance,
To him the Mother comes.[95]

---

[95] Swami Vivekananda, *In Search of God and other Poems*, (Calcutta: Advaita Ashrama, 1968), p. 25.

Sister Nivedita, one of Swami Vivekananda's foremost disciples, recorded a rare conversation she had with the Swami. Swamiji opened up and talked freely about Kali.

> How I used to hate Kali!" he [Swami Vivekananda] said, "And all Her ways! That was the ground of my six years' fight—that I would not accept Her. But I had to accept Her at last! Ramakrishna Paramahamsa dedicated me to Her, and now I believe that She guides me in every little thing I do, and does with me what She will. . . . Yet I fought so long! I loved him, you see, and that was what held me. I saw his marvelous purity. . . . I felt his wonderful love . . . . His greatness had not dawned on me then. All that came afterwards, when I had given in. At that time I thought him a brain-sick baby, always seeing visions and the rest. I hated it. And then I too had to accept Her!

> "No, the thing that made me do it is a secret that will die with me. I had great misfortunes at that time. . . . It was an opportunity. . . . She made a slave of me. Those were the very words—'a slave of me.' And Ramakrishna Paramahamsa made me over to Her. . . . Strange! He lived only two years after doing that, and most of the time he was suffering. Not more than six months did he keep his own health and brightness."

> "Guru Nanak was like that, you know, looking for the one disciple to whom he would give his power. And he passed over all his own family—his children were as nothing to him—till he came upon the boy to whom he gave it, and then he could die."

"The future, you say, will call Ramakrishna Paramahamsa an Incarnation of Kali? Yes, I think there's no doubt that She worked up the body of Ramakrishna for Her own ends."

"You see, I cannot but believe that there is somewhere a great Power that thinks of Herself as feminine, and called Kali, and Mother."[96]

[96] *The Complete Works of Sister Nivedita*, (Calcutta: Sister Nivedita Girls' School, 1967), pp. 119-120.

In Summary

The list of exalted Mother worshippers is long but, unfortunately, it has many holes in it. Many of Kali's saints are missing since they had chosen never to reveal their greatness in public and were content living obscure holy lives. M. described one such saint in the *Gospel of Sri Ramakrishna*:

> A few days after the dedication of the temple at Dakshineswar, a madman came there who was really a sage endowed with the Knowledge of Brahman. He had a bamboo twig in one hand and a potted mango-plant in the other, and was wearing torn shoes. He didn't follow any social conventions. After bathing in the Ganges he didn't perform any religious rites. He ate something that he carried in a corner of his wearing-cloth. Then he entered the Kali Temple and chanted hymns to the Deity. The temple trembled. Haladhari was then in the shrine. The madman wasn't allowed to eat at the guest house, but he paid no attention to this slight. He searched for food in the rubbish heap where the dogs were eating crumbs from the discarded leaf-plates. Now and then he pushed the dogs aside to get his crumbs. The dogs didn't mind either. Haladhari followed him and asked: "Who are you? Are you a purnajnani [a perfect knower of Brahman]?" The madman whispered, "Sh! Yes, I am a purnajnani" My heart began to palpitate as Haladhari told me about it. I clung to Hriday. I said to the Divine Mother, "Mother, shall I too have to pass through such a state?" We all went to see the man. He spoke words of great wisdom to us but behaved like a madman before others. Haladhari followed him a great way when he left the garden. After passing the gate he said to Haladhari: "What

else shall I say to you? When you no longer make any distinction between ditch water and the water of the Ganges, then you will know that you have Perfect Knowledge." Saying this he walked rapidly away."[97]

A friend once remarked sadly that we generally only hear about saints after they are long gone. Why don't we hear about them when they are alive? Well, we do. The difficulty lies in weeding out the real ones from the pretenders. There are so many holy men, gurus, babas and people who claim to know God. How can one determine whether a person is holy or not?

That's not easy, because it takes a holy person to recognize another. But, one may try the cause and effect method and begin to find out about another by first looking into one's own mind to see how it is affected by the other person. When one comes in contact with a real saint, without fail, his or her influence will increase one's hunger for God. And this hunger for God is an ingredient needful for realization of God.

Though holy company is extremely important and provides the guideposts along one's spiritual path, one shouldn't forget that holy men and women can only point us in the right direction. They cannot walk it for us. The wonderful experience Moses had when he saw God in a burning bush can never quite give me the same experience. What it really tells me is that there is hope for me, too. If it is possible for one person in this world to see God, I, too, have a chance. Thus, a real saint inspires us to try for ourselves.

In lieu of saints, one can get holy company from books and, while a book, a word, is not the thing it denotes, it helps to focus one's mind. This book on Ma Kali, the Black Goddess of Dakshineswar, is only a blueprint. Nobody can

---

[97] *The Gospel of Sri Ramakrishna*, p. 491.

define Kali. If it looks attractive and strikes a special chord within your heart, dear reader, you will have to make an effort yourself to experience her. Then, you will be the saint that still needs to be recorded in this book. And once your soul is burning with a desire to know the Great Mother Goddess, the rest will take care of itself. The Divine Mother will provide everything— teachers, money, opportunity. All will be favorable.

Throughout this book, we've talked at great length about people's love for the Divine Mother. So, we felt that an appropriate subject for the conclusion of this book would be the Divine Mother's love for all people. The more we thought about it, the less we could write. While one can fairly accurately write about our love for God, one cannot write about God's love for us. It's too much to put into words.

Therefore, the conclusion of this book will never be written.

Jai Kali!

Glossary

abharana. Jewelry.

achamanam. Purification of the mouth.

achamaniyam. Rinsing the mouth.

acharya. Religious teacher.

Advaita. Non-duality; a school of the Vedanta philosophy.

Ahambrahmasmi. I am Brahman, I am God.

alta. Red dye for Mother's feet.

amavasya. Worship during or following the darkest night of the moon every month. In Dakshineshwar, the amavasya worship is conducted after the morning worship on the day of the new moon.

amrita. Nectar.

Annapurna. A name of the Divine Mother as the Giver of Food.

apana. Downward air, or inhalation.

arati. Vesper service.

arghya. Respectful puja offering of bel leaves, red hibiscus and red and white sandalwood paste, rice, and durva grass.

asana. Seat, small prayer rug.

asura. Demon.

Atman. Self or Soul. Atman is the ultimate God manifest in the individual self. It's that thing you can't live without.

avahana. Invocation of Deity.

Avatar. Incarnation of God, God in human form.

bakshish. Money.

bali. Sacrificial place.

Baul. God-intoxicated minstrel.

beedi. Cigarette rolled in a kendu leaf.

bel. A tree whose leaves are sacred to Shiva.

Bhairava. A Tantric.

bhajan. Religious music.

bhakti. Love for God.

Bhavatarini. The name of the Divine Mother Kali in Dakshineswar (Lit. , the Savior of the Universe).

bhog arati. Offering of cooked food at noon service.

bhuta shuddhi. Purification of the old and formation of celestial body.

Brahma. God, the Creator, first God of the Hindu Trinity.

Brahman. The Absolute, the Supreme Reality of the Vedanta philosophy.

brahmin. The highest caste in Hindu society.

Brahmo Samaj. A theistic organization in India.

buddhi tattva. Cosmic Intelligence.

chakra. Each one of the six centers in the Sushumna through which the Kundalini rises.

chalkumra. A kind of pumpkin.

chamar. A fan made of the white hair of a yak's bushy tail.

Chandi. Part of sacred Tantra scripture.

chandni. An open portico at the Dakshineswar Kali Temple with steps leading to the Ganges.

charanamrita. The water in which the image of the Deity was bathed.

citta. Memory.

dakshina. A gift of money given to a priest or holy person.

Dakshina Kali. Benign Kali.

darshan. The act of seeing the image of a Deity, a holy person or place.

dashamahavidya. Ten terrible forms of the Divine Mother.

deepa. Light.

deva. A God.

devi. A Goddess.

dhoti. A man's wearing cloth.

dhup or *dhupa.* Incense.

divya. Godlike.

Durga. A name of the Divine Mother.

Durga Puja. Autumn festival.

ekadasi. The eleventh day after the full or new moon.

gandha. Fragrance.

gandha taila. Oil for body and hair.

Ganesha. The God of success, the elephant God.

Gaya. A sacred place in northern India.

Gayatri. A sacred vedic verse which is recited daily by Hindus of the three upper castes after they have been invested with the sacred thread.

ghat. Landing, bathing place.

ghee. Clarified butter.

Gopala. Baby Krishna.

Gopis. The milkmaids of Vrindaban, companions and playmates of Krishna.

gosap. Snake.

gunas. The three gunas, which constitute Prakriti, make up the universe of mind and matter; they are known as sattva, rajas, and tamas.

guru. Spiritual teacher.

homa. A Vedic sacrifice in which oblations are offered into fire.

Indra. The king of Gods.

Ishta. The Chosen Ideal, spiritual ideal of the devotee.

ishta devata. Chosen deity.

japa or *japam*. Repetition of the holy name of God, a mantra.

jilipi. An Indian sweet.

jiva. The individual soul, an ordinary person.

jnana. Knowledge of God arrived at through reasoning and discrimination.

kajal. Blackened ghee used for eye makeup.

Kala. Time, a name of Shiva.

Kali Puja. The greatest night of the year for Kali worshippers.

karma. Action, in general.

Keshab Sen. A celebrated Brahmo leader, famous orator.

khepa. Mad; an honorary title given to God-intoxicated saints.

kirtan. Devotional music, accompanied by singing and dancing.

KRĪM. Kali's seed mantra (bija = seed).

Krishna. The God of the Vaishnavas.

Kumari. Virgin.

Kundalini. Serpent power; the spiritual energy lying dormant in all individuals.

kuthi. A bungalow in the Dakshineswar Temple garden.

Lakshmi. The Goddess of fortune.

linga. Stone symbol of Shiva.

luchi. Round, thin bread which becomes very light and puffy when fried.

Mahadeva. The Great God, a title of the God Shiva.

Mahamaya. The Great Illusion, a name of Kali, the Divine Mother.

mahat tattva. Great Principle.

mahayuga. Four yugas that make up one cycle of time.

mala. Garland.

mangal-arati. Early morning services.

mangal-ghata. A pitcher made from clay and filled with Ganges water.

mantra. A sacred word or string of words.

maya. Ignorance that obscures the vision of God.

mudras. Gestures.

mukti. Liberation.

murti. Image.

nahabat. Music tower.

naivedya. Fruit and candy.

Narada. A great sage.

nirvikalpa samadhi. The highest state of samadhi, wherein the aspirant completely merges with the infinite Brahman.

nyasa. Laying hands on.

padya. Water for washing the feet.

panca-makara. Sadhana in Tantra Shastra.

panchadip or *panchapradip.* Five burning ghee lights on a brass vessel—used during arati.

panchamundi asana. Seat made of five skulls—used during Tantric sadhana.

Panchavati. A grove of five sacred trees: the banyan, peepul, ashok, amlaki and bel tree.

panisankha. A conch filled with water—used during arati.

paniya. Water for drinking.

panjabis. Indian shirt.

papa purusa. Sinful self.

pasu. Animal.

Prakriti. Primordial Nature which, together with Purusha, creates the universe.

prana. Upward air, or exhalation.

prana pratistha. Infusian of power.

pranam. Salutation.

pranayama. A process of breath control.

prasad. Sanctified food.

puja. Ritualistic worship.

pujari. Priest performing the puja.

punarachamaniyam. Rinsing the mouth again.

purna. The All.

Purusha. Soul.

pushpa. Flowers.

pushpanjali. An offering of flowers to Kali.

rajas. Activity, restlessness; see gunas.

Rani. (Literally, queen); a female title of honor.

sadhaka. Spiritual aspirant.

sadhana. Spiritual discipline.

sadhika. Holy woman who practices austerities.

sadhu. Holy man.

samadhi. Trance—union with God.

samana. Air at the navel which helps digest food.

samanya arghya. Consecrated water.

Samkalpa. Sacramental intention or resolution.

Samkhya. One of the six systems of orthodox Hindu philosophy.

sandesh. Indian sweet made of cheese and sugar.

sandhya. Worship.

sankirtan. Group singing of divine names.

sannyasin. A Hindu monk.

sattva. Balance or wisdom; see gunas.

sevak. Servant.

Shakta. Indian Mother worshipper.

Shakti. Female power of God.

Shakti pithas. Places dedicated to Mother worship.

shalagram. Stone symbol of Vishnu.

shastanga pranam. Full prostration wherein a person lies down on the floor, head down and arms stretched toward the object of worship.

Shiva. The third God of the Hindu Trinity; the Destroyer.

shona-bindu. Red dot, femaleness, menstrual blood, the ovum.

shweta-bindu. White dot, maleness, semen.

sindur. Vermillion, used to worship Kali.

Smashan Kali. Fearful Kali of the Cremation Ground.
snaniya. Water for bath.
stuti. Adoration.
Sushumna. A path in the spinal column.
Swami. A title of a monk.

tamas. Inertia, dullness; see gunas.
Tantra. A system of religious philosophy in which the Divine Mother is the ultimate reality; also a scripture.
Tantric. A follower of Tantra.
tapasya. Religious austerities.
tirthas. Holy places in different parts of the body.

udana. Air leaving the body.
Upanishad. Hindu scriptures.

Vaishnava. A devotee of Vishnu.
vastra. Clothing.
Veda. Sacred Hindu scriptures.

Vedanta. One of the six systems of orthodox Hindu philosophy.
Vedantist. A follower of Vedanta.
vedi. Altar.
vilvapatra. Bel leaf.
vira. Hero.
Vishnu. The second God of the Hindu Trinity; the Preserver.
vyana. Air within the body.

yantra. A mystic diagram.
yoga. Union of the individual soul with the universal one; also the method through which one realizes this union.
yoni. Female symbol.

Bibliography

A Bridge to Eternity. Calcutta: Advaita Ashrama, 1986.

Atmaprana, Pravrajika. *Sri Ramakrishna's Dakshineswar*. New Deli: Ramakrishna Sarada Mission, 1986.

Swami Bhajanananda. *Prabuddha Bharata*. May 1980.

Swami Budhananda. *Ramprasad: The Melodious Mystic*. New Delhi: Ramakrishna Mission, 1982.

Swami Chetanananda. *They Lived with God*. St. Louis: Vedanta Society of St. Louis, 1989.

Eastern & Western Disciples. *The Life of Swami Vivekananda*. Calcutta: Advaita Ashrama, 1974.

Graves, Robert. *The White Goddess*. New York: Vintage Books, 1958.

Swami Gambhirananda. *Holy Mother Sri Sarada Devi*. Madras, India: Sri Ramakrishna Math, 1969.

Swami Harshananda. *Hindu Gods and Goddesses*. Mysore, India: Ramakrishna Ashrama, 1981.

Isherwood, Christopher. *Ramakrishna and His Disciples*. Hollywood, CA: Vedanta Press, 1965.

Kinsley, David R. *The Sword and the Flute*. Santa Barbara, CA: University of California Press, 1975.

M. *The Gospel of Sri Ramakrishna*. Swami Nikhilananda, tr. New York: Ramakrishna-Vivekananda Center, 1969.

———. *The Gospel of Sri Ramakrishna*, the abridged version. Translated by Swami Nikhilananda. New York: Ramakrishna-Vivekananda Center, 1988.

Swami Madhavananda & Ramesh Chandra. *Great Women of India*. Calcutta: Advaita Ashrama, 1953.

Mookerjee, Ajit. *Kali: The Feminine Force*. Rochester, VT: Destiny Books, 1988.

Swami Nikhilananda, tr. *The Upanishads*, Vol. 4. New York: Ramakrishna-Vivekananda Center, 1959.

Sister Nivedita. *The Complete Works of Sister Nivedita*. Calcutta: Sister Nivedita Girls' School, 1967.

———. *Kali the Mother*. Calcutta: Advaita Ashrama, 1986.

Swami Saradananda. *Sri Ramakrishna, The Great Master*. Madras, India: Sri Ramakrishna Math, 1952.

Sinha, Dr. Jadunath. *Ramprasada's Devotional Songs—The Cult of Shakti*. Calcutta: Sinha Publishing House, 1966.

Swami Tapasyananda. *Sri Sarada Devi the Holy Mother*. Madras, India: Sri Ramakrishna Math, 1969.

Swami Vijnanananda, tr., *Srimad Devi Bhagavatam*. New Delhi: Munshiram Manoharlal, 1986.

Swami Vivekananda. *In Search of God and other Poems*. Calcutta: Advaita Ashrama, 1968.

———. *Inspired Talks*. New York: Ramakrishna-Vivekananda Center, 1970.

Walker, Barbara G. *The Woman's Encyclopedia of Myths and Secrets*. San Francisco: HarperCollins, 1983.

Waters, Frank. *Mexico Mystique: The Coming of the Sixth World of Consciousness*. Athens, OH: Swallow Press/Ohio University Press, 1975, 1989.

Woodroffe, Sir John. *The Garland of Letters*. Madras, India: Ganesh & Company, 1985.

———. *Hymns to the Goddess*. Wilmot, WI: Lotus Light Publications, 1981.

Zimmer, Heinrich. *Myths and Symbols in Indian Art and Civilization*. Joseph Campbell, ed. New York: HarperCollins, 1962.

Index

Kali Mandir

In a way, publication of the first edition of this book in 1993 started public Kali worship in the United States. When the book sparked interest in worship, Harding brought Sri Haradhan Chakraborti (seated right of the author on page 320), the main pujari of the Dakshineswar Kali Temple, Calcutta, to Laguna Beach to install an image of the Goddess Kali. This led to the formation of Kali Mandir, a non-profit religious organization that facilitates worship of the Divine Mother Kali following the purity of Sri Ramakrishna's teachings and the tradition of the Dakshineswar Kali Temple. Kali Mandir functions like a public Indian temple, with no presiding guru, no membership. Kali Mandir's annual Kali puja (generally held in the summer) performed by Sri Haradhanji has become a tradition, drawing people from all over the United States.

For further information, visit our Web site:

www.kalimandir.org

or write to:

Kali Mandir
P.O. Box 4799
Laguna Beach, CA 92652

Author sitting among Kali priests on the back steps leading to the Kali temple. Elizabeth U. Harding is a journalist who has covered the computer software industry for over 10 years. While working on a special assignment for *Software Magazine* in India, Harding visited Calcutta and had the opportunity to take rare photographs of Kali in the Dakshineswar Temple. She became interested in Kali and wanted to know more about this mysterious black goddess. When she could not find books that provided sufficient information on Kali, she decided to do research and write one herself. This book contains authentic information verified by Indian scholars, Swamis, and priests. Details of her recently formed Kali Mandir are found on page 319.